Teaching Race

Teaching Race

How to Help Students Unmask and Challenge Racism

Stephen D. Brookfield
and Associates

JB JOSSEY-BASS™

A Wiley Brand

Published by Jossey-Bass
A Wiley Brand
One Montgomery Street, Suite 1000, San Francisco, CA 94104-4594—www.josseybass.com

Library of Congress Cataloging-in-Publication Data

Names: Brookfield, Stephen, author.
Title: Teaching race : how to help students unmask and challenge racism /
  By Stephen D. Brookfield and Associates.
Description: San Francisco, CA: Jossey-Bass, [2019] | Includes bibliographical references
  and index. |
Identifiers: LCCN 2018013990 (print) | LCCN 2018021387 (ebook) |
  ISBN 9781119374565 (pdf) | ISBN 9781119374398 (epub) |
  ISBN 9781119374428 (hardback)
Subjects: LCSH: Multicultural education–United States. | Racism in higher
  education–United States. | Race–Study and teaching–United States. |
  BISAC: EDUCATION / Teaching Methods & Materials / General.
Classification: LCC LC212.42 (ebook) | LCC LC212.42 .B76 2019 (print) | DDC 370.117–dc23
LC record available at https://lccn.loc.gov/2018013990

Cover image: kyoshino / Getty Images
Cover design: Wiley

Set in 11/15pt Goudy by SPi Global, Pondicherry, India

Printed in the United States of America

FIRST EDITION
V10004724_102218

Contents

About the Authors

Pamela E. Barnett's career and research in higher education have focused on advancing diverse student bodies, faculties, and curricula. She served most recently as Dean of the College of Arts and Sciences and Distinguished Professor of English at Trinity Washington University in Washington, DC. One of the few remaining women's colleges, Trinity enrolls a student body that is majority Pell grant eligible, first generation to college, and underrepresented minority. She currently serves as Dean of the School of Arts and Sciences at La Salle University in Philadelphia. Pamela began her career as a professor of English and African American Studies at the University of South Carolina, where she was named an Outstanding Teacher of the Year in 2003.

Stephen D. Brookfield is the father of Molly and Colin and the husband of Kim. He is a white man who was born in Liverpool, England, who has spent his professional life trying to understand how to help adults think critically about their learned ideologies and how to create collaborative yet critical learning spaces. He has done this with multiple organizations, sectors, and groups, including community organizations, nonprofits, corporations, TV companies, the military, hospitals, and numerous schools, colleges, and universities. As part of this journey he has written, coauthored, or edited 18 books on adult learning, teaching, and critical thinking, 6 of which have won the Cyril O. Houle Award for Outstanding Literature in Adult Education (for the years 1986, 1989, 1996,

2005, 2011, and 2012). He currently holds the titles of distinguished university professor and John Ireland Endowed Chair at the University of St. Thomas, Minnesota. He has also been a professor at Teachers College, Columbia University; Harvard University; and the University of British Columbia.

Consuelo E. Cavalieri (Kootenai), PhD, is an associate professor at the Graduate School of Professional Psychology at the University of St. Thomas, Minnesota. Her scholarly and teaching interests focus on early childhood mental health, decolonizing psychology training, and the use of culture as medicine. She earned her PhD in counseling psychology at the University of Wisconsin–Madison in 2006. She has been an invited speaker at the Minnesota American Indian Mental Health Conference, has delivered guest presentations for the Indian Health Board in Minneapolis, and has collaborated with the State of Minnesota and the University of Minnesota to train early childhood–mental health clinicians in developmentally informed, evidence-based approaches across Minnesota.

Bryana H. French, PhD, is an associate professor at the Graduate School of Professional Psychology at the University of St. Thomas, Minnesota. Her scholarly interests include black feminism and sexual violence, and her teaching focuses on multicultural and social justice psychology. She earned her PhD from the University of Illinois Counseling Psychology Program in 2010 and is a former Fellow of the American Psychological Association's (APA) Minority Fellowship Program. She has served in APA governance in Division 17 (Society of Counseling Psychology), Division 51 (Society for the Psychological Study of Men and Masculinities), and Division 45 (Society for the Psychological Study of Culture, Ethnicity and Race), and her research on men's sexual victimization has been featured in several news outlets, including *Time*, *U.S. News & World Report*, and the Huffington Post.

Talmadge C. Guy is a retired professor of adult education who has held various positions in the fields of adult and continuing education, from instructor to administrator to professor, spanning a career of

43 years. His specializations were in the history of the education of African American adults, diversity and inclusion, and culture and education. He has published research and analysis in a variety of publication outlets in North America and internationally. He is a Cyril O. Houle Scholar in Adult and Continuing Education, a recipient of the President's Fulfilling the Dream Award from the University of Georgia, and a Carl Glickman Scholar. He has served as a consultant to organizations and in community settings to address issues of racial, gender, and class inequality. He lives in Athens, Georgia.

Susan Hadley, PhD, MT-BC, is a professor and the director of music therapy at Slippery Rock University, Pennsylvania. She is the editor of *Feminist Perspectives in Music Therapy* (Barcelona Publishers, 2006) and *Psychodynamic Music Therapy: Case Studies* (Barcelona Publishers, 2003), and the coeditor of *Our Black Sons Matter: Mothers Talk about Fears, Sorrows, and Hopes* (Rowman & Littlefield, 2016), *Therapeutic Uses of Rap and Hip-Hop* (Routledge, 2012), and *Narrative Identities: Psychologists Engaged in Self-Construction* (Jessica Kingsley Publishers, 2005). She was also the editor of volumes four and five of Barcelona Publishers' monograph series *Qualitative Inquiries in Music Therapy*. In addition, she is the author of *Experiencing Race as a Music Therapist: Personal Narratives* (Barcelona, 2013), for which she was awarded the 2016 President's Award for Scholarly and Creative Achievement from Slippery Rock University. In appreciation of her critical approach to pedagogy, she was the faculty recipient of the 2014 Women of Distinction Award from Slippery Rock University. She has published numerous articles, chapters, and reviews in a wide variety of scholarly journals and books in the music therapy and related fields. Dr. Hadley serves on the editorial boards of several journals and is coeditor in chief of *Voices: A World Forum for Music Therapy*, an open-access, peer-reviewed journal that invites interdisciplinary dialogue and discussion about music, health, and social change.

Mary E. Hess has served on the faculty of Luther Seminary as a professor of educational leadership since 2000. One of her earliest peer-reviewed journal publications was on the topic of white religious educators and unlearning racism, and since then she has continued to wrestle with the privilege she carries as a white woman in the United States. Teaching in a graduate theological school has given her the opportunity to work both with graduate students, and perhaps more importantly, the communities from which they come and to which they are sent as leaders. In the midst of the ferocious polarization and brutal neoliberalism of the United States, she finds hope in the day-to-day challenges of helping people to listen deeply to each other across various divides and in the creative energy to be found in imaginative and collaborative digital media. Her recent work includes developing the websites Storying Faith (Storyingfaith.org) and the Racial Justice Collaborative in Theological Education (https://mncts.net/2014/08/04/racial-justice-collaborative-in-theological-education-2).

Jaye Jones is the executive director of the Institute for Literacy Studies at Lehman College-CUNY and an adjunct assistant professor in the college's Department of Social Work. She received her PhD in social work from the University of Chicago. Her interdisciplinary research agenda focuses on adult learners with a history of trauma and the creation of emotionally responsive learning contexts that foster collective empowerment.

Mike Klein says, "I am from...white, middle class, male, able, middle aged, cisgender, heterosexual, blonde haired, blue eyed, and right handed...all the dominating identities of contemporary US culture. And I am from a critical and ongoing examination of the intersectional privileges and oppressions adhered to these identities so that I can work collaboratively for social justice from my particular standpoint." He is an assistant professor in the Department of Justice and Peace Studies at the University of St. Thomas, Minnesota, where he teaches the undergraduate courses Leadership for Social Justice, Qualitative Research, and Introduction to Justice and Peace Studies, and seminars on art and social change, history's future, community leadership, and coffee as a lens for interdisciplinary analysis. He also teaches graduate courses on social justice pedagogy, critical education in social movements, and the pedagogy of Paulo Freire. His research, publishing, and consulting focus on peace education, popular culture, the intersections of art and social justice, peace building, and democratizing leadership (the last is also the title of his 2017 book). He works with the Pillsbury United Communities' Art Is My Weapon initiative in Minneapolis to creatively address violence by producing art from decommissioned weapons. He expresses gratitude for the opportunity to contribute to this collaborative publication with esteemed colleagues and for the generous editorial work of Stephen Brookfield, and he hopes that this volume might inspire work for racial justice.

Elaine Manglitz is a native Georgian who earned a bachelor's degree in psychology from West Georgia College, a master's degree in middle grades education from Georgia State University, and a PhD in adult education from the University of Georgia. She has worked in the field of public education for almost 30 years, in both K–12 and higher-education settings. Her most recent experience has been serving as the vice president for student affairs at Clayton State University, where she had the opportunity to engage both formally and informally with students, faculty, and staff to address issues related to equity and white privilege, among other areas. Elaine's scholarly interests include research and writing on facilitating effective cross-racial dialogues in educational settings and on other, similar topics.

Lisa R. Merriweather is an African American woman who works in a majority-white institution of higher education. She is currently an associate professor of adult education at the University of North Carolina at Charlotte and is involved in various initiatives related to equity, diversity, and social justice. She cofounded *Dialogues in Social Justice: An Adult Education Journal* in 2015. Her primary research interests are antiblack racism in adult education, Africana philosophy as a guiding lens for issues of race and racism, and culturally responsive doctoral mentoring.

Lucia Pawlowski is a white, cis, straight woman who earned her PhD in English from the University of Minnesota, Twin Cities and has been an assistant professor of English at the University of St. Thomas, Minnesota since 2012. She specializes in the teaching of college writing, community-engagement pedagogy, literary theory, and cultural studies. In the field of writing studies, Dr. Pawlowski works at the intersections of queer theory, Marx, and post-structuralism. She has presented her work on how writing pedagogy should respond to the neoliberalization of the university at the conferences of College Composition and Communication and the Rhetoric Society of America, and at the Thomas R. Watson Conference on Rhetoric and Composition. Her scholarship has appeared in *Griot: The Journal of African-American Studies* and she is coauthoring the forthcoming book *Uncovering Whiteness* with Dr. Stephen Brookfield (Stylus, 2019). Her teaching revolves around political injustice and how to respond to it through rhetorically powerful writing. Students in her class write for social justice organizations in the Twin Cities and study how marginalized people have developed linguistic varieties that resist standard forms of English. Dr. Pawlowski facilitates workshops on antiracist pedagogy throughout the Twin Cities, and she is an active member of the Anti-Racism Coalition at the University of St. Thomas, Minnesota.

Dianne Ramdeholl has been an adult-education practitioner for over 15 years, working in community-based adult-literacy programs and, more recently, in higher education. She's committed to adult education for democratic social change. Currently an associate professor in the Master of Arts in Adult Learning program at SUNY Empire State College in New York City, the principal focus of her research has been developing educational projects that promote equitable socioeconomic and sociopolitical conditions for disenfranchised populations. Her research and practice have primarily focused on connecting adult education to increased participation in democratic decision-making. She has coedited three volumes of the series *New Directions for Adult and Continuing Education* (Jossey-Bass), which focuses on reenvisioning doctoral education in more democratic ways, decentering the ivory tower of academia, and struggling for democracy within the field of adult education. She has also authored the monograph *Adult Literacy in a New Era: Lessons from The Open Book* (Paradigm, 2011).

Salina M. Renninger, PhD, is an associate professor and the director of training in the Graduate School of Professional Psychology at the University of St. Thomas, Minnesota. Her scholarly and teaching interests include clinical supervision and training, attending to culture and other diversity variables in training and therapy, and therapy to address the needs of those who have experienced complex trauma. She earned her PhD at the University of Minnesota in 1998. Prior to joining the faculty of the University of St. Thomas, Minnesota, she worked for many years directing a practicum/internship training program and providing therapeutic services in university and community mental-health settings.

Bobbi Smith is a teacher and education consultant in Campbell River, British Columbia. She is a white middle-class housewife and minivan driver, who took a hell of a long time to do her master of adult education. Her graduate research was a self-study of her adult-education practice that teased out when and how she was performing whiteness and colonizing the indigenous students she was serving. She consequently developed a framework to help other professionals identify their own largely unconscious oppressive attitudes and behaviors, which she speaks about with government and nonprofit organizations. She can be reached at bobbipatriciasmith@gmail.com.

Buffy Smith, PhD, is a sociologist, educator, and consultant. She is the founding associate dean of Dougherty Family College and a professor of sociology at the University of St. Thomas, Minnesota. She earned her BA in sociology from Marquette University and her MS and PhD in sociology from the University of Wisconsin–

Madison. The courses she teaches include Social Problems, Race and Ethnicity, Social Stratification, and the senior Seminar in Sociology. She was an Association for the Study of Higher Education/Lumina Fellow in 2003. Dr. Smith's primary research interest is examining racial and class disparities within the higher education system. She also writes on policy issues dealing with mentoring, access, retention, equity, and diversity in higher education. For over 10 years, she has researched how colleges and universities can assist underrepresented students in understanding and navigating the institutional culture of higher education in order to achieve academic success. Dr. Smith has received several awards and grants that recognize her research on diversity issues in higher education. Dr. Smith's work has been featured in a variety of research and practice-oriented journals, such as *African American Research Perspectives* and *Equity & Excellence in Education*. In addition, she is the author of the book *Mentoring At-Risk Students through the Hidden Curriculum of Higher Education* (Lexington Books, 2013). She can be reached at bsmith@stthomas.edu.

George Yancy is a professor of philosophy at Emory University. He has authored, edited, or coedited over 18 books. He is known for his influential essays and interviews in The Stone, the *New York Times'* philosophy column. Yancy's two most recently published books are *On Race: 34 Conversations in a Time of Crisis* (Oxford University Press, 2017) and *Backlash: What Happens When We Talk Honestly About Racism in America* (Rowman & Littlefield, 2018).

Wendy Yanow is an adult educator and associate with Adult Learning Unleashed, a group of educators leveraging justice and equity through learning. She facilitates workshops on race, whiteness, and privilege through a network of interfaith organizations and other community groups in Chicagoland. Wendy works with adult university students, trains faculty educators, and has served as a popular education teacher in a bilingual adult high school. Wendy teaches a variety of undergraduate and graduate courses, including Developing Cultural Understanding, which engages adults in dialogic practices that foster a critical understanding of themselves and others.

Preface

There are some books that you write or edit because you think they're necessary, and there are some that are torn out of your heart. *Teaching Race* is a work of passion intended to address one of the greatest scars on America's soul. All the authors have activist hearts that impel them to view their classrooms as antiracist laboratories – spaces in which to raise students' awareness of the pervasive dynamics of racism and to prepare them for action. So this is not a book of analysis (though there certainly is analysis in here) but a book of *action*. We have stuffed it full of activities, techniques, exercises, and tools, and all are designed to help teachers in their project of teaching about race and racism.

Obviously, however, this is not a recipe book, prescribing models of practice to be followed to the letter. There is no neat or exact recipe for this work, and we all, to some degree, constantly invent and reinvent our practice in response to the contexts in which we find ourselves. Anyone who sells you an inventory, method, protocol, or multiple-step approach to transform your campus into an antiracist wonderland is either putting you on, making big bucks from people's understandable desire for epistemological certainty, or just incredibly naïve. But we all have to start somewhere, and for me, that's by combining a number of factors. I begin with my own learned instincts of what to do and then combine these with my read of a situation. These are then blended with actions I've seen colleagues take and things I've read about that make some kind of sense.

Building practice is a collective and collaborative effort, and we all benefit from seeing how others work and adapting the good stuff to our own situations.

To go back to the recipe analogy: Chefs tell me that recipes are only starting points for your own experimentation, as you delete ingredients, change portions, alter cooking times, or add new flavors. I think this is how the practice of any teacher or activist is built. You see people doing something, and you think "Hey, I could try that." Then, as you start to think through the particularities of your own learners, teaching goals, and environments, you strip this new idea down and reassemble it in a way that makes sense for your own work contexts and who you are as a teacher. For example, many of the contributors in this book talk about the importance of modeling a vulnerable commitment to examining your own racism in front of learners, but exactly how that general dynamic is realized in your own classroom, workshop, or community depends on your own identity and experience, who your learners are, and the culture in which you work.

Cooking involves a degree of generative creativity, and so does crime. I have always thought of myself as a burglar where teaching is concerned, a kind of pedagogic shoplifter. I enter learning environments with an acquisitive eye, looking for gems and valuables that are easy to remove but that have major payoffs for me. I'm always looking to steal (with thanks and attribution) exercises, techniques, and approaches that, with some alteration and reworking, will help me take learners where I want them to go. I build my practice on the shoulders of colleagues, authors, YouTube, Twitter, and other external resources just as much as on the analysis of my own experience. Sometimes I see a colleague doing an exercise and the only thing I'll take from it is the core impulse behind it. At other times I judge that something works so beautifully that I can lift it wholesale and just alter the organizing question or prime focus. Mostly it's somewhere in between.

Adaptations of practice are typically more substantial than, say, just changing the license plate on a Ford. You strip the engine down, recalibrate the acceleration, switch out the headlights, or add a turbo. When working with students new to considering race, you may initially be driving slowly on the equivalent of back-country lanes or dirt tracks. But with students thoroughly committed to uncovering white supremacy and their own collusion in racism you're charging down the Italian *Autostrade*. As you test-drive your new machine, you find out which parts work well, which have to be thrown out, and what needs to be replaced. You consider students' reactions to the activity, and, if you're lucky enough to team teach, you debrief what happened with colleagues.

As you read through the pages ahead I hope you will do so with a burglar's eye, always on the lookout for something to steal. Or if you think, "That's a recipe I could try," don't hesitate to throw out ingredients, add new ones, or change portions. If any of these chapters offer ideas that you can adapt and experiment with in your own contexts, then this book will have been worth it. I have stolen from my coauthors and I urge you to do so as well.

Our Audience

Our audience is anyone interested in antiracist practice. Although we work mostly in college and university settings, we have used many of the exercises described here in groups, communities, and organizations far removed from academe. These include churches, prisons, the military, corporations, hospitals, public and private schools, media companies, social movements, and numerous community groups. These exercises have been tried out in the belly of the capitalist beast and in the Occupy movement, in the armed forces and with peace groups. Given that racism and white supremacy are all pervasive, permeating every corner of our society, we as educators don't really have the luxury of choosing only to work with those who already think as we do.

Overview of the Contents

The book kicks off with an opening chapter that defines key terms (racism, white supremacy, and microaggression) and summarizes common dynamics of antiracist teaching, such as scaffolding, modeling, and community building. Chapters 2 and 3 explore, from different positionalities, the specific dynamics of teaching whites about their whiteness. In Chapter 2, George Yancy, a black philosopher and leading public intellectual on race, describes how he models vulnerability for his white students by describing his own sexism and then follows this up with race journaling. In Chapter 3, Susan Hadley, a white woman, also emphasizes the importance of modeling and the use of journals, and describes eight other techniques, including moving from right-handed privilege to white privilege, bearing witness, practicing mindfulness, and depending on accountability buddies.

In Chapter 4 we move to an in-depth discussion of how to create a brave space classroom through student writing. Brave space classrooms invite students to wade into controversy and ambiguity, and here Lucia Pawlowski describes how she uses writing assignments and social media to help students explore their racial identities. Teaching students about intersectionality and identity is also the focus of Mike Klein's analysis of the "I am from…" activity in Chapter 5.

The next cluster of chapters looks at how to build trustful learning environments in which students will commit to the risk of engaging in truthful, honest racial dialogue. Pam Barnett describes in Chapter 6 how a teacher functions as "the good doctor" in using naming exercises, hopes-and-fears feedback, and structured questioning to build trust and negotiate conflict when teaching race. Chapter 7, by Lisa Merriweather, Talmadge Guy, and Elaine Manglitz, explains how teachers can carefully research their students while trying to balance a concern for safety with the need to confront learners with productive danger. Developing a working alliance with students is the focus of Chapter 8, in which Consuelo Cavalieri, Bryana French, and Salina Renninger describe the experience of working collaboratively to take students deep into uncovering systemic racism. In Chapter 9, Buffy Smith proposes joining students together in an *ohana* community before inviting them to consider privilege and white supremacy. And in Chapter 10

I review how six specific discussion protocols can be adapted to the analysis of racial issues.

Teaching against a color-blind perspective is the focus of Chapter 11, in which Wendy Yanow builds on critical race theory to explore community writing projects, documentary analysis, and the juxtaposition of story and counterstory. Then in Chapter 12 Dianne Ramdeholl and Jaye Jones consider how to help students unearth their positionalities through learning histories, questioning, decoding media, and integrating current events into the curriculum. The practice of digital storytelling is examined in Chapter 13 by Mary Hess, who describes how the intimacy of this format brings students into an analysis of race and racism.

The final two chapters examine the role of mistakes in teaching race and urge readers to problematize the whole notion of mistakes as missteps and errors that can gradually be erased as we move to a trouble-free racialized pedagogy. In Chapter 14, Bobbi Smith describes how her world exploded when she asked participants in a workshop to conduct an antiracist power analysis of her own teaching. Finally, in Chapter 15 I build on Samuel Beckett's notion of failing well to review some common misperceptions that block white teachers' efforts to do antiracist work.

Acknowledgments

We all acknowledge the numerous students, colleagues, and activists who have formed our identities as antiracist educators and who continue to embrace the risks and dangers of teaching race. I particularly want to acknowledge my fellow authors for sharing their insights and experiences, and for providing so many suggestions for readers to steal, adapt, and shape for use in their own practices.

Stephen D. Brookfield
St. Paul, Minnesota

1

The Dynamics
of Teaching Race

Stephen D. Brookfield

The authors in this book hold these truths to be self-evident:

- We live in a time of rampant racism fueled and legitimized by racist political leaders.
- If unchallenged, racism will continue to extend its hegemony and exclude large groups of people from full participation in political, social, and economic life.
- Racism damages everyone: victims who suffer from abuse, violence, and assault, and perpetrators who live in fear of the "other."
- The roots of racism lie in the ideology of white supremacy; hence a fundamental pedagogic task is to help people unmask this ideology.
- Racism is learned; therefore, a key task for teachers is to help people recognize how they internalize racist ideas and beliefs and how these play themselves out in everyday life.
- Racism is structural, not individual. It is embedded in systems and institutional practices. A major project, therefore, is to help students think structurally and

Teaching Race: How to Help Students Unmask and Challenge Racism, First Edition.
Stephen D. Brookfield and Associates.
© 2019 John Wiley & Sons, Inc. Published 2019 by John Wiley & Sons, Inc.

systemically about racism and to go beyond seeing it as
a matter of individual choice or personal prejudice.

■ The point of teaching race is to prepare students to take
action to combat racism.

All of us have spent many years trying to understand the pedagogy of teaching race. There is well over a century's worth of experience represented in this book and our intent is to share the lessons
we've learned while pursuing this most difficult of teaching tasks.
We don't spend lot of time lamenting the existence of racism or
analyzing its history; after all, plenty of other authors have done
those things superbly. We choose instead to use this book's space to
focus on documenting activities, exercises, techniques, tools, strategies, and approaches that we find helpful to us in uncovering and
challenging white supremacy. This is a book focused on practical
ways to help students take antiracist action in their worlds.

Defining Terms

Three terms are used repeatedly throughout this book: racism,
white supremacy, and microaggression. So as to create a common
base for understanding I want to begin by defining each of these as
clearly as possible. In general conversation these terms are thrown
around somewhat indiscriminately, so it's essential that when
they're used in the following pages the meaning is as consistent as
possible.

Racism

Racism is a system of beliefs and practices that are embedded in
the institutions we move through as individuals and routinized in
the conventions of everyday lives. These beliefs and practices
legitimize the power of whites and justify their viewing all other
racial groups as inherently inferior. Organizational structures,
social policies, and institutional habits embody racism by combining to exclude people of color from access to full participation
in social, political, and economic life. In the educational sphere,

racism is glaringly evident in admissions policies, disciplinary guidelines, curricula, hiring practices, attrition rates for faculty and students of color, and the composition of boards of trustees. The point of racism is to preserve the power of one dominant racial group.

When racism is threatened it responds with a combination of overt force (police brutality, political imprisonment, state-sanctioned murder) and covert manipulation (symbolic festivals celebrating diversity, public holidays, prominent so-called success stories of black, brown, and indigenous exceptionalism). Racism is expert at reconfiguring itself by appearing to have ceded important territory while in reality maintaining its power. Hence, college application brochures feature a rainbow of different student racial identities, institutions create diversity offices headed up by the only person of color in the senior leadership team, reading lists are widened to include authors of color, and admissions offices and departments recruit students, staff, and faculty of color. In reality, these changes are often superficial. Faculty of color fail to get tenure, diversity officers have a high rate of turnover, attrition rates are disproportionately high for students of color, and new, racially based curricula are regarded as exotic and temporary diversions from an agreed-upon mainstream.

Finally, racism is both socially constructed and learned. No one is born with innate stereotypes, prejudices, and biases about other racial groups. These are acquired through the minutiae of daily interactions via jokes, asides, and parental injunctions; from media messages; in peer group conversations; and from institutional policies and practices. Because of de facto housing segregation, most people grow up in racially homogenous areas with little sustained interaction with other races. In the absence of experiences that counter dominant racial messages and challenge "official" or "stock" stories of race (Bell, 2010), people develop ever-deepening beliefs about various racial groups. Any limited interactions with those from a different race are mediated via these learned narratives so as to confirm the idea of white supremacy.

White Supremacy

Behind the structure of racism lies a set of ideas that legitimizes its existence. This is the ideology of white supremacy. White supremacy is a worldview sedimented in institutional practices to ensure that white people stay in control of the systems and structures that control our society. By white supremacy I don't mean the groups of white nationalists, KKK, and Aryan Nation members who openly espouse racial genocide, exclusion, separation, or repatriation. I mean instead the idea that whites, because of their superior intellect and reasoning power, should be in control of decision-making for society as a whole. White supremacy perpetuates the notion that whites should naturally hold the most powerful positions in business, the judiciary, the legislature, the military, and the media because they can think better than nonwhites. Whites are held to be able to use reason more effectively and think more logically, and therefore be more objective in their decision-making processes. This reflects the enduring power of European Enlightenment thought and its privileging of reason and objective analysis, seen particularly in positivism and scientism.

White supremacy views people of color, by way of contrast, as moved by passion and raw emotion, easily inflamed and therefore not to be trusted with decision-making authority. White supremacy views emotion in mostly negative ways, as an unreliable interference with coolly objective decision-making. In the case of people of color, emotion is viewed as something that is quickly converted into aggression and inflamed mob violence. So the ideology of white supremacy places *whiteness* as the preferred norm in society, *white people* as the natural authorities in any situation, and *white knowledge* (and white forms of knowledge production) as the most valid of humankind. White supremacy is frequently denied by its perpetrators (such as me) even as it's being disseminated. The authors in this book view white supremacy as the philosophical foundation of racism and believe that progress in the area of racial justice depends on dismantling this powerful and all-pervasive ideology.

Microaggressions

Microaggressions are the everyday behaviors that enact the ideology of white supremacy and keep racist systems in place. They are small acts of exclusion perpetrated by whites against people of color. Yet enactors of aggressions have no conscious, overt intent. When called on these aggressions, whites will typically reply that people of color are being too sensitive, imagining slights that aren't intended and seeing racism when it's not there. In claiming a lack of racist intent whites are actually being honest. There is no deliberate or conscious wish to diminish, insult, or exclude anyone. The perpetrators are just going about their normal daily business and doing what comes naturally.

Because I've grown up as a white man in a racist world I usually don't notice my unwitting microaggressions: After all, they're not decisions I'm consciously making. A white supremacist view of the world creates a structured blindness to one's enactment of racism where whites like myself are concerned. So when I overlook students of color, remember mostly the names of white male students, or direct my comments in meetings I'm chairing mostly to whites, I'm usually unaware these things are happening until someone challenges me. Typically, when whites are called on for committing microaggressions in multiracial groups, other whites rush in to save the perpetrator, saying he or she just had a moment of forgetfulness, was tired, made an unintended mistake, or had a brain fart. Those calling out a microaggression are often accused of taking political correctness too far and of seeing things that aren't really there.

Three Key Dynamics of Race-based Teaching

A complex mix of emotional reactions confronts teachers trying to introduce the examination of race into their classrooms. Some students display hostility and anger; others seem bored, weary, and uninterested, while still more are fearful. Even students who have deliberately volunteered to study the topic fear saying or doing the wrong thing. As I was writing this chapter I asked two different groups – one composed of students in a leadership course I was teaching and one comprising colleagues in a professional workshop I was running – to list the reasons lying behind any reluctance they felt in addressing the topic of race. Here are the rank-ordered responses, going from most to least frequent:

- I'll say the wrong thing and be called a racist.
- This will be a messy, distressing, and uncomfortable discussion.
- I don't have any experience to draw on that's relevant.
- I don't trust the teacher or leader to know what she or he is doing.
- This never goes well and always ends in tears.
- I'm fed up with the implication that I have privilege and act in a racist way.
- This is just one more example of politically correct brainwashing.

How do we navigate through these different reasons for pushing back against an engagement with racial issues? The contributors in this book suggest three approaches: scaffolding, modeling, and community building.

Scaffolding

Eighteen-year-olds who have grown up in racially homogenous neighborhoods and high schools show up at college completely unprepared to dive into racially charged curricula. They will think about race in broad, dualistic terms – "whites do this, blacks do that" – and will be challenged by any kind of contextual complexity. They will want to know the so-called right, nonracist way to behave and the behaviors they should avoid. Many white students will be firmly caught in the color-blind paradigm and sincerely believe themselves to be good-hearted people who focus on the content of people's character and not on skin color.

So students who have never thought much about this topic (who will mostly be white) should be eased into it, if possible, in ways that feel invitational. In this book, Lisa R. Merriweather, Talmadge C. Guy, and Elaine Manglitz describe how they research students' backgrounds, preconceptions, and experiences (partly through their Race Literacy Quiz), and how they choose instructional strategies based on that inquiry (Chapter 7). Susan Hadley talks about how she switched her approach to teaching about the constructed nature of racial disadvantage by focusing initially on the less emotionally charged benefits of being right-handed (Chapter 3). Buffy Smith describes how she decided to start race-based discussions with the language of power and institutional privilege after researching her young students' reactions against the charged language of white supremacy (Chapter 9). Similarly, George Yancy publicly examines his own unconscious sexism as a precursor to asking students to examine the racism that lives within them (Chapter 2). Another important element in scaffolding race pedagogy is to start by inviting students to tell each other about themselves. Mike Klein's use of the I Am From exercise leads students into considering their racial identity and positionality by having them share the experiences that have shaped who they are (Chapter 5). Pam Barnett uses the My Name exercise and her Hopes and Fears activity to do the same thing (Chapter 6). Dianne Ramdeholl and Jaye Jones ask students to write a personal learning history paper (Chapter 12). Exercises like these are a prelude to the more intensive, personal journaling described by George Yancy, Susan Hadley, Pam Barnett, Lucia Pawlowski, and Wendy Yanow.

It also seems to be useful to immerse students in doing some preliminary reading or viewing of testimony by people of color before moving gradually into a direct examination of their own experiences. Consuelo Cavalieri, Bryana French, and Salina Renninger; Pam Barnett; Mary Hess; Dianne Ramdeholl and Jaye Jones; Wendy Yanow; Susan Hadley; and Lisa Merriweather, Talmadge C. Guy, and Elaine Manglitz all emphasize the value of students hearing stories detailing the experience of being on the receiving end of racism. Several of these authors argue strongly for using feature films, documentaries, and video to present compelling images and representations of how white supremacy operates.

As Wendy Yanow points out, the point of scaffolding is to begin instruction at the point where many students are – the color-blind paradigm – and then move them into understanding the operation and pervasiveness of racism. Students new to this area of study often need an initiation period during which they stretch their cognitive and emotional hamstrings by doing the warm-up exercises described above. As they develop a basic grasp of the reality of systemic racism and start to trust their peers and teachers, the level of dissonance, contradiction, and discomfort can be ratcheted up. Students can be confronted with more complex ideas of privilege and white supremacy and invited to examine how these manifest themselves in their own lives.

Modeling

Modeling racial disclosure seems to be a dynamic that almost everyone in this book describes. One of the prime tasks of teachers of race is, as much as possible, to normalize the topic. By that I mean making the acknowledgment and discussion of racism as unremarkable as possible. When teachers tell stories of their own learned racism and disclose how white supremacist ideology still lives within them despite all their efforts to push back against it, this accomplishes several objectives. First, it provides students with an example of what an honest discussion of race can look like. Second, if the teacher is happy to provide current examples of how he or she engages in racist thinking or actions, this legitimizes students' attempts to do this.

Third, telling a story of a racially charged event in your own life offers an opportunity to link what seem like abstract concepts (privilege, supremacy, racism, critical race theory) to actual experience. It's so easy to keep the discussion of race at a level of generality that most are comfortable with. We can all condemn racism and laugh at the buffoonish actions of political leaders and right-wing media figures. But when I, Stephen Brookfield, describe my momentary surprise at seeing a senior leader, pilot, doctor, or academic who is black, I can illustrate how white supremacist ideology operates within me at a preconscious and subconscious level. George Yancy reveals that his students are shocked when they find out their philosophy professor is black, since philosophy is typically viewed as a Eurocentric white discourse. In his autobiography, Nelson Mandela (1994) provides a pertinent example of internalized racism when he discloses his alarm at seeing a black pilot enter the cockpit of his plane and immediately wonders if the plane will crash. Tim Wise noted the same reaction in his book *White Like Me* (Wise, 2005).

Community Building

The more students feel that they belong to a community of inquirers united in exploring a significant topic, the more they're emboldened to enter into racial discussions. Consuelo Cavalieri, Bryana French, and Salina Renninger describe how they build what they call a working alliance with students that's intended to foster mutual trust and rapport. Pam Barnett and Lucia Pawlowski both encourage students to develop their own norms and ground rules. Buffy Smith attempts to create a classroom *ohana*, a community in which no one is left behind and all experiences are valued.

The modeling described earlier is crucial in any effort at community building. If people are to start trusting each other, they need to know that they are encountering authentic selves. This requires people to open up about their own racism and give honest accounts of how they struggle to fight against learned instincts and biases. George Yancy shows how difficult this is for whites to do in *Backlash* (Yancy, 2018), his analysis of whites' responses to his letter titled "Dear White America" (Yancy, 2015) that was published as an op-ed piece in the *New York Times*.

Students need to see teachers talking about their experience of, and struggles with, racism as a precondition to doing this themselves. When teachers disclose their own passions, enthusiasms, frailties, and errors, this encourages students to do the same. Interestingly, when white students openly admit to their own learned racism and their struggle to identify and challenge this, students of color are appreciative. Instead of blaming whites for their unearned privilege and blindness to white supremacy, students of color give a sigh of relief that the elephant in the room – their peers' own racism – has been named.

Students who are digital natives frequently use social media to create cyber communities. They share details of their lives on Facebook, Instagram, Snapchat, Twitter, and so on. Lucia Pawlowski and Mary Hess point out that in real-time instruction, the anonymity of platforms such as TodaysMeet (https://todaysmeet.com) allows students to raise contentious issues in ways that can hasten the formation of community norms. This is particularly important when the credibility and authenticity of teachers are concerned. If students are skeptical of you because of your positionality, or if they just don't know enough about you to be able to judge whether or not you can be trusted to lead a group in the discussion of raw and explosive topics, a tool like TodaysMeet can be enormously helpful. Using this anonymous feed, students can challenge you and question your legitimacy with no negative consequences for them. If you can respond to a student's comment on your apparent racism in an open and nondefensive way, this demonstrates your willingness to delve deep into your own biases and microaggressions.

Watching Out for Repressive Tolerance

In one of the most formative influences on my thinking about how white supremacy maintains itself, Herbert Marcuse (1965) explicates the concept of repressive tolerance. Put very simply, repressive tolerance is the process by which institutions manage threats to their authority and legitimacy so that they appear to be changing while keeping things as they are. Instead of opposing the challenge by directly rebutting or discrediting those issuing critiques, institutions respond in a far subtler and ultimately more effective way. They appear to take the challenge seriously, creating working parties, task forces, and advisory committees to document the grievances being brought to their attention. They then make small, symbolic changes to institutional functioning and present these as substantive and important. But as all these things are happening, the fundamental structure remains unchanged. White supremacist consciousness remains in place and whites continue to hold the levers of power and determine institutional culture and policy.

The easiest repressively tolerant change to make is change the bodies that appear on your public documents. Find the minority of students and faculty of color at your institution and plaster their faces on your website, publicity materials, and billboards. Make sure you have a nicely balanced racial equation of African, Asian, Latin, and indigenous faces on your brochures so that your student body looks like a rainbow coalition. In the alumni magazine make sure you disproportionately profile students and faculty of color who have achieved something of note so that it looks like you devote considerable institutional resources to ensuring their success.

Playing this game of representational identity politics is the cheapest and most immediate move in the repressive tolerance jig. In a very short time, with some simple photoshopping and image manipulation, you can present to the world a dramatically altered version of the kind of institution you are. But the manipulative beauty of this strategy is that you don't actually have to do anything of importance. The numbers of students and faculty of color can stay exactly the same, even as it looks as if a relative equity of representation is in place.

But image manipulation can only go so far. Sooner or later institutions are pressured to increase the representation of different racial groups at all levels of the institution. Money is allocated specifically for scholarships to encourage a higher proportion of students from racial minorities to apply and search committees are urged to ensure that people of color are well represented in the candidate pool. The problem is that without addressing the ideology of white supremacy and attempting to uncover its presence at all levels of institutional functioning, members of minority racial groups admitted to the institution find themselves negotiating what they perceive as a hostile and unfriendly environment. The *Journal of Blacks in Higher Education* (2006) reported national data showing a 42% graduation rate for African American students compared with the 62% for white students and cited the unfavorable racial climate at some institutions as the first of several possible explanations for this statistic. An even worse 24-point difference was reported by the National Student Clearinghouse Research Center, with African American students demonstrating a 38% graduation rate compared with the 62% rate of whites (National Student Clearinghouse Research Center, 2017).

The same dynamic pertains to hiring faculty of color, especially at predominantly white colleges and universities. Myers's (2016) analysis of the racial identities of professors at all higher education institutions found that only 5% were black, 4% Hispanic, and 0.4% Native American. An analysis of how faculty of color experience college and university campuses across the United States and United Kingdom reports widespread feelings of alienation, of being outsiders drowning in a sea of whiteness, and of perceiving themselves as assailed on all sides by practices and policies steeped in white supremacy (Bhopal, 2016). Women faculty of color are particularly disregarded, often initially assumed by white students to be secretaries or administrative assistants (Cole Robinson and Clardy, 2010). Additionally, their appointment to the faculty is typically viewed only as a response to the mandatory imposition of affirmative action. Consequently, these women have to work twice as hard to establish their academic legitimacy. Both male and female faculty of color are also expected to take on a second unpaid teaching job of teaching white faculty colleagues about the nature of racism (McKinley Jones Brayboy, 2003).

Admitting larger numbers of students of color without a corresponding investment in administrative and academic support services for those students only serves to set many of them up for failure. If there is no effort at curricular change, and if faculty continue to work in a mostly color-blind way, then students of color will feel isolated, strangers in a strange land. There will need to be an institution-wide effort to identify practices and policies framed by white supremacy and a willingness by those in the most public positions of institutional authority and power to model their own commitment to examining how they too live out aspects of this ideology and how they struggle to fight it.

The final repressive tolerance strategy is to make a high-profile appointment of a person of color to the leadership team. The most common example is to create a diversity office, staffed by a chief diversity officer or senior vice president for diversity. That person is often the only person of color on the leadership team, and is assumed, by virtue of his or her racial identity, to have the authentic experience of being on the receiving end of racism. This is taken to qualify him or her as someone who is uniquely positioned to address white supremacy.

But chief diversity officers are often set up to fail. The fact that no other high-level leader is a person of color makes it harder for them to develop the network of personal relationships and support that whites enjoy. They are positioned as the exotic other, the voice of authentically racialized experience whom presidents and provosts can turn to and ask, "How does diversity play into this decision?" If the strategy developed to address the need for diversity is essentially to "add, mix, and stir" people of color into a mostly white environment, then difficult questions of racism and white supremacy can be kept at bay. But the real experts on how white supremacy as an ideology is learned and deeply internalized so that it frames daily actions, interpretations, and decisions, are whites. People like me are the learners and enactors of this ideology, so instead of turning to the only person of color on the senior leadership team for awareness of racial issues, the white members need to be examining the way that they are complicit in retaining whiteness as the unquestioned norm and standard of legitimacy.

The Ontology of Teaching Race – Nothing Works

A consistent theme explored in the forthcoming chapters is the fact that anyone engaged in this work constantly feels that they have made the wrong choice or could have done better. There's a constant desire to rewind the videotape and go back to the beginning of a class session for a do-over. So the basic ontology of race-based teaching – the fundamental nature and reality of engaging in this work – is that you continually feel things are spiraling out of control as your plans misfire. Chapters by Bobbi Smith and by me focus specifically on making and learning from mistakes, but almost all the other authors somehow refer to the regular experience of feeling surprised, disturbed, and discombobulated by events and, in the moment that crises occur, of not having any clue what to do next.

The first few times this happened in my career I was mortified and felt like a complete charlatan. Someone (sometimes I myself) would say or do something that produced palpable anxiety and anger. Because I had been socialized to assume that overt conflict in the classroom was something to be avoided at all costs, I would leave the class with an overwhelming sense of failure and shame at my incompetence. There would be two voices contending in my head. One would say, "I'm never doing that again! Why risk messing about in stuff you're unqualified to engage with?" The other one would say, "Hey, don't be so hard on yourself. This was your first time doing this. You'll get better with time and experience."

In the 1980s and 1990s there was a sort of fluctuation for me between building up the nerve to introduce race as an issue in class, seeing my efforts to do this apparently backfire in unforeseeable ways, backing off for a while after having been burned by a scarring classroom event, and then coming back and trying to do it again. Two decades into this work, in the late 1990s, I sort of got it: Teaching about race is not like teaching about other critical and controversial issues that critical theory explores (Brookfield,

2005). Its rawness means that you will probably constantly feel out of your depth and a total novice. I began to accept that I would leave every race-based class feeling that I had screwed up and lost control. So although I've been doing this to a greater or lesser degree for four decades, I know that I will never feel as if I really know what I'm doing.

This is when the ontological realization kicks in: The fundamental reality and experience of teaching race is feeling as if you're not getting it right. Once you accept that things will never go the way you anticipate, you start to reframe what success and failure means. I had grown up as a teacher believing that a successful class was one in which everyone left feeling equally valued, bonded in a common learning project, and enjoying equal opportunities to participate. A failed class, on the other hand, was one whose emotional tenor was out of control. By this I meant that heated emotions were present, and that people left feeling angry, even bitter, or that the discussion got off topic by veering wildly into uncharted waters. If we walked out of the room with some people feeling annoyed because we hadn't settled on a conclusion or view that everyone agreed with, and others accusing me of not giving them sufficient time to speak or complaining that the classroom was not a calm, safe space, then in my mind I had failed.

Lucia Pawlowski's chapter on brave space classrooms unpacks this notion of so-called safety very nicely, and I remember her one day saying to a group of colleagues, "There are two ways to teach about race – badly, or not at all." Once you understand that this pedagogic project is challenging and usually leaves people feeling disturbed, you gradually accept that feeling like an impostor is the nature of the beast. You start to reframe notions of what constitutes good and bad class sessions and come to understand that classroom success is, at a very basic level, simply having the conversation. Moreover, keeping a conversation going in the face of long periods of awkward silence; expressions of hurt, pain, and anger; tears; and the frustration being voiced that we're not reaching a solution is actually a raging success! I say again, simply having the conversation is an indicator of classroom success and keeping it going is a sign that you are an exemplary teacher. If teaching-evaluation forms had an item asking students to rate the degree to which they were discomfited, disturbed, or made to feel like their worldviews were shattered, then teachers of race would typically be ranked as stars instead of being punished in the way Buffy Smith describes. To help students become productively disturbed is the point of teaching race, and the rest of this book explores how we might do that.

References

Bell, L.A. (2010). *Storytelling for Social Justice: Connecting Narrative and the Arts in Antiracist Teaching*. New York, NY: Routledge.

Bhopal, K. (2016). *The Experiences of Black and Minority Ethnic Academics: A Comparative Study of the Unequal Academy*. New York, NY: Routledge.

Brookfield, S.D. (2005). *The Power of Critical Theory: Liberating Adult Learning and Teaching*. San Francisco, CA: Jossey-Bass.

Cole Robinson, C. and Clardy, P. (2010). *Tedious Journeys: Autoethnography by Women of Color in Academe*. New York, NY: Peter Lang.

Journal of Blacks in Higher Education. (2006). Black student graduation rates remain low, but modest progress begins to show. *Journal of Blacks in Higher Education* 50: 88, http://www.jbhe.com/features/50_blackstudent_gradrates.html (accessed 19 October 2017).

Mandela, N. (1994). *Long Walk to Freedom: The Autobiography of Nelson Mandela*. Boston, MA: Little Brown.

Marcuse, H. (1965). Repressive tolerance. In: *A Critique of Pure Tolerance* (ed. R. P. Wolff, B. Moore, and H. Marcuse), 95–137. Boston, MA: Beacon Press.

McKinley Jones Brayboy, B. (2003). The implementation of diversity in predominantly white colleges and universities. *Journal of Black Studies* 34 (1): 72–86.

Myers, B. (2016). Where are the minority professors? *Chronicle of Higher Education* (14 February), http://www.chronicle.com/interactives/where-are-the-minority-professors (accessed 19 October 2017).

National Student Clearinghouse Research Center. (2017). *Completing College: A National View of Student Attainment Rates by Race and Ethnicity*. Herndon, VA: National Student Clearinghouse Research Center.

Wise, T. (2005). *White Like Me: Reflections on Race from a Privileged Son*. New York, NY: Soft Skull Press.

Yancy, G. (2015). Dear white America. *New York Times Opinionator* (December 24), https://opinionator.blogs.nytimes.com/2015/12/24/dear-white-america (accessed 9 January 2018).

Yancy, G. (2018). *Backlash: What Happens When We Talk Honestly About Racism in America*. Lanham, MD: Rowman & Littlefield.

2

Guidelines for Whites Teaching About Whiteness

George Yancy

I am an African American philosopher who critically engages questions regarding race and its phenomenological, or *lived*, embodied and spatial dimensions, especially in terms of how certain processes of racialization violently impact black bodies and bodies of color. I am also part of a critical cadre of black philosophers and philosophers of color who have importantly shifted – through the important work of making more visible the philosophical voices and perspectives of black philosophers and philosophers of color – the Anglo-American philosophical metanarrative that holds that philosophy transcends race. In terms of whiteness, more specifically I am one of an even smaller group of philosophers of color who has written about whiteness as a site of power, privilege, hegemony, and, yet, paradoxically, a site of lived invisibility vis-à-vis white people. I also write about white identity formation, white embodiment, and the complexities and subtle contradictions involved in white antiracist praxis, especially as I theorize white antiracist praxis as a process, *not an arrival.*

As a black male, my work theorizes and critically engages primarily the black/white binary, but I don't see this as a philosophical or political restriction, especially as I argue that whiteness is structurally binary. The racialized other is structurally integral to whiteness.

Teaching Race: How to Help Students Unmask and Challenge Racism, First Edition. Stephen D. Brookfield and Associates.
© 2019 John Wiley & Sons, Inc. Published 2019 by John Wiley & Sons, Inc.

Who is constituted as other vis-à-vis whiteness isn't just restricted to black people of African descent. Yet, I take it as an important assumption that whiteness has significantly taken a racialized Manichean shape. Hence, while I don't argue for it here, I agree with Feagin and Vera (1995) when they argue that "white-on-black racism is thus a – if not *the* – crucial paradigmatic case of racism historically and in the present" (p. xii).

Let's be clear. When I enter a classroom, when I go shopping, when a white police officer sees me driving, or when on elevators with white people, they see a *black* man first: What they "see" is distorted through the prism of the white racial frame (Feagin, 2013). That reality informs how I pedagogically engage race and racial cognizance or the lack thereof, especially within the context of predominantly white institutions of higher learning. I bring such experiences to bear on my pedagogy, to show that the latter is inextricably linked to the former. So, the question of race, for me, is not simply about philosophical abstraction or the mastery of a set of key philosophical concepts. Rather, race involves and raises importantly lived, personal experiences of exclusion, marginalization, and even trauma.

More generally, race, for black people and people of color, involves life and death existential situations. Within the American context – a country founded upon white hegemony – race pertains to the subtle and not so subtle ways in which I am subjected to habituated and historically sanctioned white gazes that misrepresent me. There are white discourses and white microaggressions that assault me, and white meta-philosophical assumptions that refuse to recognize my lived experiences within an antiblack America and that thereby occlude the *philosophical* significance of my lived experiences. What I delineate up front in this section are important epistemological precursors for any good-intentioned white teachers to understand that from the start, before we enter the classroom to teach about race, we are already differentially situated in terms of race. You are white and I am black. That makes a hell of a difference.

I recall once that a white student said to me that she had expected that I would be a white male philosopher teaching the course. So, even prior to my arrival, there are racial assumptions about who I am or who I ought to be. Once I do arrive, however, what do the majority of my white students see? Do they see incompetence, inferiority, an exception, or perhaps the embodiment of the "violent" black male? What they see need not be conscious, but this neither minimizes how those unconscious assumptions unfold in terms of classroom dynamics, nor mitigates the sense of trauma that black students and teachers have come to experience within the context of mundane, apparently benign encounters with white students in class. The white student who spoke about what she expected had already placed me under erasure. She expected a "philosopher" (that is, a "real" white philosopher).

That I am embodied as black can function against me within the context of teaching about race and whiteness, as many white students have already been inculcated with assumptions that what I have to say about race and whiteness is primarily ideological. They assume that I have a personal ax to grind, that I will play the race card throughout the semester, or that I want them to feel guilt. One white male student on a visit home told his father that we were discussing white privilege and he shared with the class that his father said, "Watch out for that Dr. Yancy; he wants you to feel guilt." That could have been the reactionary message that completely shut down my white student's openness to undergoing processes of potential transformation regarding his own whiteness and the ways he had just begun to think about whiteness as an historical and contemporary systemic phenomenon. Luckily, in this case, there was nothing about my pedagogy that suggested that my aim was to generate in my white students a paralyzing sense of white guilt.

However, if you are a *white* teacher who seriously teaches about race you will be granted a level of unquestioned epistemic credibility by white students, you will be seen as a white ally, and you will bring, pedagogically, to the classroom your whiteness and the ways in which it insidiously constitutes your cognition, affect, and assumptions. In short, as a white teacher you will have already been problematically impacted by the very subject (that is, race) that you are trying to teach. Students of color, by the way, will rightly question your integrity and sincerity. Yet, as a white, you *must* accept their skepticism.

Even some black students and students of color will grant unquestioned epistemic credibility to white teachers in ways that they will not grant credibility to black teachers and teachers of color. They have come to internalize the white gaze, a gaze that, in this case, has negative implications for how they see their own epistemic credibility. As I have only taught at predominantly white institutions of higher learning, it is important that black students and students of color, especially within the field of philosophy (the whitest field within the humanities), are exposed to black academics and academics of color. Such students are not witnessing racially diverse people in positions of academic authority; indeed, they are not seeing themselves in those who teach them.

Lastly, what I have discovered is that predominately white classrooms and academic institutions function as microcosms of the larger white societal ethos. I've had situations where white students have told other white students that "Dr. Yancy hates white people!" When false claims of this sort make their way to the dean's office, especially if one doesn't have tenure and is a scholar of color, this can potentially negatively impact one's academic career and one's larger livelihood. White students, unfortunately, don't get how, within these contexts, they are actually exercising their white privilege and how they are benefitting from the protection of white institutional mores that also distort and evade the importance of critically naming whiteness, both individually and institutionally.

So, as a philosopher who engages whiteness within the classroom and who engages whiteness within the framework of doing public philosophy, there are potential dangers. In terms of public philosophy, I wrote a letter called "Dear White America" (Yancy, 2015a). In the letter, I maintained that the letter was a *gift* to white America, a gift that was designed to invite levels of honesty and critical consciousness regarding *their* racism, a potential gift of liberation. Immediately after it appeared in the *New York Times*, however, the letter went viral and I began to receive a huge number of vitriolic responses from white readers in the form of electronic messages, voice messages, and physical letters that were filled with nauseatingly white racist epithets and threats. One would have thought that I wrote an asinine article entitled "Why I Hate White People."

There was, however, a specifically important pedagogical offshoot, as many professors from around the country had their students read the letter. Even high school teachers had their students read the letter, some of whom encouraged their students to write to me personally, though with respect. I also received quite a large number of messages from white readers who spoke to me about how the letter had transformed their lives, touched their hearts (their words), and encouraged them to take a hard look at their racism. They thanked me for the gift.

So, why the inclusion of the story about "Dear White America"? I share this story, and provide one of the responses below, to make it clear that there are real *existential* risks when, as a black philosopher, a black citizen of a so-called racially inclusive polity, I decide to address a larger white audience outside the classroom proper. Think of the cumulative impact of the existential stakes outside the classroom along with the frustrations experienced within the context of the classroom – the intimations that I hate white students, accusations of my racist biases and generalizations toward white students, and assumptions that I'm protecting my own narrow (antiwhite) ideological interests. While I have never had a white student, to my knowledge, call me a nigger or threaten my life, I want to mark clearly the shared vociferous defensiveness and obfuscation that many white students express toward me as I critically engage and expose *their* whiteness in the classroom, and the deep defensiveness and bad faith expressed by the larger white public regarding *their* whiteness.

All of this can and does negatively impact one's pedagogical enthusiasm and one's aspirations as a public intellectual. While there is overlap, unabashed public white racist attacks obviously don't take the form that they do within relatively "respectful" white classroom spaces. Hence, there is also the need to mark how, when assaulted by white readers who disagree with my views, I have been discursively assaulted in *racist* terms. Keep in mind that my white public intellectual colleagues have also written controversial articles, and participated in public philosophy, but they have not been, to my knowledge, *racially attacked*, though some did receive threats. The above-mentioned response, sent to my university email address, read:

> I read your rant regarding white people, and I'm proud
> to inform you that I will never feel any guilt or shame
> for being white or who I am. FUCK YOU you race
> baiting piece of shit! You're just another nigger with a
> chip on his shoulder that's looking for excuses to justify
> his hatred, and guess what asshole NOBODY WHITE
> GIVES A FUCK WHAT YOU THINK. My only regret
> is that I didn't hear your bullshit in person so that I could
> call you a FUCKING NIGGER to your face you worth-
> less bitch, and then kick your black ass until you were
> half dead. FUCK OFF BOY.

This response speaks to so many complex layers of the white imaginary, levels of white obfuscation, white discursive violence, and a desire to carry out actual white violence. My aim is not to discuss all of this here. The email, one of many, speaks to America's race problem; indeed, I would argue that it speaks to America's whiteness problem.

It is important here to reiterate to well-intentioned white teachers that you are *privileged not* to talk about race and your whiteness. Personally, you can just walk away. You have that privilege just as you have the privilege not to have "the talk" with your white children about white police brutality. There is no necessity or even second thought about how you must warn your children about their so-called furtive movements in the presence of white police officers and their proxies. I don't have such privileges, and the stakes are too high for me to pretend that I do. This brings me back to the point about being differentially situated in terms of race. I was asked recently by a Latina philosophy graduate student, "Why do you do this? Why do you teach white people about their whiteness given the level of threat?" I could only respond by saying that I must do it for my black sons and for those white people who are young enough and willing enough to be transformed so that they might vigorously resist white anti-black racism, white privilege, and white inordinate power. The subtext of my response is that to be black in America is to be trapped. If I critique whiteness, I incur forms of hatred from white people. If I don't critique whiteness, I incur forms of hatred from white people. So, I *must* act pedagogically within the classroom to teach about race and teach about race within larger public spaces of learning; each space has potential for important acts of liberation.

Pedagogical Approaches

In this section of the chapter I will describe two pedagogical approaches that I have found to be very effective within contexts of teaching white students about race. First, I show the importance of vulnerability and frank speech that is necessary on the part of white teachers who work to get white students to understand their own whiteness. Pedagogically performing vulnerability and frank speech helps white teachers to mark whiteness, to show how race isn't something that marks only black people and people of color, and to challenge the fact that white students have accepted a false neoliberal conception of themselves as free from inheriting and perpetuating white privilege and power. This is a pedagogical practice in which white teachers must be prepared to foreground their own whiteness.

Second, I offer a practical exercise of requiring white students to keep a journal of white racist encounters that take place within the context of exclusively white people. I have found that this practice helps white students to be acutely attentive to white racist situations, discourses, practices, and stereotypes that are pervasively manifest within their encounters with friends and family. The exercise facilitates awareness of just how white racism operates within their everyday social spheres of transaction and encourages critical self-reflectivity regarding their problematic silences and the extent of white racist assumptions that they possess.

The Pedagogy of Vulnerability and Frank Speech in the Classroom

In the context of classrooms where I critically engage race and whiteness, I find that white students enter those spaces with a false understanding of themselves as autonomous (as if presocial), free from the weight of white racist history, and exempt from perpetuating systemic white oppression, which devastatingly impacts black people and people of color, and which has deep implications for their sense of white moral "innocence." They firmly believe in meritocracy and fully embrace the Horatio Alger myth; that is, they believe that it is through hard work and ability alone that people achieve and make it in America and that their white ancestors achieved what they did by pulling themselves up by their bootstraps. They see themselves as neoliberal, atomic subjects who are untouched by the forces of white history and white social structures. They see themselves as not raced at all: For them, to be white is to be human as such.

In short, my white students have been inculcated by a white racist ideology that is so taken for granted that how they see themselves is taken as an a priori truth. Yet, isn't this the function of ideology? Peggy McIntosh (1997) writes, "My schooling gave me no training in seeing myself as an oppressor, as an unfairly advantaged person, or as participating in a damaged culture. I was taught to see myself as an individual whose moral state depended on her individual moral will" (p. 292). Her schooling, in my view, was complicit with and helped to sustain an ideology of white privilege, which renders such privilege invisible.

Because I obviously can't claim white privilege, I use sexism to illustrate how ideology inserts itself into my consciousness to frame how I regard the other – in this case women. With respect to sexism, I was also taught *not* to see myself as an oppressor, but to see my moral will as something separate from what was true about the larger sexist, hegemonic context within which I was, upon later critical reflection, indeed an oppressor. The point here is that the ways in which I've come to relate to women – how I look at women, how I fantasize about them, how I feel this impulse to open doors for them and pull out chairs, and how the woman that I would marry would presumably take my last name without any questions asked – are deeply informed and shaped by patriarchal, misogynistic assumptions and practices that are systemic and performed privately and publicly. In fact, these practices could be viewed as acts of violence against women. Yet, through a sexist and patriarchal ideology I was inculcated to believe that such ways of interacting with women involved what it meant to be a male, pure and simple.

So, there is the truth of the matter. I am complicit with the sexist oppression of women. When I came to realize this, it was hard, especially as it brought to my awareness the ways in which I helped to perpetuate a damaged culture consisting of sexist violence that is responsible for the denigration of women. That realization is extremely difficult to bear. And, yet, I must bear it and try not to flee in bad faith, which is a continuous struggle. Critically tarrying with the gravitas of my sexism, not trying to flee, rationalize, or normalize it, not only deepens how I conceptualize the world in gendered oppressive terms but also heightens the urgency for forms of personal and collective liberation praxes that interrogate hegemonic conceptions of masculinity, challenge structural sexism, and thereby create just and safe spaces for women in and outside the classroom.

So, how does the social, relational, and embodied marking of
the reality of my sexism pedagogically impact my classrooms, especially my white students? And how can the critical consciousness
about, and disclosure of, my sexism in my classrooms function as a
model for white teachers to engage in acts of vulnerability and
frankness when it comes to critically discussing race/whiteness?
Well, within the context of my classrooms, where I teach about
race and whiteness, I tell the truth. I risk vulnerability: "I am a sexist!" While this declaration is meant for all of my students, I specifically have in mind my white students. I want to communicate
to them the importance of vulnerability and the importance of
accepting how social and historical structures impact our lives in
ways that we didn't ask for and yet in terms of which we help to
sustain and therefore for which we must take responsibility.

It is through the process of marking my own sexism that I pedagogically model for my students how to engage critically, openly,
and boldly their whiteness as a site of racism. They initially look at
me in silence. Many are stunned. Many are no doubt thinking,
"Why would a male professor say such a thing, indict himself?" Yet,
my white students have later confided in me that it was my pedagogical practice of vulnerability regarding my sexism and my use of
frank speech that emboldened them to think differently and more
insightfully about their whiteness, to speak in class about their
whiteness, to lay claim to their own white racism. The objective is
to explain to my white students that I am not a horrible human
being, but that this doesn't free me from oppressing women and,
thereby, doesn't exempt me from taking responsibility for perpetuating that oppression. I'm not a horrible human being as such, and
certainly don't abuse women, but I explain that being a sexist has
implications that are directly related to questions of my "violence"
against women. It is this oppressive treatment of women that negatively implicates the status of aspects of my ethical standing.

Once I have called myself out, as it were, as a sexist, and even
shared personal examples of how sexism gets performed both consciously and unconsciously in my daily life, many of the students

begin to get it, to comprehend how we are all defined and structured by social and historical forces that exist beyond our *complete*
control. More importantly, for me, in terms of the aim of this disclosure regarding my sexism, my white students' vocabulary, their
theoretical orientation, and how they think of their embodied
existence begins to shift in terms of highlighting how they are
socially embedded, not simply autonomous, but heteronomous.
Hence, their understanding of themselves as fundamentally
socially relational beings emerges. Concurrently, their understanding of white responsibility shifts toward a collective one, a
conceptual shift that provides insight into their own complicity
with white racism.

This process of relearning is not easy. White students often
persist in their denials, they shift in their seats, their faces contort
in great discomfort. As one white female student disclosed before
the entire class, "This feels like choking, but I am a racist." Some
white students even miss class because of the level of discomfort.
Some have teared up. And a few leave at the end of the semester
apparently unmoved. Yet, many undergo a form of conceptual
and embodied disorientation that leaves them ethically disturbed
and eager to engage in acts of liberation. I am then reassured
that "to educate" is, as bell hooks (1994) says, "the practice of
freedom" (p. 13).

By openly declaring the truth about my sexism I hope to change
my white students' understanding of racism so they can begin to
see themselves as racist. They see me as a decent human being, but
come to understand that that sense of decency is complicated once
theorized through a relationally embedded conception of sexism.
They realize that within a systemic sexist society, what I do or fail
to do has implications for the safety or lack thereof regarding
women. I've introduced a counterintuitive understanding of what
it means to be embodied. I explain to them that our bodies have no
edges, no outside limit within sexist and racist hegemonic sociohis-
torical matrixes. Mine is an ontology that argues that we are always
already touching. The aim is to find radically new ways of touching

that involve mutually liberational forms of being in the world; it is about radically rethinking our social, institutional, and existential phenomenological being.

By engaging theory, and introducing rich conceptual metaphors, there are also implied aims. For hooks (1994), theory fulfills the function of liberation "when we ask that it do so and direct our theorizing towards that end" (p. 61). For me, pedagogically, through vulnerability, honesty, and frank speech regarding my sexism, I've been able to establish an *affective* space, a pervasive mood, that enlarges and deepens how students previously *felt* about the world, their social locations, and their complicity with white racist forms of oppression. What occurs, pedagogically, in the process of my white students modeling my vulnerability and frankness of speech is the accomplishment of reciprocal *trust* – fragile, but powerful.

My pedagogical advice, then, if you are a white teacher, is to risk vulnerability, engage in frank speech – offer a gesture of trust in advance. Say it: "I am a racist!" Sure, there is the risk of eliciting from black students and students of color a range of intense emotional reactions, but you are required to explain what you mean by the declaration. Be prepared for the initial reaction from white students who might attempt to distance themselves from you, "the white racist." Your aim is to contextualize the declaration. One way of thinking about such a declaration is in terms of ideology critique, where the pedagogical function of the declaration helps white students come to an awareness of how whiteness shapes oppressive social relations (Brookfield, 2005) that are not predicated upon intent or voluntary action, but yet implicates them. As their white teacher, through your open declaration, you have modeled vulnerability and frank speech. You've exemplified that your classroom will function as a courageous space within which students should not be afraid to be vulnerable.

As their teacher, you're also complicating their understanding of white racism, especially for those who associate white racism with the KKK or with a few whites who belong to a "lunatic fringe, not with the everyday life of well-meaning white citizens"

(Wildman and Davis, 2008, p. 12). More specifically, in this way, you model for them that white racism is not simply restricted to the show of overt racist hate or prejudice (Olson, 2004, p. 104) and that *benefitting from* white systemic racism is connected to *contributing to* the maintenance of that system. You further trouble the "good white/bad white" distinction. You explain to them that you are not a horrible white person, but that this does not exempt you from the relational dimensions of white privilege and power. It implicates you in socially, politically, and economically oppressive relations.

I have had white students say to me that they understand that they possess white privilege, but refuse to admit that such privilege is oppressive to black people and people of color. Here it is important to engage pedagogically the work of white scholars who also model forms of white vulnerability and frank and bold speech, who are courageous to lay bare the complex ways in which systemic racism works. In this way, they come to realize that there are many well-intentioned, well-educated white people who refuse to avoid the ways in which white privilege implicates them in oppressive systems. Within this context, silence not only supports white power, but violates the epistemic and lived integrity of black students and students of color who have been negatively impacted by everyday forms of white racism as they move through predominantly white institutions, your place of employment. Many black students and students of color have said to me, outside the earshot of their white teachers and peers, that they wish that their white teachers would just tell the truth and admit their racism. They imply that this act could lead to greater trust from them. Many of those students are crying out, to little or no avail, to have their suffering validated within such white academic spaces.

Rarely have my white students, even my philosophy graduate students who are white, previously engaged in open forms of vulnerability regarding their own racism. And frank speech, more generally, about white racism was out of the question. This is why there is so much visible discomfort and deep silence when I've asked white students: "Are any of you racists?" I once overheard one white undergraduate student as she left the room say to another white student, "Did you hear what he asked us?" There were elements of shock and indignation.

To educate as the practice of freedom is by no means easy. So, it is important to incorporate the voices of other white thinkers who take seriously the aims of creating a brave pedagogical space. For example, introduce them to the work of Stephanie M. Wildman, who writes, "Some readers may be shocked to see a white person contritely acknowledge that she is a racist. I do not say this with pride. I simply believe that no matter how hard I work at not being racist, I still am. Because part of racism is systemic, I benefit from the privilege that I am struggling to see" (Wildman and Davis, 2008, p. 114). Or share with them the critical pedagogical work of Barbara Applebaum (2010), which argues that the white complicity claim "maintains that white people, through the practices of whiteness and by benefitting from white privilege, contribute to the maintenance of systemic racial injustice" (p. 3).

It is important to point out that your pedagogically courageous declaration regarding your own white racism is not about performing "white gallant" acts of self-confession. The concept of confession may have problematic ties to forms of white self-flagellation. Your black students and students of color don't need confessions, but demonstrations of your critical consciousness regarding how your whiteness has implications for their oppression. Your white students are in need of white teachers to emulate what it means to critique the taken-for-granted white order of things. There is no need for white savior figures. It is not about you or seeking your students' praises; after all, that just reinscribes whiteness as the "glorified" center. Rather, it is about your capacity to bring painful attention to the complexity of racism, of modeling for your white students and helping them to understand how critically engaged education (*educare*, "to lead out") is about their practice of freedom, their resistance to white hegemony, and their practice of ideology critique.

White students need white teachers who are prepared to *un-suture* (Yancy, 2015b, pp. xi–xxvii), which is my term for white people critically and honestly exposing the ways in which they have both internalized whiteness as normative and exposing the ways in which they are fundamentally, even if unconsciously, cooperative with oppressive structures of racist violence without the immediate temptation to cover over such disturbing realities. Within such a pedagogical context, un-suturing is about modeling white vulnerability, frank speech, and processes of mourning or lamenting the horrors that white racism has created and continues to generate. Lament, within the classroom, can function as a form of speech that talks back to oppressive orders. As hooks (1989) writes, "It is that act of speech, of 'talking back,' that is no mere gesture of empty words, that is the expression of our movement from object to subject – the liberated voice" (p. 9).

Race Journals: The Pedagogical Importance of Chronicling Backstage White Racism

At the beginning of my courses on race, I assign my white students the task of keeping a journal or diary of their everyday encounters with white racism, many of which they would normally simply overlook or interpret as of no significant meaning for themselves or for their white friends and family members whom they are required to record. I acquired the idea for this assignment from the significant and insightful sociological work done by Joe R. Feagin and his colleagues. As Feagin (2013) writes, "I have found that much blatantly racist thought, commentary, and performance has become concentrated in the social 'backstage,' that is, social settings where only whites are present" (p. 124). I typically instruct my students, over the course of 12 to 15 weeks, to record anything that they witnessed in the "backstage" that had racist implications.

This is an unusual assignment for undergraduate philosophy courses, and perhaps too empirical. Many of my white students are skeptical. They assume that their diaries will be short and sparse. However, the assignment pushes them to new levels of attentive acuity and troubles their illusions about how racism is not an inti-mate part of the fabric of their everyday existence. White students often come in believing that racism is basically over, that we live in a post-racial America, and that if racism does exist it is episodic and infrequent. Keeping a journal of backstage racism is consistent with the assumption that racism permeates America in the form of microracist acts, subtle racist sensibilities, beliefs, discourse, and perceptual practices that white students have come into contact with on campus, in their homes, and in other social settings. Moreover, through frank speech, I encourage white teachers to tes-tify on behalf of the epistemic integrity of black students and stu-dents of color who know about the existence of hidden forms of racism that play out on the backstage of white social life.

Yet, even here, I think that white teachers should openly mark the ways in which they have been silent when present during those contexts where only white people were present. White teachers need to speak to how that silence makes them complicit with backstage racism. In this way, white teachers don't convey false distances between themselves and the subtle ways in which they have been exposed and participated in, even if indirectly, common practices of racist tendencies and assumptions. I have found that well-intentioned white people are often ambushed by racist tendencies and assumptions that they would otherwise deny that they have when asked (Yancy, 2017).

Typically, in any given semester, white students will attempt to convince me that they constitute a new generation that has funda-mentally changed when it comes to treating black people in racist ways. They assure me that they are different from their parents and grandparents. I have yet to be convinced. As a white teacher, it is incumbent upon you to raise the fact that de facto white racism is alive and well. While optimistic, I have found that my white stu-dents have not really understood the social and existential dynam-ics of what it means to be black in America; they have not come to terms with white America's embedded and recalcitrant racist his-torical past and present. Richard Wright (1996) writes, "I feel that for white America to understand the significance of the problem of [the vast majority of black people] will take a bigger and tougher America than any we have yet known. I feel that America's past is too shallow, her national character too superficially optimistic, her very morality too suffused with color hate for her to accomplish so vast and complex a task" (p. 213).

In the journal entries shared here, the reader will note the overwhelming and pervasive themes of antiblack racism, racist imagery, racist jokes, hatred and fear of miscegenation, use of the term *nigger*, and racist stereotypes. The journal entries belie the bad-faith discourse about our so-called post-race moment in American history. Consider the following:

> I was with my family and we were discussing my Super Bowl plans. My dad mentioned how he didn't want me to go downtown after the game because it could get crazy. Someone else agreed and said I shouldn't go off campus because it will be dark and there are black people.

> I was sitting in my guy friends' room while they watched a movie. One friend poured half his Monster energy drink into a cup for another friend. I told him I was taking a sip, grabbed the glass, and did so. When I sat the glass back down he looked mortified. I asked what was wrong and he pointed to saliva left on the side of the glass and replied, "You nigger-lipped it!"

> I was on the phone with my boyfriend and he asked, "What's the difference between a large pizza and a black man?" I told him that I didn't know, and then he answered that "A large pizza can feed a family of four, but a black man can't."

> I was out to dinner with my friend and my text message notification went off on my cell phone. My ringtone is a P. Diddy song, and my friend, joking around, said, "...I didn't know you liked nigger music."

Yesterday alone I can count many instances where I heard the word nigger, or a variation (niglet, nig-nog, nig). I was playing video games with my friend, not of African American background, and he would say the word nigger after throwing an interception or when I would score. Another instance was when I received a text message from my friend, also a Caucasian, and after I answered his question, he said, "Alright, thanks nig-nog."

I went to get my nails done with one of my friends, and while we were picking out our nail polish colors I asked her what she thought of a dark purple. Jokingly, she said that that dark of a nail polish would make my nails look like nigger nails.

A couple of friends and I were talking about guys we liked. One girl had a black guy who asked for her number. She said she was afraid because he was so intimidating, so she gave it to him. Later on in the conversation, she said she could never marry him because "if we had kids, I wouldn't know how to take care of their hair."

My friend and I were discussing ways to become rich. She suggested that she should adopt an African baby so he will be a sports star and share his millions with her once he grows up.

Last night, a group of friends were drinking in [M] and [G]'s room. I picked up a stuffed raccoon off of [G]'s bed. One of the boys in the room said, "Oh [M], that's something you and [G] have in common: you both sleep with coons.

One white girl was talking about why she could not date a black guy and she mentioned the black hands. "When they turn over their hand, that is really gross – they look like gorilla's hands."

One white guy told me his secret [thoughts] while he was boxing…he always imagined his girlfriend being banged by some really big black guy and this [makes him] so pissed that he could go all out in boxing.

My friend's grandmother, while driving through a bad part of town, spotted some black people. "The neighborhood is going downhill," she sighed.

Some of my friends at [university] were talking about Wiz Khalifa before our class started and the one girl made the comment that "black people have two goals in life – sell drugs or try to be a rapper."

My mom and I [were] watching Teen Mom on MTV and one of the girls on the show started dating a black man. My mom made derogatory comments about a white girl dating a black guy, and said that he looked like he was "no good."

My dad and I were watching the Grammys and throughout the show there were a few different black rap and hip-hop artists that performed. When one of the artists was performing…my mom said she thought that he had already performed a song and my dad said that he was pretty sure this was [a] different guy but you can't be sure because they all look the same. I just gave my dad a look and he said he was just kidding but for some reason it bothers me more when my family make[s] jokes than when my friends make jokes.

I was at a house party for St. Patrick's Day and a guy walked in and greeted his friend by saying "Sup nigga" [and] then stops, looks around and says, "O good there aren't any black people here, I can say that."

Pedagogically, after a respectful discussion with black students and students of color about how they might feel uncomfortable having the entries read aloud, have your white students read their entries out and ask them to think critically about what the entries say about the dynamics of race/whiteness within our contemporary moment. Ask them how many times prior to the assignment must they have witnessed backstage racism and yet remained silent.

This journaling assignment encourages critically engaged forms of listening and unmasking taken-for-granted racism and can also encourage new ways of thinking about complicity on their part. White teachers should encourage white students to call out their white friends and white parents on their racism. "I don't find that funny at all." "That was so racist and offensive." "I refuse to tolerate any use or variation of the word *nigger* in or outside of my company from you." "I didn't know that you held such racist beliefs." Encouraging your white students to call out their friends and parents is consistent with hooks's powerful practice of talking back, but it also reveals how you, as a white teacher, understand the importance of engaged pedagogy outside of the classroom. Paulo Freire (2000) writes, "Human existence cannot be silent, nor can it be nourished by false words, but only true words, with which men and women transform the world" (p. 88). The objective is to model for your white students the fluidity between the classroom and the larger social and political world; to teach them that critical education must impact larger liberation efforts. Yet, you must also communicate to your white students that having them call out their friends and family members can be very uncomfortable and risky. Indeed, it can result in the potential loss of friendships and rebuke from family members. In some cases, it can cost the loss of parental love.

This is when, as a white teacher, you pedagogically draw from your own experiences of having found it necessary to engage in frank speech and openly discuss the risks involved when it comes to friends and loved ones who continue to perpetuate antiblack racism in your presence. Feagin (2013) writes, "… what is particularly striking here and in numerous other student diary accounts is how the participants describe friends who do these blatantly racist performances as 'nice,' 'fun to hang out with,' or 'not a racist'" (p. 124).

He maintains that the concept of *white virtue* and a colorblind ideology, which are deeply embedded within what he calls a white racial frame, both play a role in preventing white students from labeling as racist what is so clearly the case. This is where a pedagogy of unmasking is so important. Articulate for your white students how the insidious assumptions about white virtue occludes their marking the racism of their friends and family members. This will involve a deeper discussion about how such terms as *goodness*, *cleanliness*, and *purity* function as tropes of whiteness and have impacted the consciousness of your white students. Also, a larger critical pedagogical discussion of colorblind racism – the refusal to see not only forms of white racism that is evident within the racial structural arrangement of the larger society, but also the racism of their friends, relatives, and themselves – is imperative.

At the end of her journal, one white student entered a personal reflection that was unsolicited and that summarized her feelings about the assignment, one that was both insightful and validating:

> When I was given this assignment, I thought that I would have a really hard time getting journal entries, but I really have not, which was very surprising to me. Until you really listen to what people are saying and are making jokes about, you don't always realize how racist or negative the outcomes really are. This assignment really opened my eyes up to how many people I surround myself with are racist. I don't think that this means that they are horrible people, but I do think that it shows how ignorant they can be. I think that being white in America can really make someone racist without them even knowing. This is something that needs to be changed, but it will take time and effort to do that. Keeping this journal has also made me think twice sometimes about ideas in my head that I had about other people. This assignment was very interesting to do, and was very eye-opening to things that I never realized were occurring around me every day.

I will end here. It is so important pedagogically to get our students to think twice, to really open their eyes, to be attentive to the ideas in their heads. For me, the white student's unsolicited message brought home the importance of hooks's (1994) understanding that a classroom remains a location of possibility and a space of radical openness. As educators, we must transgress and oppose all manifestations of oppressive structures. We must affirm our fallibility and yet constantly recommit to radical educational practices that translate into liberation for all. Within the context of predominantly white institutions, white educators as allies are necessary to demonstrate for their white students what it means to be brought to the edge of vulnerability and frank speech and then be instructed to leap.

References

Applebaum, B. (2010). *Being White, Being Good: White Complicity, White Moral Responsibility, and Social Justice Pedagogy*. Lanham, MD: Lexington Books.

Brookfield, S.D. (2005). *The Power of Critical Theory: Liberating Adult Learning and Teaching*. San Francisco, CA: Jossey-Bass.

Feagin, J.R. (2013). *The White Racial Frame: Centuries of Racial Framing and Counter-Framing*, 2nd ed. New York, NY: Routledge.

Feagin, J.R. and Vera, H. (1995). *White Racism*. New York, NY: Routledge.

Freire, P. (2000). *Pedagogy of the Oppressed*, 30th Anniversary Edition. New York: Continuum International.

hooks, b. (1989). *Talking Back: Thinking Feminist, Thinking Black*. Boston, MA: South End Press.

hooks, b. (1994). *Teaching to Transgress: Education as the Practice of Freedom*. New York, NY: Routledge.

McIntosh, P. (1997). White privilege and male privilege: A personal account of coming to see correspondences through work in women's studies. In: *Critical White Studies: Looking Behind the Mirror* (ed. R. Delgado and J. Stefancic), 291–299. Philadelphia, PA: Temple University Press.

Olson, J. (2004). *The Abolition of White Democracy*. Minneapolis, MN: University of Minnesota Press.

Wildman, S.M. and Davis, A.D. (2008). Making systems of privilege visible. In: *White Privilege: Essential Readings on the Other Side of Racism* (ed. P.S. Rothenberg), 109–116. New York, NY: Worth Publishers.

Wright, R. (1996). *Eight Men*. New York, NY: Harper Perennial.

Yancy, G. (2015a). Dear white America. *New York Times Opinionator*, https://
opinionator.blogs.nytimes.com/2015/12/24/dear-white-america (accessed
9 January 2018).

Yancy, G. (2015b). Introduction: Un-suture. In: *White Self-Criticality Beyond
Anti-Racism: How Does It Feel to Be a White Problem?* (ed. G. Yancy),
xi–xxvii. Lanham, MD: Lexington Books.

Yancy, G. (2017). *Black Bodies, White Gazes: The Continuing Significance of Race
in America*. Lanham, MD: Rowman & Littlefield.

3

Teaching Whiteness in Predominantly White Classrooms

Susan Hadley

This chapter outlines the 10 strategies that I have found to be most effective in getting students to become aware of how they are racialized as whites. The majority of my students are white, and I want them to become more aware of the ways in which they are positioned and the way they unintentionally position others as a result of their white racial formation. Some of these strategies are sequential, others simultaneous. Many of these have been borrowed or adapted from others who have impacted my thinking in profound ways through their writings and teachings. Although I write as a white music therapy professor teaching race to predominantly white music therapy students, I trust that the strategies that I describe can be utilized by teachers in a wide variety of settings.

When I "Became" White

It is my first day of grad school at Temple University. I am both nervous and excited to be in a new city, Philadelphia, in a country halfway around the world from Australia. As I get onto a crowded bus at 26th and Girard, I look around to find a seat. They are all taken. I put my arm up and hold on to the strap for support. As I take in my surroundings,

Teaching Race: How to Help Students Unmask and Challenge Racism, First Edition.
Stephen D. Brookfield and Associates.
© 2019 John Wiley & Sons, Inc. Published 2019 by John Wiley & Sons, Inc.

I am suddenly acutely aware that I am white. I feel hypervisible for the first time in my life. Of course, I've been white all my life, but now I'm much more aware of my whiteness. Here I am, living in a predominantly African American neighborhood, the only white person on the bus, no longer surrounded by a familiar sea of whiteness.

Moving to Philadelphia meant, for the first time in my life, that I was in the racial minority. In my new neighborhood, I was constantly aware of the color of my skin. I felt that negative assumptions were being made about me based purely on my skin color, and I felt angry that I was not being seen for the person I felt I was. At the time, I thought it gave me empathy for those who were so often in the minority. However, what I came to learn was that even though I was temporarily in the minority for those moments, I was in a larger society that privileges whiteness. In the wider world, whiteness is the norm against which standards of beauty, achievement, and morality are judged. Racial depictions on magazine covers, on television, in the news, on radio, and in films only confirmed that. In politics, stores, my music, other classes, and the textbooks I read, the subtleties of whiteness were embedded in many forms. I have witnessed countless ways in which my whiteness affords me unearned advantages, while people of color are systemically disadvantaged.

While studying and working in Philadelphia I met my husband, who is African American. Now my whiteness gets performed in so many of my everyday encounters. Through our relationship and our regular conversations about race, I have become significantly more aware of the dynamics of whiteness, racialization, and racism. Being in an interracial relationship has opened me up to a whole new way of seeing the world. I found myself in more honest conversations about race. I learned from mistakes I made. I began to realize how unaware I was regarding the dynamics of race. There were many times when I felt, and sometimes still feel (almost 25 years on), defensive. There are times still when I want a break from thinking and talking about race. But that is coming from a standpoint of whiteness. I can't afford not to think about it. We now have four boys who need me to be aware all the time.

As I became more aware of how whiteness operates in my daily life and in our society generally, I realized I needed to bring these new understandings into my work as a music therapy educator, training future music therapists. In music therapy, race and culture were rarely discussed, and when they were it was mostly in terms of finding ways to work effectively with people from "other" cultures. The focus was almost always in an outward direction from a central point of whiteness, with little or no explicit naming of whiteness as normative and problematic. I felt that it was very important to turn the focus inward. My aim was to engage music therapists in critically exploring ways in which their race impacts their values and beliefs, and in turn the therapeutic relationship and the therapeutic process. The 10 strategies described below represent some of the ways I have tried to do this.

Strategy 1: "I Am..."

As an introductory experience, I ask students to complete an "I am..." worksheet. This strategy comes from psychologist Beverley Daniel Tatum (2003) who asks students to respond to the "I am..." prompt with as many descriptors as they can think of in 60 seconds. After years of doing this she noticed that while students of color often included their racial or ethnic group, white students rarely mentioned being white. She noticed similar patterns in terms of gender, religion, sexuality, and, I assume, disability. She notes:

> Common across these examples is that in the areas where a person is a member of the dominant or advantaged social group, the category is usually not mentioned. That element of their identity is so taken for granted by them that it goes without comment. It is taken for granted by them because it is taken for granted by the dominant culture.
>
> (Tatum, 2003, p. 20)

This exercise is a great way to begin exploring intersectional identities as well as introducing conversations about what aspects of their identities students did and did not write down. It becomes apparent fairly quickly that they are more likely to write down things that hold a lot of meaning for them, based on marginalization and issues of subjugated social positioning, and less likely to name descriptors related to the unearned privilege and dominant group membership that they hold. In Chapter 5, Mike Klein shows how this exercise can be adapted and extended.

Strategy 2: Moving from Right-handed to White Privilege

Teaching students about the structured nature of racial advantage is difficult and complex. I begin by trying to help them understand that because of the way our society is structured, there are unearned advantages that are granted to some groups of people based purely on group membership. One of the most successful approaches I have found to get this premise across is to begin with right-handed privilege. A useful resource is Stephen Jones's handout – "The Right Hand of Privilege" (Jones, 2003) – which discusses the idea of unearned privilege and the widespread resistance to acknowledging its existence. Jones provides multiple examples of how the world is wired for right-handed people and how right-handers rarely give a second thought to their advantage (unless they have a left-handed child or sibling).

The example of handedness has far less historical baggage than whiteness, and white students are usually open to considering it. When contemplating right-handedness, students don't blame individuals for this systemic problem or constantly look to the past; instead, they focus on recognizing the problem and taking responsibility for reducing its power. After providing examples, Jones returns to statements (quoted at the beginning of his piece) regarding responses to claims of male and white privilege. He substitutes right-handed and left-handed for "whites" and "people of color," or alternatively for "men" and "women," in the quotes. With powerful insight, he questions how many people would deny their right-handed privilege with comments such as, "As a right-handed person, I don't have any privilege. I'm just an individual who works hard every day to make ends meet. This is America. Everyone gets the same opportunities. If left-handed people don't make this an issue, there is none." And, "I am tired of hearing that right-handed people have privilege. I am not going to feel guilty or be blamed for what has happened in the past. The playing field has been leveled. Being left-handed has nothing to do with it anymore."

Once students grasp the overall concept of unearned advantage or privilege, we move to consider male privilege, heterosexual privilege, and able-bodied privilege before finally moving to white privilege. My choice to proceed in this manner is based on the fact that by the time we get to white privilege, my white students have explored the concept through many different avenues, thus breaking through some of their resistance. I put the list of white privileges outlined by McIntosh (1997) on slides in VoiceThread and ask students to comment on which ones they were particularly struck by and why. I also instruct students to add privileges they have noticed over the past week to the list. The VoiceThread list is available throughout the course for them to continue to add to.

Even so, white privilege remains difficult for my white students to grasp and accept fully. A complicating twist arises in my work when my white students and colleagues learn that I am married to a black man and have biracial children. Interestingly, it's as if some of my advocacy for teaching about white privilege somehow becomes tainted, because I am now seen as advancing a racial agenda. Some white students and colleagues argue that my passion for racial justice is driven by my familial circumstances only, and in a strange way this justifies their skepticism about taking the idea of white privilege seriously. The unspoken assumption is that if I were married to a white man and had white children I wouldn't be teaching students that racism was a problem.

Once the reality of white privilege is acknowledged, the next step is to name it as often as possible and to discuss its impact on our relationships. Of particular importance for my music therapy students is for them to start exploring its impact on therapeutic relationships. This is where narratives and stories start to become more prominent.

Strategy 3: Modeling Vulnerability

As a way of reducing the hierarchical teacher–student power dynamic in the classroom, I use a healthy amount of self-disclosure in my approach to teaching race. This includes telling stories of my experiences and openly sharing mistakes I have made and continue to make (Hadley, 2013). I have found that being vulnerable myself is a necessary first step in opening up a space for greater risk-taking by my white students. When I am perceived as not having mastered my own racism (as if such a thing were even possible!) students seem more prepared to share their experiences. Seeing the supposed expert apparently failing regularly communicates to students that getting it wrong comes with the territory of racial conversations. I want my students to understand that whites engaging perfectly with race and privilege (if perfect is defined as never having people misunderstand you or be angry with you) is impossible.

Furthermore, when students of color call me out in class about something I have said and when I am able to hear them without defensiveness and take ownership of my mistake, I am providing a model to white students of how to respond when they screw up. My intention of genuinely thanking students of color for their courage in calling me out on my actions is to encourage them to continue to speak up when they recognize something as racist in the classroom. I want to show how important it is to cultivate a habit of self-reflective watchfulness when you are slipping into the false safety of imagining that you are now free of racism.

I have found, however, that some of my students of color don't speak up when they could. When I talk to them about this in private, it is because I am concerned that they perceive my class as an unsafe space to do this. In response, they often express that they tend to give me a pass because they know that I am continually reflexive about issues of white privilege and racism. I assure them that I appreciate the honesty they bring and that I don't desire to be given a pass, but I still feel they are more forgiving than they perhaps ought to be. At times they don't speak up out of fear of how the white students will respond to their honesty or because they are tired of explaining racism to white people. I honor their choice to be silent in these situations.

Strategy 4: Bearing Witness

Giving full, focused, and sustained attention to someone's testimony of experiencing racism is an important step in learning to understand the full depth and breadth of its reach. So in addition to sharing my experiences, I have found it important for white students to bear witness to the experiences of people of color in our society. I provide them with a variety of books and articles to read and videos to watch, and encourage students to suggest resources and share links for them with all class members. Given that I teach music therapy students, it is important for them to hear the stories of other music therapists. Thus, my students read narratives of music therapists from various racial groups across the world who discuss how their own racial identities affect their therapeutic work with differently raced clients (Hadley, 2013).

I believe that it is important for students to witness courageous discussions about race between people of different races. One of the most powerful ways I have found to do this is to have them watch Lee Mun Wah's (1994) documentary *The Color of Fear*, which is a film in which eight men of different racialized backgrounds talk about the state of race relations in North America. This film covers many issues related to race and racism, and is produced in a way that helps the viewers to connect in important ways with the men on a personal level. Each year that I have shown *The Color of Fear*, I see the profound impact it has on students. In fact, many of them have mentioned the impact of the documentary even a decade after they have graduated.

Strategy 5: Exploring and Challenging Values and Beliefs Through Inventories and Journals

Becoming aware of their values, beliefs, and biases in relationship to race is an essential, yet incredibly difficult, process for students to undertake. Of course, we are not born with our sociocultural values and beliefs, but they are already forming and taking hold long before our ability to self-reflect develops (Jun, 2010). These sociocultural values and beliefs are nurtured and cherished, and shape our understandings of ourselves and of others. They become a central component of our developing identity, and, over time, become almost invisible to us, taken as givens. Given that our values and beliefs are so entrenched, it is no surprise that students find it difficult to bring them into awareness and to challenge them.

One approach that I employ to help students to access unconscious values and beliefs is to develop an inventory of common claims made about race that are embedded in what Feagin (2013) calls the white racial frame. This inventory contains a list of typical contentions about race that whites are taught overtly and covertly as they grow up. These are the kinds of assertions and unchallenged opinions students might have heard spoken by family members, at school, and in places of worship, or disseminated via the media. I ask them to think about the "official" stories and values that they were taught overtly, such as treating everyone as equals, achieving anything you put your mind to, putting others before yourself, rooting for the underdog, and so on. I also ask them to identify things that were taught covertly: the unofficial curriculum of their childhood and adolescence. These include who typically entered their houses and in what capacity (friends, family, service provider), the demographics of the family place of worship, who they were taught about in school, and who was regularly featured in the news media they consumed. Then I create a blank document in the group locker on the course shell in our university's learning management system for the students to create a list of values and beliefs about race.

This document is anonymous for a reason. I want all students to access the document with no record of who is contributing which items to the list. My rationale is that because it can be challenging to students at first to acknowledge these values and beliefs, I want them to feel complete freedom to post things that they would be embarrassed or reluctant to disclose publicly. Furthermore, I can add some values and beliefs to the list that are difficult to own, and the students won't know that it was the teacher who added these items. Articulating clearly problematic and contentious claims on the list can encourage students to go deeper and stimulate them to take more risks. Once the list is developed, I put it on VoiceThread so that the students can discuss values and beliefs that are in direct contradiction to each other. This exercise can be difficult for students as they begin to unpack what they have long held dear, but it is one of the most eye-opening classroom activities I conduct.

Another technique I employ is to have the students maintain a reflexive journal during the entire course about things related to race and racism that they notice in their everyday encounters and in their clinical practices. This journaling is modeled on Barry and O'Callaghan's (2008) approach, in which there are "four steps which [alternate] in a back and forth manner: descriptive journal writing, extending self-critiquing and understanding, integration of new insights into practice, and reflexive evaluation" (p. 58). The students begin by just describing their encounters and experiences. Then they try to apply a critical lens to the situations they describe by reflecting on how they did or did not respond and what shaped their particular choices and decisions. They examine the thoughts, emotions, and even bodily responses they had at the time, and also at the present moment as practitioners reflecting back on those situations. Once they have explored these thoughts and feelings, they then discuss what they think now about how, ideally, they could have responded. This provides them with options in the future, when they are likely to have similar encounters or experiences. Finally, all of the students share their journals with me in a Google Doc. This way, I can add comments and ask questions to help them to be more reflexive and connect their experiences to what we are learning in the course.

One challenging aspect of exploring beliefs and values is that students often feel distressed about the implications for their love for family members and close friends whom they come to realize hold racist values and beliefs. Even more difficult is owning that they too have held, and continue to hold, racist values and beliefs. This new insight challenges their understanding of themselves and their family and friends as "good people." As a teacher, what becomes important is to help them stay in this tension and discomfort and work through it, rather than running for cover.

Strategy 6: Uncovering and Challenging One's Intrapersonal Communication

Intrapersonal communication comprises the back-and-forth inner dialogue that happens continually as we process things that happen around us and manage the minutiae of everyday life. As we try to make major decisions concerning relationships, commitments, and the crises we face, these dialogues become more prominent, and we can usually recreate them long after they've occurred. But most intrapersonal communication takes place at a deeper, more subliminal level.

Heesoon Jun (2010) states that "Intrapersonal communication is a mirror image of one's own cultural values, beliefs, and biases" (p. 19). Given that our interpersonal communications grow out of our intrapersonal communication, it is imperative to begin to take more notice of our inner dialogue as a way to understand our values and beliefs more clearly.

One of the challenges of our internal dialogue is that "there is no feedback loop for a reality check because the sender and the receiver are the same person, the self" (Jun, p. 21). Because of this, there is no challenge to the thoughts swirling around in our mind, no reality check to the claims and contentions that occur to us.

After all, because the sender and the receiver are the same person, they (that is, we) are inevitably in agreement! Depending on how often these messages are repeated to ourselves, they become automatic thoughts, sedimented in our consciousness. Yet these thoughts, beliefs, and unreflexive assumptions are often the result of cognitive distortions that have grown out of negative messages we received as children.

Consequently, an important practice is to externalize these inner dialogues and to write them down in an uncensored and unfiltered way in the reflexive journal described above. Students can then go back over these inner dialogues and identify which of Jun's thinking styles they embody: hierarchical, dichotomous, linear, or holistic (Jun, 2010, pp. 27–29). Hierarchical and dichotomous thinkers tend to see individuals and groups as superior or inferior to others – better or worse, more or less. These kinds of thinking styles support practices and systems based on inclusion and exclusion. Linear thinking leads us to project and generalize future actions based on past events or experiences. While this can sometimes be useful, it is very damaging when beliefs passed from generation to generation, or an analysis based on only one experience, lead to personal and systemic discrimination, stereotyping, and marginalizing others.

Holistic thinking, in contrast, is multilayered and multidimensional, requiring a nonjudgmental attitude and a stance that is not defensive. People who practice this kind of thinking listen carefully to others and try to understand and appreciate multiple perspectives. As such, holistic thinking requires mindful practice. Most of my students, and I myself, were raised in societies that tend to privilege hierarchical, dichotomous, and linear thinking over more holistic thinking. Depending on context, all these thinking styles are useful and appropriate to one degree or another. Equally, however, it's important for students to understand when these patterns of thinking become problematic and to learn ways to disrupt automatic thinking patterns that contribute to ethnocentric, racist beliefs and values.

Strategy 7: Recognizing and Working to Eliminate Microaggressions

In the early 1970s, African American psychiatrist and Harvard University professor Chester M. Pierce first described what he named racist microaggressions. More recently, cross-cultural counselor Derald Wing Sue has examined these as the "daily verbal, behavioral, and environmental indignities, whether intentional or unintentional, that communicate hostile, derogatory, or negative racial, gender, sexual-orientation, and religious slights and insults to the target person or group" (Sue, 2010, p. 5). These comments, tones of voice, looks, gestures, actions, and inactions leave recipients feeling invalidated, demeaned, overlooked, devalued, excluded, undesirable, inferior, dangerous, or even abnormal, purely because of their race, class, gender, sexuality, disability, religion, ethnicity, and so on. Microaggressions imply that all people of a particular group are the same and also that they do not belong. Because these behaviors are so widespread, they are often unrecognized or dismissed as innocent and harmless. Yet continually being on the receiving end of these can be very damaging psychologically (in terms of self-esteem), emotionally (in terms of the anger and frustration they foster), and physically (in terms of health and well-being).

Microaggressions are most often unconscious, unintentional, and automatic. Because they are largely fueled by unconscious biases they are often perpetrated by well-intentioned people, and therefore are difficult to identify and navigate. In our society our values and beliefs are structured within the oppressive system of white supremacy, so perpetrators of microaggressions are members of groups that historically have had power and privilege over those not in the dominant group. Consequently, racist microaggressions are typically perpetrated by well-intentioned white people on people of color.

Microaggressions can occur at multiple levels: the individual (from one person to another), the institutional (policies, practices, procedures, and structures), and the cultural (when one group sees itself as superior and has the power to impose its values and standards on other groups). These aggressions can be expressed verbally as direct or indirect comments to targets or nonverbally through the use of body language or other more direct physical actions. Sometimes they are environmental and embedded in physical structures, or they can be reflected in the numerical imbalance of one's own group, inaccurate media portrayals, inclusion or exclusion in educational curriculum, signs, symbols, statues, and sports mascots.

It is important that white students become very aware of racist microaggressions. As with white privilege, I find it easiest for students to understand the concept of microaggressions by beginning with their own standpoints. As the majority of my students are female, I begin by exploring gender microaggressions. As I begin to share some of my experiences of gender microaggressions, they readily start to share theirs. I have also been fortunate to have students who are nonbinary and who frequently experience gender microaggressions. This happens in class when incorrect pronouns are used for them, or when in the reading materials gender is only conceptualized as the male–female binary. Exploring the impact of gender-based microaggressions on each of us personally, along with sharing stories of how our experiences of microaggressions are often minimized and negated by the dominant group, provides a bridge for becoming more aware of how we perpetrate, minimalize, and negate racial microaggressions.

As my students learn more about racist microaggressions, they are able to recognize instances of these in their daily experiences and to include these in their reflexive journals. It is easier, of course, for them to recognize when these microaggressions are perpetrated by others than when they perpetrate them. In time, however, they are better able to recognize ways in which they unwittingly commit racial microaggressions and to increasingly listen without defensiveness to accounts of microaggression by people of color. Once this level of awareness is reached, there is a greater chance of reducing the frequency and intensity of racist microaggressions and making amends when they occur.

Strategy 8: Practicing Mindfulness to Navigate Difficult Dialogues

One of the most challenging situations that white students find themselves in is navigating difficult dialogues as they become more aware of everyday racism (Hardy and Bobes, 2016). At some point in their process of transformative learning, they realize that by staying silent they are remaining part of the problem. But, as they begin to speak out about racist comments, racist jokes, and racist microaggressions, they often become the target of scorn. Exacerbating their feelings of discomfort is the fact that these comments, jokes, and microaggressions are coming from their parents, siblings, grandparents, aunts, uncles, cousins, friends, teachers, mentors, and other significant people whom they hold dear. When students speak out against these microaggressions they are accused of being overly sensitive, overly reactive, lacking a sense of humor, or even being aggressive. My white students are made to feel bad about themselves, as if they are the ones with the problem. This invariably makes students doubt themselves; after all, these accusations come from the people they love and respect, the people who raised them.

Consequently, I feel it is important to prepare students to stay with these difficult conversations with families and friends. I discuss how to get in the habit of using "I" statements instead of making generalizations that are perceived as more accusatory. We explore how to tap into values that we know that their family members cherish and to share our personal curiosity about how those values can be in place when comments and jokes are made that directly contradict them.

Another technique I use is a mindfulness exercise that encourages softening around discomfort. I have them sit in a comfortable position with their eyes shut and instruct them to stay in that position without moving throughout a music and meditation experience. I ask them to notice any desire to move and anything that provides them with discomfort but remind them that they must remain still. As they notice feelings of discomfort, I ask them to allow themselves to soften around it, to relax any muscles that may tighten in response, but to remain still. I ask them to focus on the sensation of discomfort as it emerges and to stay with it without trying to move away from it. Again, I prompt them to allow themselves to soften around the discomfort, to relax any muscle tension that occurs in response to the discomfort. Once the music and meditation experience has ended, I allow them to move into whatever position they have been wanting to sit in and to focus on the sensations as they do this. Does it provide relief? Is the relief immediate or gradual? In what way do their bodies feel better? They are told to release any remaining tension they may feel.

After this experience, we discuss how people usually respond to discomfort by trying to build a solid wall of tightness around it, attempting to block off the feeling or avoid it. We talk about the alternative strategy of sitting in the discomfort, acknowledging its presence, being mindful, sitting with oneself compassionately, and softening around the feelings of discomfort. By doing this, we can focus on the discomfort without all the resistance we usually summon to combat it. I say that while we work on becoming more aware of how power and privilege permeate our everyday encounters and our therapeutic relationships, I want them to remember this exercise in mindfulness and how they practiced softening around the discomfort. My hope is that they will find ways of practicing the strategies that we used in this experience as they encounter feelings of discomfort and start to build the wall of resistance they want to protect themselves with.

Strategy 9: Response/Ability

My aim as a teacher is not only for my students to be better citizens, but also to be more effective music therapists. According to Nisha Sajnani (2012), as creative arts therapists we need to encourage *response/ability* in our practices – that is, the *ability* to *respond* amid suffering and against oppression. She states that we need to form "collaborative relationships based on respect for our clients' wisdom about their own lived experiences" and we need to be willing "to make our values and assumptions transparent" (p. 189). Sajnani encourages us to think about the politics of representation (how bodies and histories are signified in various arts media) and the politics of witnessing (how we honor the experiences of those who have experienced personal and social trauma). In her words:

> A critical race feminist paradigm also challenges us to think through the politics of representation and witnessing. Through our various modalities, we are able to provide a platform and an artform through which human experience can be communicated and heard. However, art is never neutral. Representation refers to how bodies and histories are signified in print, on canvas, on stage, [in music,] and on video. Witnessing, in this context, refers to how we support our audiences, especially those who may feel emotionally or socially alienated by what they are presented with to respond to and possibly even enter into alliance with those performing (or exhibiting, etc.).
>
> (Sajnani, 2012, p. 190)

Thus, I explore with students the concept that to be authentic in their work as music therapists they need to seize the ability to respond to issues of racial oppression and suffering within their practices. We examine the implicit and explicit messages in the music we use and how these reinforce or challenge racial oppression. We consider ways of creating music with our clients that bear witness to their experiences of racial oppression, support expressions of outrage and resistance, and provide vehicles for empowerment.

Furthermore, we unearth issues of race in clinical supervision by getting students to talk about their work as music therapists. Given the whiteness of my profession, I feel that it is my responsibility (and the responsibility of my white colleagues and students) to explore its impact on therapeutic relationships. Whiteness is foregrounded in our supervision sessions, not just when it is seen as getting in the way of the therapeutic relationship, but as something permeating the therapeutic relationship. Students are encouraged to explore how their white identity frames their practices in their supervision sessions, clinical journals, clinical research, and clinical assessment, treatment, and evaluation. Even when we don't see a direct connection between our own actions and the root causes of racial injustice, I stress the importance of making it our responsibility to work together in an effort to dismantle racist power structures that continue to oppress some and privilege others.

Strategy 10: Accountability Buddies

Continually exploring the systemic nature of racism in our society is far too significant and far too challenging to do alone. White supremacy has a way of reinserting itself even as we work against its powerful hold on us. One suggestion I provide is for students to find what I call *accountability buddies* – people who are willing to call them out when they make mistakes or when they seem to be lulled into a state of inaction in the presence of racial injustice. Much as in a 12-step program for addictions, I explain that they will fall off the wagon, and that they need to find a community of people who will help keep them on the path of recovery. These accountability buddies must be people whom they trust and who have the strength and determination to challenge them and not let them off the proverbial hook – people who are able to see through and withstand their defenses and resistance.

Ongoing Journey

At the conclusion of one of my courses, one of my students wrote:

> Although my awareness has increased, I must say that
> I often still do not view myself as privileged. In the same
> way, I still do not view myself as racist although I am.

> I realize that as a white person I do not view myself as raced. I realize that I view myself as the norm and view others to be outside the norm. It is difficult to admit that I am racist. It is difficult to accept that I have earned things in my life through no merit of my own. It is difficult to accept stories of oppression from [people of] other races because of the implications to myself. If their experience of racism on a daily basis is true, what does that say about me? What does it say of my character as a good, responsible, respectable, and deserving white person? It destroys it. It is so much easier to deny its existence and sweep it under the carpet. It is the denial surrounding these issues that empowers them. I believe that as we recognize and give voice to that which is silent and face our fears, we can begin to move forward.

Throughout my courses, I continually remind my students that we are merely scratching the surface and that working against racist structures in our white supremacist society is an unending process. I explain that hegemony works to build up power structures continually, even as people are trying to tear them down. I remind students that once we begin to notice these invisible systems around us that parade as normal and neutral, we need to remain vigilant and ever-mindful of their presence. We need to provide alternative narratives as well as alternative unoppressive and non-discriminatory social structures that will minimize or even eradicate the damage that these oppressive racist social structures cause people of color. That is the reason for establishing unoppressive practices in creative arts therapies (Baines, 2013).

Given that dominant racist narratives have a way of repairing themselves even as they are challenged, working against them is a never-ending process, much like cleaning a house. It is something that we need to work at daily, because if we let things go for a while and don't pay attention to them, they become much larger and require much more work to clean up. Because there is no point of arrival per se (Yancy, 2012, p. 169), we must continue to work at this project. Some students will argue that it seems pointless to try if we will never get there. The same can be said for cleaning, but we have to do it if we don't want to live in the funk.

References

Baines, S. (2013). Music therapy as an anti-oppressive practice. *The Arts in Psychotherapy* 40: 1–5.

Barry, P. and O'Callaghan, C. (2008). Reflexive journal writing: A tool for music therapy student clinical practice development. *Nordic Journal of Music Therapy* 17 (1): 55–66.

Feagin, J.R. (2013). *The White Racial Frame: Centuries of Racial Framing and Counter-Framing*, 2nd ed. New York: Routledge.

Hadley, S. (2013). *Experiencing Race as a Music Therapist: Personal Narratives.* Gilsum, NH: Barcelona Publishers.

Hardy, K.L. and Bobes, T. (2016). *Culturally Sensitive Supervision and Training: Diverse Perspectives and Practical Applications.* New York: Routledge.

Jones, S. (2003). The right hand of privilege. Global LeaderSHIFT ThoughtPaper. San Diego, CA: Jones & Associates Consulting, www.jonesinclusive.com/ The_Right_Hand_of_Privilege.pdf (accessed 31 May 2018).

Jun, H. (2010). *Social Justice, Multicultural Counseling, and Practice: Beyond a Conventional Approach.* Thousand Oaks, CA: SAGE.

McIntosh, P. (1997). White privilege and male privilege: A personal account of coming to see correspondences through work in women's studies. In: *Critical White Studies: Looking Behind the Mirror* (ed. R. Delgado and J. Stefancic), 291–299. Philadelphia, PA: Temple University Press.

Sajnani, N. (2012). Response/ability: Imagining a critical race feminist paradigm for the creative arts therapies. *The Arts in Psychotherapy* 39: 186–191.

Sue, D.W. (2010). *Microaggressions in Everyday Life: Race, Gender, and Sexual Orientation.* Hoboken, NJ: John Wiley & Sons, Inc.

Tatum, B.D. (2003). *Why Are All the Black Kids Sitting Together in the Cafeteria? And Other Conversations About Race.* New York, NY: Basic Books.

Wah, L.M. (dir.). (1994). *The Color of Fear.* Running time 90 min. Stir Fry Productions.

Yancy, G. (2012). *Look, a White! Philosophical Essays on Whiteness.* Philadelphia, PA: Temple University Press.

4

Creating a Brave Space Classroom Through Writing

Lucia Pawlowski

As a white, cis, straight professor working at a predominantly white university, I am working to discover my own privilege and to fight for racial justice as part of a coalition of faculty, staff, and students who aim to make our institution not just inclusive, but explicitly antiracist. In this institutional environment I have found the concept of the "brave space" classroom to be pedagogically generative. In contrast to the oft-quoted injunction that classrooms should be safe spaces, brave space assumes that tension, conflict, and risk are at the heart of the cognitive and personal transformation integral to learning about race and racism. In this chapter, I argue that any brave space classroom requires an extensive writing curriculum. This is because writing facilitates processes integral to unpacking racism, particularly self-discovery, privacy, and accountability. I advocate both anonymous writing exercises that allow dissent to more easily surface, and self-identified writing to make students responsible readers and listeners. I also examine how instructors can write their own way into brave pedagogy.

The Course

The course in which I implement brave space writing pedagogy is a freshman- and sophomore-level English course. It is the second

Teaching Race: How to Help Students Unmask and Challenge Racism, First Edition.
Stephen D. Brookfield and Associates.
© 2019 John Wiley & Sons, Inc. Published 2019 by John Wiley & Sons, Inc.

literature and writing class in a two-course sequence required of all undergraduates in our midsized, Midwestern, urban university. I have been teaching this course since 2014, and there have been two sections each semester (for a total of 40 students). For three of the four years I've taught the course I have experimented with brave space writing pedagogy. Although I developed this curriculum for an English course, the writing exercises I present here can be used across contexts.

My section of the course sequence is called Race, Gender, Sexuality and Language. Here we learn how marginalized linguistic variations (women's discourse, gay men's coding, African American Vernacular English, Chicano Spanish, Native American languages, and L2 English in former African colonies) develop, and how they represent both a history of oppression for these marginalized groups and the creativity and resistance that these marginalized groups enact through these linguistic variations.

Brave Space: When, What, and Why

Brave space is a term that had not surfaced before the past five years, and it has done so in leftist activist – especially online – spaces. The term was imported from activist contexts into educational contexts with the publication of "From Safe Spaces to Brave Spaces: A New Way to Frame Dialogue Around Diversity and Social Justice", a chapter in *The Art of Effective Facilitation* (Arao and Clemens, 2013).

But even before brave space emerged as an alternative paradigm to safe space, the problems outlined in many critiques of safe spaces anticipated the development of a contrasting idea. Boostrom's (1998) critique of safe space contends that "learning necessarily involves not merely risk, but the pain of giving up a former condition in favour of a new way of seeing things" (p. 399). Within educational contexts, the strongest critiques of safe spaces were issued in the early 1990s by feminist and queer educators, and especially feminist educators of color. These critiques contend that explorations of oppression and social change are inherently fraught with risks that are to be negotiated, not neutralized.

Some such scholars have tried to name a replacement paradigm. However, the terms from feminist critiques of safe space – such as Jeannie Ludlow's (2004) contested space and Megan Boler's (1999) pedagogy of discomfort – have not been cited enough to popularize them in scholarship or practice. One parallel development in K–12 education that has gained tremendous popularity, however, is the protocol for courageous conversations (Singleton, 2005).

Arao and Clemens (2013) developed the term *brave space* from what they observed in social justice facilitation work as students' "defensive tendency to discount, deflect, or retreat from a challenge" (p. 135). My experience with my own students is similar, in that they often report staying safe by shying away from engagements with those who hold opposing views. Arao and Clemens (2013) argue that "authentic learning about social justice often requires the very qualities of risk, difficulty, and controversy that are defined as incompatible with safety" (p. 139). I contend that if risk is at the heart of learning, then learning about race – itself a project fraught with risk – requires brave space.

I want to acknowledge, however, that safe spaces certainly have their place in both education and activism. Safe spaces began in activist groups for marginalized organizers to encourage a sharing of common values, experiences, and intellectual premises as a step in planning political action to combat this marginalization (Rosestone Collective, 2014). In these spaces, participants don't need to explain themselves and defend their perspectives, and one can engage in deeper and more nuanced conversations because of what participants share. Safe spaces are essential to college campuses for marginalized students. However, I contend that the safe space paradigm does not fit for most college *classrooms*, given that we can't assume that all students in the same classroom share the same experiences, values, intent for political action, or intellectual premises.

Brave space is not just a trendy new term. It represents a significant departure from some familiar platitudes guiding much received knowledge today. These platitudes are often not explicitly identified as being part of the safe space movement, but according to Arao and Clemens (2013) they seem to consist of agreements that it is fine to:

- Agree to disagree
- Opt out of challenges that make you uncomfortable
- Avoid personal attacks
- Don't take it personally
- Respect each other

Brave space problematizes each of these platitudes and offers alternatives, such as:

- Invite and embrace controversy – wade into the difficulty.
- Critically interrogate reasons why we want to opt out, and ask: "Why am I hesitant to engage? How is my daily life affected by the choice to opt out of these challenges? How is the daily life of the group we're talking about affected?"
- Honestly acknowledge when a perceived attack is in fact just a challenge.
- Own your intentions and your impact on others in the room; reject the expectation of detachment when this material affects your lives directly.
- Unpack the common wisdom of respect to investigate whether our concrete expectations of respect perpetuate social hierarchies in the classroom.

Developing Classroom Norms for Collaborative Writing

We start writing on the first day of the semester. The opening collaborative writing activity I'll introduce here has students explore what they think our classroom engagement norms should be.

They work in small groups to draft a list of some proposed norms. I ask them to designate one spokesperson per group, and that student reads what the group wrote aloud to the class.

Usually, their initial thoughts repeat platitudes they've heard in their other classrooms, the most common of which is to "show respect." But when I ask them how this plays out in the classroom, they respond: "Don't interrupt. Don't get emotional. Don't raise your voice. Don't be biased. Don't point at someone when you talk to them."

This is when we start to question where these rules come from, and what their implications are – especially for students who have a personal stake in the course material. Emotions are a great place to start. Why do we assume that learning always requires the performance of emotional detachment? In this conversation, I begin to introduce research on emotions in the classroom from feminist, whiteness, and queer scholars who question why "respect" is conflated with emotional detachment.

Brave space rejects the relativism that safe spaces too often embrace. In this exercise I acknowledge all contributions, but we critically evaluate each one. Not every contribution becomes a guiding principle for classroom norms. This helps set the stage for the semester, when students will have to reject relativism and not let problematic comments go unchecked. My students report to me that it is far more damaging to a class dynamic to see a classroom stay silent in the face of a student's racist comment, or hear that comment uncritically validated, than to hear that comment in the first place. It's in the response, not in the original comment, where we as teachers need to show up.

We end the exercise by students breaking back into their small groups, where they are asked to brainstorm what connotations "brave space" and "safe space" have for them (at this point, students have not yet read the syllabus statement on brave space). I make two columns on the board, and a spokesperson from each group reads what the group has written. Together, we tease out the differences and overlaps between "brave" and "safe," and begin to draft our classroom norms collaboratively.

Establishing brave space in the classroom aligns with the four recursive stages of the writing process: invention (often called *prewriting*, which includes brainstorming), drafting, revision, and assessment. To scaffold students' understanding and implementation of brave space throughout the semester, I use several writing tools. In order to "invent" brave space in the classroom, we do the aforementioned brainstorming activity on the first day of class. This allows us to draft brave space guidelines together. Students then continue to think about their own accountability in building brave space by completing a form they fill out every day at the end of class. One of its questions is, "Did you participate? If not, why not?"

Finally, students reflect on how we're doing with brave space on the anonymous midsemester evaluation. I identify major themes in their comments and project these on the board the day after they complete the midsemester evaluation. Then we brainstorm (using anonymous digital platforms that I'll introduce here) about how to revise our brave space guidelines for the remainder of the semester. Finally, at the end of the semester, we spend half of one class period writing about how brave space went, what role each of us played in creating it (including when we opted out of action), and what we learned from practicing it or pulling back from it.

Establishing brave space is so akin to the writing process that calling brave space a *space* as opposed to a *process* holds the danger of making it appear to have fixed, stable boundaries. Instead, it is a fundamentally precarious and unstable classroom structure that requires continual revision and assessment throughout the semester, and writing facilitates this.

Uncovering Power Relations in Brave Space

Hierarchies of power are always at work in the classroom. In addition to the clear positional authority between students and professors, there are important differing positions of power *among students*. Another reason why brave space should resonate for teachers focusing on privilege is because of its acknowledgement of these power relations. Trying to create a brave space helps demonstrate that a classroom is never a safe space due to the differing levels of power and privilege students import into it from outside. Because of their politically marginalized positions, women, working-class students, queer students, and students of color, for example, typically have less access to the floor in class discussion. On the other hand, however, they are often tokenized by being asked to speak for their entire group, as in: "Tell us, what's the black perspective on this?"

These differing positions of power and privilege have concrete consequences on class dynamics. Crickets – extended periods of silence – are particularly common from both my students of color *and* my white students in discussions of race. But the reasons for these periods are very different for each group of students. My white students are sometimes silent because they are afraid of "saying the wrong thing," "offending anyone," or "looking racist." My students of color are silent for different reasons. They don't want to have to speak for their race, they're exhausted by the tax on them to educate white students, or it is downright painful to be the object of racist views and microaggressions that inevitably rise to the surface in these conversations.

For my white students, if we don't get them to say the "wrong thing" and they continue to walk on eggshells, we'll never get to confront and intervene in the problematic views they secretly harbor. For my students of color, there is no such thing as a safe space to begin with when they are in mixed company. As Leonardo and Porter (2010) insist, safe spaces are actually for white people's comfort and they solidify white supremacy. They ask, "Who feels safe and toward what ends?" (p. 152). hooks's (1994) argument that classrooms are enactments of bourgeois democracy makes the point that the idea of classrooms as calm, reasonable, even-tempered analytical havens means that white students are never confronted with the raw anger and hostility expressed by students who have spent their lives being insulted and dismissed by racism.

This is why students of color "may, in fact, react with incredulity to the very notion of safety, for history and experience has demonstrated clearly to them that to name their oppression, and the perpetrators thereof, is a profoundly unsafe activity" (Arao and Clemens, 2013, p. 140). For folks in power – including white professors – safety is a misplaced value and insisting on it only indexes their privilege. As Jeannie Ludlow (2004) argues, "It is only from privileged perspectives that neutral or safe environments are viable and from empowered positions that protecting others is possible" (p. 45). For marginalized people, safety is a daily impossibility.

Given the already uneven playing field, I raise expectations of vulnerability for my white students. They're required to put their views out there so that all students can examine them more closely and systematically. In turn, students of color are empowered to perform this examination in productive ways. The mantra of my brave space classroom is "surface and intervene." We have to tear off the veneer of polite discourse in order to get to the racist sentiments we harbor underneath the surface and to challenge these beliefs, and productively intervene. This often requires anonymous writing, which is a cornerstone of my brave-space writing curriculum.

It may seem at first to a white teacher that students of color would always feel unnecessary pain upon hearing racist views expressed in the classroom. But my students of color, for the most part, report relief when what they long suspected white students were thinking is actually confirmed. As one African American student of mine exclaimed to me after class privately: "Thank God someone finally admitted they feel this way! *Now* we can talk!" Another student of color reported that she felt our class time was productive because we didn't beat around the bush. Students of color often feel that the classrooms in which racisms remain beneath the surface are unproductive classrooms.

As Leonardo and Porter (2010) state: "A comfortable race dialogue belies the actual structure of race, which is full of tension. It is literally out of sync with its own topic" (p. 153). Teaching the structures of race is the topic of my course, and it takes time to teach.

As previously emphasized, brave space guidelines must not be taught just once, but scaffolded throughout the semester. In order to understand the *need* for brave space, a student must understand that there are such things as privilege and power disparities. Therefore, students will not fully understand brave space when we introduce it the first day, but, as they learn about power and privilege throughout the semester, they will also deepen their understanding of brave space. In this way, brave space is not just (pedagogical) form; it is also (course) content.

Writing: What, Why, and When

Writing is essential to learning about race for three reasons: First, writing facilitates the cognitive process of self-discovery foundational to the identity work required for studying race; second, writing offers a private space in which students can more freely explore the scariest pieces of their own racisms; third, writing compels students to be rigorously accountable to both each other and the assigned text. These elements of self-discovery, privacy, and accountability also comprise central tenets of brave spaces. After all, these spaces are designed to assist students in probing the learned racism that many of them would prefer to deny. Brave space also recognizes that privacy and anonymity are sometimes necessary to encourage students to take the risk of engaging seriously with deeply uncomfortable ideas. Finally, brave space is intended to call students to be accountable for their own commitment to surfacing and intervening in racism in the wider world. As a writing teacher, this is why I see such clear connections between what writing is designed to accomplish and the dynamics of creating brave spaces.

The Self-discovery of Racial Identity

Writing is a process not just of transcription (recording what we already know) but of discovery (figuring out what there is to know) – especially *self*-discovery. And, of course, self-discovery and discovery of the world are intimately tied. Writing scholars, feminist scholars, and cultural theorists have long held that discovering one's own positionality in relationship to new course content is foundational to learning that same material. Students must reflect on their own identities as they work through material about race; students must do identity work.

Beverly Daniel Tatum (1992, 2003) insists that an essential part of learning about race is the process of teachers and students identifying where we are in what is called our racial identity development. She draws from the work of psychologist Janet Helms (1993), who presented a six-stage model of racial identity development for whites and a five-stage model for African Americans. Scholars have subsequently presented stages of racial identity development for other groups of color (Wijeyesinghe and Jackson, 2001).

Importantly, I emphasize identity work as a corollary of, and not a prerequisite to, students' examination of the course material on race. I try to explain that identity work must be ongoing and recursive throughout the course. In my course, understanding racial identity is not the first step in my work with students. I present racial identity development halfway through the semester because I want to be sure that I've built enough community and trust in the classroom for students to feel sufficiently prepared to tangle with their own identities. And, because doing identity work is a process, we return to racial development theory throughout the rest of the course.

Writing – both student writing and instructor writing – is the heart of the lesson on racial identity development. First, students read Helms (1993) on racial identity development and, on their own, draft summaries in their notebooks of each of the stages she describes. Then each student writes one anonymous blog post on our class learning-management system in response to this prompt: "Think of an incident/belief/action of yours that demonstrates you being in one particular stage of your racial identity development. Describe the example, then tell us what it is about that example that makes you think it fits into that particular stage."

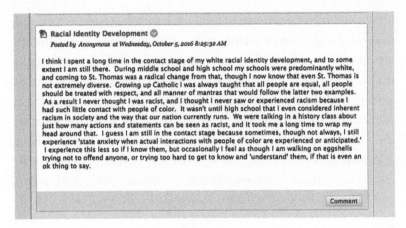

Racial Identity Development
Posted by *Anonymous* at Wednesday, October 5, 2016 8:25:32 AM

I think I spent a long time in the contact stage of my white racial identity development, and to some extent I am still there. During middle school and high school my schools were predominantly white, and coming to St. Thomas was a radical change from that, though I now know that even St. Thomas is not extremely diverse. Growing up Catholic I was always taught that all people are equal, all people should be treated with respect, and all manner of mantras that would follow the latter two examples. As a result I never thought I was racist, and I thought I never saw or experienced racism because I had such little contact with people of color. It wasn't until high school that I even considered inherent racism in society and the way that our nation currently runs. We were talking in a history class about just how many actions and statements can be seen as racist, and it took me a long time to wrap my head around that. I guess I am still in the contact stage because sometimes, though not always, I still experience 'state anxiety when actual interactions with people of color are experienced or anticipated.' I experience this less so if I know them, but occasionally I feel as though I am walking on eggshells trying not to offend anyone, or trying too hard to get to know and 'understand' them, if that is even an ok thing to say.

Comment

Figure 4.1   Student writing: Racial identity development.

You can see in the blog entry in Figure 4.1 how a student discovers his/her/their own racism *as* the student is writing – the writer is kind of feeling around in the dark.

At first, the student reports that stage one – the contact stage – was in the past ("I spent") and tentatively offers that he/she/they might still be there ("to some extent"). By the end of the blog post, it's clear that the student recognizes that this stage is current ("I guess I am still in the contact stage"), and even ventures to say something considered taboo ("if that is even an okay thing to say"). It was the act of writing that allowed this discovery to be made, and, as I will contend later, allowed the student to be so vulnerable as to say something that the student is worried might be taboo.

The Importance of the Instructor Writing on Racial Identity Development

When we ask students to be this vulnerable, we must be ready to be vulnerable too. Vulnerable disclosure must be reciprocal. So, before asking student to do their blog posts, I read extracts in class from my own racial identity development journal in which I have tried to describe an event from each stage of my own racial identity development as a white person. It is painful to admit publicly what

I have said or done whenever I fall back into stage one or two, but how can I expect my students to lay it on the line when I am not myself willing to do so? Throughout the semester, I also try to make it a habit to do all the writing assignments I assign and present that writing to the students. Again, the intent is not only to give them an idea of what that assignment asks of them but also to reciprocate the vulnerability I'm asking of them. As multiple authors have acknowledged (Brookfield 2014; Trout and Basford, 2016), teachers modeling their own commitment to uncomfortable disclosure is crucial to encouraging students to engage in this process.

Creating Student Privacy

It may seem strange to emphasize the importance of privacy in a course devoted to developing students' collective commitment to antiracist action. But, as critical theorist Herbert Marcuse (1978) argued, "in all areas of our lives we are subject to aggressive and exploitative socialization" (p. 5) that forces us into constant association with those who believe things are working just fine. In a white supremacist world, the dominant ideology holds that racism is a thing of the past and that meritocracy has assured that the most capable are in positions of authority based purely on talent and effort. To Marcuse, time alone away from the enactment of white supremacist attitudes and behaviors is crucial if people are to start questioning their taken-for-granted beliefs. He argues that the more time people spend in group-learning contexts, the more difficult it becomes for them to achieve the detachment from everyday experience necessary to the development of a truly critical perspective. Time spent with peers and teachers often impedes what he called the development of rebellious subjectivity.

Support for Marcuse's argument is found in Cale and Huber's (2001) analysis of two attempts to create a critical perspective on dominant, racist ideology. As part of their analysis Huber summarized a distance teacher-education course focused on understanding diversity and promoting antiracist practice. This course was run as a fast-track summer institute with no requirement for students to meet, either for formal classes or informal study. Huber records the surprising fact that "the assignments students completed that were most thoughtful and critical of their own positions of power were the ones that were completed alone" (Cale and Huber, 2001, p. 15). In these assignments students "discussed openly the racism and sexism that they experienced in their families, their lack of contact with people of color, and their own passive racism" (p. 15).

However, when these same students formed an informal study group to work collaboratively on confronting racism "the autonomous learning and thinking that manifested itself during their self-study disappeared after they completed the next two assignments together" (p. 15). As a consequence, "students who openly addressed the inherent racism in their classrooms and expressed a desire to end the racist practices that were a part of their hidden and overt curriculum did not complete a significant plan for change within their classrooms" (p. 15). Huber suggests that dominant ideology reproduced itself automatically in the informal group setting, whereas it could be kept temporarily at bay when participants inhabited the private space of autonomous, distanced thought.

My experience parallels Cale and Huber's. When I first introduced racial identity development into my course a few years ago, I had students doing the writing exercise *in class*, sitting in their usual seating arrangement. Back then, I always ended up with all my students proudly announcing that they were in the last stage. Ah, the journey is over! Everyone is enlightened, and we can all go home now.

So it occurred to me that students needed more privacy in order to be more honest. This is when I started hearing more ambivalence, exploration, and anxiety in students' writing, as in the blog post in Figure 4.1. Students needed privacy in order to discover what they needed to discover. By "private," I mean either writing to oneself alone, or writing to just the professor – as opposed to the whole class.

So a brave space classroom requires moments of privacy. Moreover, even those moments of privacy require brave space, as writers make painful discoveries about themselves and the world. Discovering racial oppression and one's position relative to that reality is invariably extremely unsettling for students. Writing exercises offer students a way to manage these disruptive discoveries without suffering the public shaming that they anticipate would accompany their journey if the writing was shown to the rest of the class.

Helms (1993) teaches us that an important element of stage one of racial identity development for white people is naïveté. This is typically followed in stage two by a disturbing dissonance between the views students once held and their sobering new knowledge of racism. Because writing is private, it offers the ideal space to work through this unsettling dissonance. Writing offers a private ante-room to ponder these personal discoveries before students jump into a more public forum, such as oral discussion. A brave, private space makes it more likely that students will not hold back from plumbing the depths because they are too embarrassed by their racist views to do so.

Writing can also be extremely useful for stage three of racial identity development, a stage Helms characterizes as retrenchment, the strong urge to move back into stage one. Helen Fox (2009) writes that "white students need extra encouragement to move beyond stage three" (p. 91). Because the tensions wrought by their new selves and social awareness deeply complicate their lives, there's a desire to go back into the matrix, to experience again the naïve understanding that one is color blind and free of learned racism. At this stage it is helpful if another person – the instructor or a peer – walks them over the bridge. One way to do that is through using the private writing exercise of the daily End-of-Class Reflection.

The End-of-Class Reflection

As I open every class session I hand out a half sheet of paper called the End-of-Class Reflection (Figure 4.2), which students complete throughout the class session. They turn it in to me privately as they leave the room once the session is done. This writing

```
┌─────────────────────────────────────────────────────────────────┐
│ End-of-Class Reflection                                           │
│                                                                   │
│ Name_____             │
│                                                                   │
│                                                                   │
│ Topic_____             │
│                                                                   │
│                                                                   │
│ Did you participate today?          YES          NO               │
│                                                                   │
│                                                                   │
│ If not, why not?                                                  │
│                                                                   │
│                                                                   │
│ What struck you the most about today's class? In other words, what are you │
│ taking away from today?                                           │
│                                                                   │
│                                                                   │
│ OPTIONAL: What remaining questions do you have about this topic?  │
│ _____          │
└─────────────────────────────────────────────────────────────────┘
```

Figure 4.2   Student writing: Class reflection template.

semiprivate: It is shared, but only with me. This daily form tells me where they are in their learning and where they want to go next.

Sometimes I get pretty vulnerable responses to the questions posed, as some students reveal that they are in the riskiest phase of struggling with dissonance and are contemplating retrenchment. In one session focusing particularly on language, one white male student wrote the following in response to the "What struck you?" question: "Is this all really my fault? This class makes me embarrassed to be a male." What I find so interesting about this comment is that it clearly borders precariously on understanding privilege (stage four) while still displaying denial (stage two). This student was just on the threshold of understanding, so I felt it was important to follow up with him to encourage him to cross that threshold.

To me, his comment called for another form of instructor writing: the follow-up email. Through some self-disclosure I attempted to address his concern. Part of my follow-up email read:

> ... I so appreciated reading your honest class reflection today about how these conversations make you feel embarrassed to be a guy. I can relate. As a white person, I experience a lot of "white guilt." It sounds

like you might be experiencing a little "male guilt"...
Like you didn't have a choice in being a dude, I didn't
have a choice in being white, but I can take responsibility for white privilege, and fight for racial justice...
So I just wanted to say both "I feel you" but also "let's
work through this" and also "you can talk to me about
this anytime!"

If students are to do the transformative work of moving past
blame and denial – whether it be in regard to sexism or racism – there is a place for private writing *to* the instructor, and a
place for private writing *from* the instructor, especially when
students are precariously straddling stages of racial identity
development.

I often use the metaphor of the writing process itself to illustrate
to students how the movement to an antiracist identity is a recursive, not linear, process. This was especially resonant for one student of color who reported in the privacy of an end-of-class
reflection feeling overwhelmed and hurt as she heard problematic
views expressed in my classroom. Through writing, I worked with
her on finding productive ways to respond to these views. It reassured this student of color to know that these other students who
expressed problematic views were undergoing a transformation
that wouldn't happen all at once, and that the views they expressed
were not an end point but a place on a journey (much like the
writing process).

The synthesis of student responses in the end-of-session paper
is another important practice. When there is a special circum-
stance I see in a set of end-of-class reflections – for example, a
so-called elephant in the room that a student names, or a few
students dissenting with the voices that prevailed in the class discussion – I will write a synthesis, occasionally including directly
quoted phrases from individual reflections (with names retracted).
This is then projected onto the board at the beginning of the next
class period. This way, we can acknowledge dissenting views and

unspoken concerns. That provides a starting point that day to continue the conversation, using the tools I will introduce here.

Anonymous Polling

I often begin a course unit or discussion of a reading by taking a quick, online, anonymous poll to get a snapshot of the experiences students bring to a particular unit. Figure 4.3 is a poll for a unit on gender and sexuality that I created using the Poll Everywhere tool to prepare students to read an article on homophobic slang.

This poll affords a panoramic view of students' exposure to homophobic slurs and demonstrates to students the real extent of the problem. In a sense, it justifies that particular curricular unit.

The next step is to drill down into specific responses from individual students while still preserving their anonymity. To do this, we use a tool called TodaysMeet, a digital "room" that publicly displays student writing that they do on laptops or smart phones. TodaysMeet is a tool that needs no subscription and is free and quick (about 20 seconds) to establish. As students are filing into the class, I set up a room on TodaysMeet that is named for the class topic that day. Students have 140 characters either to pose critical questions that they brought to class about the assigned text or to

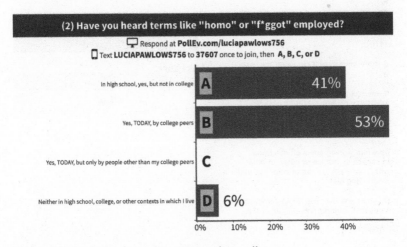

Figure 4.3 Anonymous prediscussion student poll.

respond to one of the critical questions someone else posed. I have students respond anonymously by having them use numbers as nicknames when they enter the digital room.

The room displayed in Figure 4.4 represents responses to the general question, "What critical question do you have about the text?" The text was Mary Bucholtz's (1996) article about black women's linguistic patterns, written from a black feminist perspective. Bucholtz is white, and students know this because I include a biography and photo of each scholar we read.

Typically I allow about a minute for 20 responses (one from each student) to populate the screen, and then I read each response out loud. Next, I ask students which of the responses, or set of responses, they'd like to tackle next, which we do either through Coggle (a digital mind map-application discussed below) or oral discussion.

The TodaysMeet responses to this article were much more vulnerable than the responses obtained through oral discussion of it. For example, in the TodaysMeet posts about it, the most provocative question raised was: "Can a white person be a black feminist?" This student may have been talking about him/her/themselves, or about me. In oral discussion, no one brought up the

TodaysMeet

Bucholtz

Listen	Talk
Is there any impunity in using the "wrong" words? a day ago by 2119	Nickname: 22345
If one has grown up in a heterogeneous environment, wouldn't it be easy to obfuscate words? a day ago by 2319	Join
Can someone be transracial? a day ago by 1123	
do white women come off as strong in speech as women of color, in other words, why are women of color put under a magnifying glass. a day ago by 937374	
Do you think the term "black feminism" has a negative connotation outside of this course? Why? 	
Room Tools	

Figure 4.4   Anonymous student writing on TodaysMeet.

question of what authority white academics do or don't have to write about black philosophy and black issues, and I know at least one reason why they wouldn't: Because their white teacher is teaching about black cultural productions. They might have thought that the question would be too confrontational or too sensitive for oral discussion. Anonymous, public writing makes these brave encounters possible, and here it led to a fruitful discussion about the intersection of identity and political commitments.

Coggle

TodaysMeet is very useful in getting a panoramic, surface view of students' questions about a text, but it is not a tool built for lengthy responses or responses to each other's writing. In order to have a deeper discussion, in which we tease out nuances, students can benefit from a tool such as Coggle, which is a digital mind map. The biggest benefits of Coggle over TodaysMeet are that responses are not limited to 140 characters and students can respond to each other's responses. Students can also synthesize responses by responding to several comments at once. Figure 4.5 is the Coggle for a session we spent on the ethics of cultural appropriation. This was initiated after one student wrote on TodaysMeet: "I am white. My mom bought me an Indian costume for Halloween. Is it ok for me to wear it?" This led to the question I posed at the center of the map: "Under what circumstances is cultural appropriation okay?" You can see from the Coggle in Figure 4.5 how students were experimenting with possible criteria and even intervening in each other's responses ("NOT OKAY EXAMPLE") using the ethos of brave space.

Encouraging Student Accountability: Student-constructed Quizzes

Although the previous sections describe anonymous writing exercises, self-identified writing is essential to any brave space. At some point each member of the space must demonstrate accountability to each other and to the assigned text. Fundamental to accountability is correctly understanding what each member of

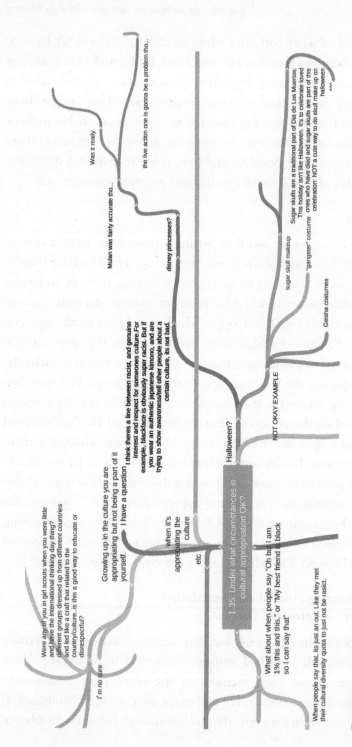

Figure 4.5 Coggle example.

The figure contains the following text:

1.35: Under what circumstances is cultural appropriation OK?

Were any of you in girl scouts when you were little and have the international thinking day thing? different groups dressed up from different countries and led like a craft that related to the country/culture...is this a good way to educate or disrespectful?

I'm no sure

Growing up in the culture you are appropriating but not being a part of it yourself.

I have a question

when it's appreciating the culture

etc

I think theres a line between racist, and genuine interest and respect for someones culture. For example, blackface is obviously super racist. But if you wear an authentic japanese kimono, and are trying to show awareness/tell other people about a certain culture, its not bad.

Halloween?

What about when people say "Oh but I am 1% this and this" or "My best friend is black so I can say that"

When people say that, its just an out. Like they met their cultural diversity quota to just not be rasict.

Was it really

the live action one is gonna be a problem tho...

Mulan was fairly accurate tho...

disney princesses?

NOT OKAY EXAMPLE

sugar skull makeup

Sugar skulls are a traditional part of Dia de Los Muertos: This holiday isn't like Halloween. It's to celebrate loved ones who have died and sugar skulls are part of this celebration: NOT a cute way to do skull make up on halloween

"gangster" costume

Geisha costumes

the group says and getting the facts of a text correct. Both these considerations fall under the purview of reading comprehension.

Reading comprehension as an act of absorption requires engagement with the text and with each other. In this way, interpretation and response are a part of, not a prerequisite to, understanding the facts of a text. To facilitate this engagement, I have students create a make-up-your-own-take-home quiz or some form of digital, public, self-identified text annotation on assigned readings. These exercises require self-identification and a different level of accountability. Because accountability is an important prerequisite to the vulnerability required of the writing exercises that I have introduced up to this point, we start the semester immediately with these reading comprehension exercises.

For the student-constructed quiz, students compose quiz questions (and include answers) in response to an assigned reading. They are asked to design a quiz that pulls out *important* points from the texts rather than asking questions about obscure passages designed to stump each other. Students write one of their questions on the board at the start of class and sign it. Then we go around the room and each student attempts to answer someone else's question. If the student on the spot cannot answer the question, we put the question to the entire class. If no one can answer the question, we put the question to its author and try to discern where in the text the answer can be found. This results in us all being accountable to the reading through trying to read a text closely, and it also teaches us how to engage a text in a public forum. I consider public, self-identified quiz questions and answers to be appropriate for self-identified writing (as opposed to anonymous writing) because reading comprehension questions and answers require less vulnerability than asking and answering critical questions of a text.

Encouraging Student Accountability: Hypothesis

An alternative tool used to build accountability to the text and each other is Hypothesis. Hypothesis is an add-on to your web browser that puts a "screen" over part of a digital text. On this

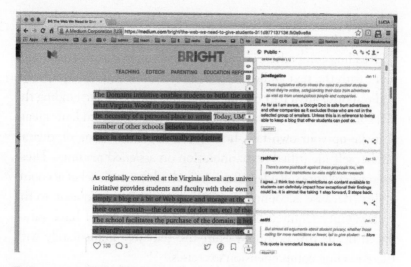

Figure 4.6 Self-identified annotations using Hypothesis.

screen, readers can write responses to a web text and to each other. It is a uniquely *public* form of text annotation, where students can engage each other's responses to the text. It too is self-identified, not anonymous. Figure 4.6 is an example of a Hypothesis conversation about an article on the web.

As you develop your own brave-space writing curriculum, consider designing the course "backwards" by answering these questions in the following order:

1. Which course concepts will require bravery to learn?
2. What major assignments will get students to be brave in learning these concepts?
3. Which minor assignments and daily activities will scaffold toward these major assignments?

As a final note, brave space requires bravery on our parts too. Annette Henry (1993–1994) notes, "For me, as a black woman, my pedagogy is not only a political act, but an act of courage" (p. 2). As we work on establishing brave spaces, we must remember that we ourselves must be on a journey to bravery. Students are not on their own; we are not just modeling brave space through writing *to* them but using writing to go through the process of brave space *with* them.

References

Arao, B. and Clemens, K. (2013). From safe spaces to brave spaces: A new way to frame dialogue around diversity and social justice. In: *The Art of Effective Facilitation: Reflections from Social Justice Educators* (ed. L. Landreman), 135–150. Sterling, VA: Stylus.

Boler, M. (1999). *Feeling Power: Emotions and Education*. New York, NY: Routledge.

Boostrom, R. (1998). Safe spaces: Reflections on an educational metaphor. *Journal of Curriculum Studies* 30 (4): 397–408.

Brookfield, S. (2014). Teaching our own racism: Incorporating personal narratives of whiteness into anti-racist practice. *Adult Learning* 25 (3): 89–95.

Bucholtz, M. (1996). Black feminist theory and African-American women's linguistic practice. In: *Rethinking Language and Gender Research* (ed. V.L. Bergvall, J.M. Bing, and A.F. Freed), 267–290. New York, NY: Routledge.

Cale, G. and Huber, S. (2001). Teaching the oppressor to be silent: Conflicts in the "democratic" classroom. *Proceedings of the 21st annual Alliance/ACE Conference: The Changing Face of Adult Learning*, Austin, TX (10–13 October 2001).

Fox, H. (2009). *When Race Breaks Out: Conversations About Race and Racism in College Classrooms*. New York, NY: Peter Lang.

Helms, J.E. (1993). *Black and White Racial Identity: Theory, Research, and Practice*. Westport, CT: Praeger.

Henry, A. (1993–1994). There are no safe places: Pedagogy as powerful and dangerous terrain. *Action in Teacher Education* 15 (4): 1–4.

hooks, b. (1994). *Teaching to Transgress: Education as the Practice of Freedom*. New York, NY: Routledge.

Leonardo, Z. and Porter, R.K. (2010). Pedagogy of fear: Toward a Fanonian theory of "safety" in race dialogue. *Race, Ethnicity and Education* 13 (2): 139–157.

Ludlow, J. (2004). From safe space to contested space in the feminist classroom. *Transformations* 15 (1): 40–56.

Marcuse, H. (1978). *The Aesthetic Dimension: Toward a Critique of Marxist Aesthetics*. Boston, MA: Beacon Press.

Rosestone Collective (2014). Safe space: Towards a reconceptualization. *Antipode* 46 (5): 1346–1365.

Singleton, G.E. (2005). *Courageous Conversations About Race: A Field Guide for Achieving Equity in Schools*. New York, NY: SAGE.

Tatum, B.D. (1992). Talking about race, learning about racism: The application of racial identity development theory in the classroom. *Harvard Educational Review* 62 (1): 1–24.

Tatum, B.D. (2003). *Why Are All the Black Kids Sitting Together in the Cafeteria? And Other Conversations About Race*. New York, NY: Basic Books.

Trout, M. and Basford, L. (2016). Preventing the shut-down: Embodied critical care in a teacher educator's practice. *Action in Teacher Education* 38 (4): 358–370.

Wijeyesinghe, C. and Jackson, B. (eds.). (2001). *New Perspectives on Racial Identity Development: A Theoretical and Practical Anthology*. New York, NY: New York University Press.

5

Teaching Intersectionality Through "I Am From…"

Mike Klein

Recently a student in my undergraduate Introduction to Justice and Peace Studies course chose to introduce herself by saying, "I am from…my family's history of war in Liberia and the conflict that continues to impact my family and my community here in the United States, where I grew up." In this brief and reflective disclosure she raised issues that were already on our syllabus, and she helped the class glimpse the reality of war beyond any academic abstraction by humanizing it through her own story. She complicated the identity categories of black and African American by identifying herself as a first-generation immigrant from an African nation who is fleeing war and dealing with the ongoing impact of violent conflict.

"I am from…" is a tool for analyzing the social construction of intersectional identity that addresses racism and other inequities in the classroom. The earliest reference to it that I've located is in a poem by George Ella Lyon, who explains:

> "Where I'm From" grew out of my response to a poem from *Stories I Ain't Told Nobody Yet* (Orchard Books, 1989) by my friend, Tennessee writer Jo Carson. All of the People Pieces, as Jo calls them, are based on things

Teaching Race: How to Help Students Unmask and Challenge Racism, First Edition. Stephen D. Brookfield and Associates.
© 2019 John Wiley & Sons, Inc. Published 2019 by John Wiley & Sons, Inc.

folks actually said, and number 22 begins, "I want to know when you get to be from a place." In the summer of 1993, I decided to see what would happen if I made my own where-I'm-from lists, which I did, in a black and white speckled composition book. I edited them into a poem – not my usual way of working – but even when that was done I kept on making the lists. The process was too rich and too much fun to give up after only one poem. Realizing this, I decided to try it as an exercise with other writers, and it immediately took off. The list form is simple and familiar, and the question of where you are from reaches deep (Lyon, n.d.).

I learned the current version from a spoken word artist and former student named Ryan Kopperud (n.d.; http://ryankopperud. com), who learned of the exercise from Lyon. He uses the exercise to ground himself in his own history and identity, in order to write and rap authentically.

"I am from…" helps students recognize their own constructed identities, enhances their ability to articulate the complexities of their identities, and encourages them to engage in a more critical analysis of power and privilege from the plural standpoints of intersectionality. This is very different from using the simplistic and abstract categories of introduction – *name, major, year in school* – so common in college classroom icebreakers. These categories position students as passive participants with little opportunity to distinguish themselves from each other or to acknowledge lived experiences that might be pertinent to the course. By humanizing and complicating those abstract categories, educators can promote the agency to claim their own identities in students while setting the stage for future critical analysis. In this chapter I explain the "I am from…" activity, describe applications for its use through examples focused on race and racism, and explore its implications for addressing other identity issues related to power and privilege.

The Context for "I am from..."

I often tell my justice and peace studies students that our class will complicate their lives as we examine a complex and interdisciplinary field through a four-step Circle of Praxis pedagogy: insertion into injustice, descriptive analysis, normative analysis, and action planning (Klein, 2013). Our analysis begins with insertion into situations of violence, oppression, or marginalization through direct field experiences or through the indirect experiences of literature, film, news media, or guest speakers. To accomplish this insertion effectively and ethically, we have to know ourselves, cross boundaries of identity and power, and encounter others with respect while avoiding harm. Self-knowledge heightens critical awareness of disciplinary standpoints for descriptive analysis of the insertion experience. Self-knowledge also grounds our normative analysis, helps us understand how other worldviews are different from our own, and spurs us to recognize our blind spots and biases. The exercise thus opens "possibilities for mediating agency" (Holland et al., 1998, p. 4) by helping students understand that how they see themselves shapes how they act in the world.

I also use the "I am from..." activity with master's- and doctoral-level students studying critical pedagogy. We examine the role of education in perpetuating or challenging racism in formal, nonformal, and informal teaching and learning environments. As practitioner-scholars, self-knowledge is essential in order to problematize and evaluate identity construction, and to understand unexamined biases, prejudices, and racialized assumptions. We recognize that we are on a lifelong journey to unearth racism that is rooted in the formative institutions of family, school, church, and community. We approach this work as critical pedagogues: not to assign blame or wallow in guilt, but to critically assess normative assumptions and to free ourselves from racist social constructions so we can pursue education as the practice of freedom (Freire, 1976; hooks, 1994).

As I write this chapter about intersectionality, I must acknowledge my own identity. While I engage in this analysis because it is urgent and important for education, I am certain to misappropriate aspects of intersectionality because my identity is neither a person of color nor female. In fact, my identities represent most of the dominant and dominating categories in the society I inhabit. I will, however, risk teaching about intersectionality and advocating for racial justice and feminism because – as an educator and activist – I do not see an alternative. So, I qualify this writing as an attempt to reach beyond the limitations of my identities in a continuing journey toward liberation from white supremacy, patriarchy, and other biases.

Teaching about intersectionality moves students beyond simplistic and binary distinctions of *black* and *white*, *male* and *female*, *rich* and *poor*. I explore more complex categories and introduce complex dynamics of power and privilege among these categories. When approaching many topics in the classroom I often prompt students by saying, "We are going to complicate this now." This is a way of helping them recognize the complexity of social justice phenomena beyond news headlines, political slogans, and Facebook memes. My undergraduate and graduate students tend to view discussions of identity as potentially divisive and may adopt a defensive rhetoric implying clear distinctions between *us* and *them*. Recognizing that the construction of identities is ongoing and complicated allows us to move beyond easy responses such as, "Everybody's oppressed, so get over it and get on with it," or, at the other end of the response spectrum, what I've heard students refer to as "the oppression Olympics": a competition over who can claim the greatest level of oppression. Both responses shut down conversations that might provide a more nuanced understanding of oppression and what to do about it.

How It Works

The "I am from…" activity requires 2 or 3 minutes for an introduction, 10 to 12 minutes for written responses, and approximately 15 minutes for students to read their responses aloud, for a total of 20 to 30 minutes. The length of time allocated for reflection and discussion following the activity depends on the amount of time the educator is willing to invest. The majority of students in my undergraduate college classroom – located in a medium-sized metropolitan area of the midwestern United States – are white, middle class, cisgendered, abled, and young. But there are also students in every class who represent very different identity categories, sometimes outwardly and proudly, and sometimes inwardly and without disclosure. I have found meaningful outcomes in using this activity with both very diverse groups and seemingly homogenous groups.

The activity begins with you, the instructor, passing around worksheets and pencils or pens. You can use a worksheet modeled on the one shown in Table 5.1 or simply use blank sheets of paper and instruct students to write the phrase "I am from..." at the top. Ensure that everyone has a place to write comfortably and with some privacy, preferably tables with chairs or desks. Begin with the directions that follow.

This exercise is about introducing yourself after reflecting individually on many different parts of your identity. It is anonymous except for the parts you are willing to share. Please do not write your name on the worksheet as you will not hand it in to me, and please do not look at others' worksheets. The phrase "I am from..." sounds like geography and might be completed by naming the place you were born, where you grew up, or where you live now. But in addition to geographic places we are also from families and ideas, histories and ethnicities, hopes and fears. Sometimes we choose where we are from. Sometimes the choice is made for us. Complete the phrase "I am from..." in as many different ways as you can in the time we have. When you are finished, you will not hand it in; no one else will see your answers. You will only read aloud the three (or four) answers you choose to speak, to identify yourself to others in this particular time and place.

Table 5.1   Sample "I am from…" worksheet.

If our identity shapes our agency, how do we give voice to our *being* to inspire our
  doing?
I am from (geography)
I am from (gender)
I am from (class)
I am from (ethnicity/race/nationality)
I am from (sexual orientation)
I am from (ability/disability)
I am from (religion/spirituality)
I am from (politics)
I am from (family)
I am from (education)
I am from (travel)
I am from (heroes/role models)
I am from (nature)
I am from (conflict/loss)
I am from (social movement)
I am from (movies/music/art/literature)
I am from (…)
I am from (…)
Or…*colonialism, hegemony, dominant culture, globalization, left-handedness,*
  outsider status, doubt, transition, liminality, crisis, love…

You should then introduce yourself with several different "I am
from…" responses to model the activity and set expectations for
the quality of responses. My responses could be:

*I am from…a lower middle-class family who made me feel rich with-
out having material wealth, substantial income, or financial resources.*
  *I am from…an education in a homogenous community with very
little difference between us, and I am from appreciation for differences that help me to learn and to grow.*

I am from...an extended family that values freedom and equality yet chooses to remain isolated from people of different ethnic and racial backgrounds.

I am from...the desire to work for social justice and create a more peaceful world, now and for generations to come.

I then model my own critical reflection in this exercise by voicing a normative response to my constructed identity:

I represent nearly every dominant and dominating category in US culture: white, male, middle class, middle aged, heterosexual, cisgendered, Christian, blonde haired, blue eyed, even right handed... but I continue to learn about the unearned privileges I am afforded by my identities and the responsibilities implied by these privileges to address personal and structural manifestations of racism and oppression.

I find that my reflection at the start of this activity draws students deeper into their own self-reflection; some of them begin writing before I finish my introduction. By addressing the personal and the structural, I also foreshadow the analysis to come in my courses on justice and peace studies or critical pedagogy. I finish the instructions by saying:

The only right answers are the ones that are true to you. Complete the phrase "I am from..." as many times as you can, in the categories you wish to address, until I ask you to finish.

When the allotted time is over (approximately 10 to 12 minutes, or as soon as most participants are finished), ask the students to complete their final phrases and to circle the three (or four) phrases they are willing to share. Ask that students begin each introductory phrase by saying "I am from..." and complete the phrases with their own responses.

The reflective time afforded for students to consider responses to the phrase "I am from...," and the context of an academic class, seem to promote positive self-identifications. I have yet to encounter a student who resisted the activity by responding with a negative or sarcastic response, although some students reply with nondescript or short answers that they perhaps see as safe responses. Contrasting the responses of students can lead to interest in, and tension over, differences. This is the point of the activity: to raise up shared or distinct identities and to welcome them all into the classroom. Some students disclose personal identifications that are deeply felt, such as "I am from...struggles with depression and finding strength in simple, daily victories." Others disclose identifications defiantly, such as "I am from...black and female and lesbian and pride and the activism it takes in this society to stand up for my rights!"

Student responses should be affirmed in the self-identification categories they are claiming and willing to express to the class. I say thank you to each student after he/she/they finishes to affirm what that student chose to share. This also prompts the next person to begin. When all students have spoken, I also acknowledge that this level of personal connection is a gift that contributes to the development of our learning community. I also suggest that this is a glimpse of what democracy looks like: learning how to live together across our differences.

The "I am from..." activity can be a profound experience for students and educators. As Myles Horton of the Highlander Folk School said, "You only learn from experiences that you learn from" (Horton, 2003, p. 120). Reflective writing and discussion about the activity can help individual students think again about their own responses, reflect on the responses of others, and deepen the sense of connection and tension between similar and diverse identities.

Following Up with Discussion

After the writing of the initial part of "I am from...," you can move into a discussion phase, with the intent of shifting students away from voicing their own identities and toward learning about the oppressions associated with those identities and the realities of overlapping and interlocking privileges. The prompts you use set the tone for these personal and perhaps vulnerable reflections of your students. Prompts should shape discussion to meet the learning objectives of your class, such as beginning to frame your learning community and creating a safe yet brave space for students to contribute. Some examples of such prompts are the following:

- What surprised you about your responses to the phrase "I am from..."?
- What surprised you about the responses of others?
- What connections or common themes did you notice? What different or contrasting themes came up?
- How might this deeper consideration of others' identities change the way you interact with them?
- What categories did you choose to share, and why? What categories did you choose not to share? (This second prompt often leads to a discussion of risk and safety.)
- How do these choices reflect the context for these introductions (in our class)? How would you identify yourself differently in other settings?
- How might our diverse identities promote or complicate our work for social justice?
- How might this activity help us view ideas about race or racism differently?

Because this activity can raise identity questions in any of the categories that have been listed, or because students may decide to add other identity categories, be prepared to have participants uncover unanticipated identity issues that might lead to emotional reactions, both positive and negative. The activity is intended to surface structural issues beyond racism that exist in society at large, such as classism, sexism, homophobia, ableism, and ageism. So the educator must expect to address unexpected responses and controversial issues.

The discussion risks leading to negative outcomes if identities are not respected by students or educators, or if an expression of intolerance goes unaddressed by the educator. For example, in response to the "I am from..." sexual orientation prompt, a student at my Catholic university said their theology professor had categorically equated homosexuality to bestiality. In that moment, I felt compelled to pause our activity and discuss how such an abstract analysis might affect people – including, perhaps, people in our class – in very real ways. It felt like an important, yet difficult and incomplete, way to address this topic. As educators, it takes some courage to step in rather than avoid or ignore such moments. The act of stepping in provides some structure for such discussions and sets the stage for deeper exploration later in the term.

When racism and other identity topics emerge unplanned in a class discussion, I sometimes opt to delay a conversation until the end of class or move it into the next class period. For example, shortly after the 2016 release of Beyoncé's "Formation" video, a white female student asked in class, "Why does Beyoncé's new video slander the police?" Half a dozen hands shot into the air as students, including several students of color, sought to confront this question. In this case, instead of opening an unstructured discussion on a potentially inflammatory question, I used the four-part, nonviolent communication framework (Rosenberg, 2003) that is part of our curriculum:

> When I *hear* you say the word *slander*, I *feel* concerned about the judgment implied in that word, and as an educator I *need* to encourage a classroom in which we think

critically about interpretation, so *I'm going to ask* that we all watch the video as extra homework and discuss it on Thursday.

The class agreed and I moved up our unit on nonviolent communication. Doing so allowed several students to express their interests and concerns prior to exploring the racial and the broader social-justice implications of the video. Students of color could decide in advance how much – if at all – they wanted to be educators to their white peers, and all students had a chance to reflect on the video in light of the plural and intersectionalized identities uncovered in the "I am from..." activity earlier than they ever had in my classroom.

What "I am from..." Accomplishes for Students

The "I am from..." exercise raises identity issues that are often neglected in the classroom. It complicates the role of educator by requiring us to introduce students to new and challenging ideas about the construction of pluralistic identities and the intersections of power, oppression, and privilege connected to those identities. This invariably raises difficult issues, feels risky, and happens imperfectly. But where better to discuss, learn, and grow than in higher education? In fact, "I am from..." accomplishes multiple tasks in its execution:

- It prompts students to begin class as active learners by replacing typical formulaic introductions or generic icebreaker questions.
- It provides a low-stakes (ungraded) writing assignment that promotes student voice and creative expression in the classroom.
- It asks students to reflect on the complex nature of their identities and where various identifiers are rooted.
- It enhances student agency by requiring active participation in the social construction of identity.

- It practices critical thinking about the construction of identity and how different identities sustain, reproduce, and sometimes challenge privilege and oppression.

Replacing Formulaic Introductions and Icebreakers

Typical first-class-meeting formulaic introductions ask students to identify themselves by narrow and abstract parameters. They often reduce students' identities to the names given to them by parents or guardians, even if an allowance is permitted for nicknames or name preferences. They are asked to share the meritocratic identity of year in school or the broadly defining choice of a major field of study. Simplistic introductions can conceal more than they reveal and imply that students should leave most of their identities outside the classroom. Investing time in more thorough and reflective introductions can enhance students' critical thinking, as active participants in the class who teach and learn from each other.

Sara Ahmed (2014) notes, "Histories are bound up with emotions precisely insofar as it is a question of what *sticks* [emphasis in the original], of what connections are lived as the most intense or intimate, as being closer to the skin" (p. 54). "I am from..." surfaces both intellectual and affective responses as students disclose the unexamined histories behind their identities. Students can share emotional responses regarding the relative significance of identity categories and enter into some productively contentious discussion about the degree and meaning of privilege and oppression associated with identity categories.

Promoting Student Creativity

"I am from..." allows for a degree of improvisational creativity that sometimes extends to a powerful form of testimonial. Claiming one's identity is a form of improvisation (Holland et al., 1998; Lederach, 2004) that stands in stark contrast to the rote memorization that typifies highly structured classroom environments. I believe that this kind of improvisation can liberate students from overly deterministic identity categories and strengthens students' ability to articulate their complex identities.

I've personally experienced creative outcomes from the "I am from..." activity over the years. As an example, this poem was sent to me after I presented the activity to AmeriCorps Fellows at a conference marking the end of their yearlong service:

Met a Man
Where we are from is more than,
WHERE we are FROM,
so said the man from justice,
the man calling us to be
FROM aware.
Reveling at revelation,
I met a man from epiphany,
shining the bright light of insight,
the man calling us to be
FROM introspection.
Loving through her orphan confusion, fear, insecurity,
I met a man from child-in-need,
always running toward another,
the man calling us to be
FROM empathy.
Teaching the ways of the wise inheritors,
I met a man from the road less traveled,
blazing new paths through forests of apathy,
the man calling us to be
FROM sacrifice.
Speaking of giving he said: give fully, artfully,
I met a man from original,
blending new with tried and true,
the man calling us to be
FROM service.
Inspiring, collaborating, creating,
I met a man from living,

seeing the need, filling the need,
the man calling us to be
FROM do.

Joseph M. Pendal, AmeriCorps Promise Fellow, 2015

In and through the freedom of creative expression, there is potential for liberation from the constraints of unexamined racism and perhaps some healing from what Wendell Berry (1989) calls the "hidden wound of racism." The opportunity for students to find and use their voices, and to claim their own identities, can be empowering as a form of testimonial. By claiming their identities, students can engage in testimonial as truth telling, which, according to Sara Ahmed, "makes demands on the others to hear, but which does not always get a just hearing" (Ahmed, 2014, p. 200). Even if some students fail to respond to the "I am from…" identity claims by fellow students, Ahmed argues that "We should not conclude that testimonial forms of politics fail in such failures to hear, or in such refusals of recognition. Testimonies about the injustices of colonisation, slavery and racism are not only calls for recognition; they are also forms of recognition, in and of themselves" (p. 200). When racism is uncritically internalized, voicing identity claims can be an emancipatory act, no matter the response.

Getting Students to Reflect on the Complexity of Identity

"I am from…" asks students to reflect on the complex nature of their identities and the social and political locations of their various identifiers. It addresses racism by encouraging participants to think about the pluralistic nature of their constructed identities, including the social construction of race. This has particular resonance for those placing identity as one color in a spectrum or mosaic comprising a beautifully diverse rainbow. Weak understandings of diversity may define "us" as the dominant or majority group in the act of including, tolerating, or accepting "them" as the other. These monolithic and conformist categories presume inclusion to mean an assimilation of minority identities into a single dominant identity with a concurrent loss of distinction and an ignorance of the operations of power and privilege. This state might be captured by the phrase "I don't see color," which judges racial categories as unimportant or neglects associated privileges and oppression. "I am from..." complicates identities and questions students' assumptions so they can work across differences without erasing important distinctions.

When students contemplate the roots of their identities in predetermined and socially reproduced categories, this helps to depersonalize the analysis of racism. Identity categories can be seen as social constructs with overlapping oppressions, rather than as given and fixed identities. This is enormously helpful in moving discussions beyond individual guilt to examining the influence of social structures. When students regard their multiple identity categories as contingent, and when they start to view racism as structural, they can begin to address racism in terms of what can be changed. In popular culture, discussions of racial identity are often premised on binary, even black and white (pun intended), categories. Complicating students' identities by rooting them in social influences helps students understand the social construction of race and the related but differential categories of ethnicity, nationality, and hybridity. It then becomes easier to link these conceptions of race with analyses of power and privilege, and how identities are "oppressed and produced" (Brown, 1997, p. 87) by social relations that construct, maintain, or challenge identity.

A student's response to the "I am from..." exercise often changes as he/she/they proceed through the term, from class to class, or in co-curricular activities, or in the context of family, religious, and social gatherings. Classrooms of a particular discipline may call very particular identity categories to prominence. For example, in my peace studies classroom, experiences of conflict and violence may cause students to create identities of mediators or troublemakers for themselves. In another discipline, such as sociology, categories based on ethnicity or race will likely rise to the surface. Helping students recognize their changing responses to "I am from..." may help them to understand how the significance or power attached to identity alters depending on context, which is itself a useful touchstone for further discussions.

"I am from..." invites students to reflect on the rootedness of different identity categories. Distinguishing among identity categories that are chosen, earned, inherent, or inherited can lead to a greater awareness and analysis of common understandings or misunderstandings. This often creates a degree of internal cognitive dissonance that manifests itself in conflict between students who are struggling to come to terms with their underlying values and assumptions about identity. For example, if you have consistently seen yourself as a good white person (Sullivan, 2014), any suspicion that you might be enacting structural racism is going to lead you to vigorously protest your allyship. So educators should anticipate – and when possible cultivate – contentious discussions about the tensions between individual agency and social determination, the diversity in gender or sexual identity, distinctions between earned and unearned privilege, and issues of class consciousness and socioeconomic status.

When these discussions happen, you should be prepared for some highly emotional responses. In the *Cultural Politics of Emotion*, Sara Ahmed writes, "emotions are not [something] simply 'I' or 'we' have. Rather, it is through emotions, or how we respond to objects and others, that surfaces and boundaries are made: the 'I' and the 'we' are shaped by, and even take the shape of, contact with other" (2014, p. 10). In other words, our identities and our feelings about them are formed socially, in relation to the identities of others. Unless examined, oppression and privilege function uncritically within this emotional topography. Ahmed describes "emotions as performative: they both generate their objects, and repeat past associations. The loop of the performative works powerfully: in reading the other as being disgusting, for example, the subject is filled up with disgust, as a sign of the truth of the reading" (p. 194). Discussions following the "I am from..." activity can benefit from the teacher preparing students to deal with the emotions associated with racism and other inequalities. They should affirm the role of affective learning in classrooms that might otherwise deny emotions as inappropriate and create structured settings and protocols to help students sit with strongly emotional expressions of anger and hurt, rather than seeking to move quickly past them.

Involving Students in the Active Construction of Their Identities

Students who see identity as fixed are subject to the socially imposed limitations of those same identities. When students introduce themselves to classroom peers who might be friends, acquaintances, or strangers, and when they introduce themselves to the educator, they have the chance to shape their own – and others' – conceptions of their identity. For instance, a student recently responded to this activity by stating, "I am from...a Latinx ancestry and white-passing," which allowed her to assert an identity that might otherwise be overlooked. Another student responded to the activity by declaring, "I am from...mild autism that leads to struggles with traditional educational approaches, but also gives me unique insights through my different ways of thinking." This student claimed the category of "mild autism" to proactively describe his noticeably different behavior and to name it as a strength before others might make their own deficit-based interpretations.

Making such identity claims was an exercise of student agency. They structured the recognition of identity on their own terms, rather than being subject to predetermined categories or unspoken biases. These "I am from..." responses might be rooted in previous misunderstanding or discrimination that might now be pre-empted before the next harm occurs. Such identity claims are an act of recognition and a naming of biases based on assumptions about identity. As Ahmed states, "The visibility produced by recognition is actually the visibility of the ordinary and normative or the invisibility of what has been concealed under the sign of truth" (Ahmed, 2014, p. 200). "I am from..." promotes visibility of implicit bias in the face of identity claims made by students who are discovering their agency to shape the social construction of their own identities.

"I am from…" also allows students to decide which identifiers they won't share, so that disclosure is not forced. Too often, when discussing race and racism in classes that are predominantly white, students of color are asked to teach white students about their experience, when their only obligation in class should be learning. For students of color who have reflectively taken on the responsibility to educate their peers, the opportunity to teach and learn can enhance their sense of agency. If, however, students of color are assumed to possess the self-knowledge, interest, and willingness to teach their peers about race and racism, educators are exercising a coercive pedagogical power. When race and racism is explicitly on the syllabus, I invite (in advance) anyone with questions or concerns (whatever the student's identity) to visit me during office hours or to set up an appointment. Only a few students accept this invitation, but it has led to powerful conversations about race and racism in the classroom and on campus.

Promoting Critical Thinking

Finally, and perhaps most importantly, "I am from…" frames the course within the overall project of critical thinking. Students are told that they will be examining the construction of race and identity and the connection of these constructions to the functioning of social structures that sustain, reproduce, or challenge the privilege and oppression associated with different racial identities. This complication of simple identity categories is foundational to moving students from personal and individual conceptions of bias and prejudice to seeing racism as structural and systemic. "I am from…" depersonalizes personal guilt over racial biases by grounding analysis in the structural production of privilege and oppression.

In my own field of peace studies, Johan Galtung (1969) problematizes an individualist analysis of race through the terms *structural violence* and *cultural violence* that are seen as complementing the notion of *direct violence*; all of these are viewed as elements of organized violence. Structural violence "shows up as unequal power and consequently as unequal life chances" (Galtung, 1969, p. 171), while cultural violence includes "those aspects of culture...that can be used to justify or legitimate direct or structural violence" (Galtung, 1990, p. 291). For example, the violence of racism is evident in the housing policy known as redlining. When the US Federal Housing Authority developed policy on urban housing values, it racialized access to credit so that mortgages would be approved for predominantly white suburban housing and denied for urban housing where most people of color lived. This structural violence of unequal power and unequal life chances reinforced the association between race and poverty that has its roots in institutionalized slavery, segregation, discriminatory laws, and the like.

The cultural violence of racism then assigns individual characteristics and behaviors (being inferior, lazy, stupid, or inherently violent) based on racial identity. White supremacy maintains itself by disregarding the overwhelming history and present practices of prejudice, bias, and bigotry that typify cultural violence. Add these together, and structural and cultural violence are used to justify direct violence, as housing is destroyed in gentrification, calls for justice are repressed as riots, and unarmed people of color are disproportionately killed by police. Asking where identity comes from in the "I am from..." activity helps set the stage for an examination of racism as historical and societal, in terms of structural, cultural, and direct violence. It is a small step in the process that Paulo Freire (2000) refers to as *conscientização*: learning to perceive social, political, and economic contradictions, and then taking action against oppressive elements of a society. Acknowledging the difference between what is natural or given and what is constructed is the start of understanding what can be differently constructed.

Theorizing the "I am from..." Activity

Exploring pluralistic identity relies on a number of theoretical analyses. Most foundational is the conceptualization of intersectionality first articulated by Kimberlé Crenshaw (1989, 1991) in her analysis of the ways racial and gender dynamics combine to complicate the understanding of black women's oppression. Intersectionality has since been developed and extended to address multiple overlapping identity categories that also convey overlapping oppressions (Anzaldúa, 1987; Collins, 1989; hooks, 1984; Sandoval 1991). More recent writing on intersectionality, such as the powerful volume *Intersectionality* by Hill Collins and Bilge (2016), also frames "I am from…"

Wendy Brown's work on the role of different discourses in identity construction is also influential, particularly her assertion that "We are not simply oppressed but *produced* [emphasis in the original] through these discourses, a production that is historically complex, contingent, and occurs through formations that do not honor analytically distinct identity categories" (Brown, 1997, p. 87). In complicating our plural identities and their attendant power dynamics, Brown reminds us that identity categories are constructed and malleable, socially determined yet also shaped by our own agency, and aligned to different degrees with aspects of oppression and privilege.

Writing on identity is a significant opportunity for students to explore intersectionality through a tangible and iterative process. Repetitive completion of the "I am from…" phrase evokes multiple and varied responses to a list of possible identity categories and helps students proactively claim their identities. This is in direct opposition to the standard power relations and practices of higher education, where students are often told what to learn and invited to use their voices only to ask clarifying questions or produce the expected answers to educators' questions. Voice in this context is, "the praxis of self-concept in action; the theory of our own identity in relationship to the way we enact that identity in the world" (Klein, 2016, p. 46). As a simple performance, rather than just a written assignment, the "I am from…" activity can be empowering to students. As ritual theorist Tom Driver (1998) states, "If you can perform, you are aware that you *could* [emphasis in the original] perform differently, and this is the beginning of freedom" (p. 236).

Conclusion

My experiences with "I am from..." have been overwhelmingly positive. The activity allows students to bring more of themselves into the classroom on the first day of class. It helps develop a richer learning community by acknowledging the plural and complex identities of its members. For undergraduate college students, it can promote the developmental task of distinguishing and claiming their identities separate from the influence of peers, parents, and other groups, such as churches and paramilitary groups. I have used this activity to address social justice issues with graduate students, grassroots community leaders, and youth groups. It is powerful as a stand-alone activity and more powerful when integrated into developing and deepening critical reflection and the analysis of racism and other identity constructions. I hope you will adapt the "I am from..." activity to your own needs and context, and that it will contribute toward your lifelong journey of self-discovery and understanding.

References

Ahmed, S. (2014). *The Cultural Politics of Emotion*. Edinburgh: Edinburgh University Press.

Anzaldúa, G. (1987). *Borderlands/La Frontera: The New Mestiza*. San Francisco, CA: Aunt Lute Books.

Berry, W. (1989). *The Hidden Wound*. San Francisco, CA: North Point Press.

Brown, W. (1997). The impossibility of women's studies. *differences* 9 (3): 79–101.

Collins, P.H. (1989). The social construction of black feminist thought. *Signs* 14 (4): 745–773.

Crenshaw, K.W. (1989). Demarginalizing the intersection of race and sex: A black feminist critique of antidiscrimination doctrine, feminist theory, and antiracist politics. *University of Chicago Legal Forum* 1: 139–167.

Crenshaw, K.W. (1991). Mapping the margins: Intersectionality, identity politics, and violence against women of color. *Stanford Law Review* 43: 1241–1299.

Driver, T. (1998). *Liberating Rites: Understanding the Transformative Power of Ritual*. Boulder, CO: Westview Press.

Freire, P. (1976). *Education as the Practice of Freedom*. London: Writers and Readers Cooperative.

Freire, P. (2000). *Pedagogy of the Oppressed*, 30th Anniversary Edition. New York: Continuum International.

Galtung, J. (1969). Violence, peace and peace research. *Journal of Peace Research* 6: 171.

Galtung, J. (1990). Cultural violence. *Journal of Peace Research* 27 (3): 291–305.

Hill Collins, P. and Bilge, S. (2016). *Intersectionality*. Malden, MA: Polity.

Holland, D., Lachicotte, W. Jr., Skinner, D. et al. (1998). *Identity and Agency in Cultural Worlds*. Cambridge, MA: Harvard University Press.

hooks, b. (1984). *Feminist Theory: From Margin to Center*. Cambridge, MA: South End Press.

hooks, b. (1994). *Teaching to Transgress: Education as the Practice of Freedom*. New York: Routledge.

Horton, M. (2003). *The Myles Horton Reader: Education for Social Change*. Knoxville, TN: University of Tennessee Press.

Klein, M. (2013). Cell phones, t-shirts and coffee: Codification of commodities in a Circle of Praxis pedagogy. *Peace Studies Journal* 6 (1): 31–45.

Klein, M. (2016). *Democratizing Leadership: Counter-hegemonic Democracy in Organizations, Institutions, and Communities*. Charlotte, NC: Information Age Publishing.

Kopperud, R. (n.d.). Ryan Kopperud. http://ryankopperud.com (accessed 31 July 2017).

Lederach, John Paul. (2005). *The Moral Imagination: The Art and Soul of Building Peace*, 2nd ed. New York: Oxford University Press.

Lyon, G.E. (n.d.). Where I'm from. Georgeellalyon.com. www.georgeellalyon.com/where.html (accessed 31 July 2017).

Rosenberg, M.B. (2003). *Nonviolent Communication: A Language of Life*. Encinitas, CA: Puddledancer Press.

Sandoval, C. (1991). U.S. third world feminism: The theory and method of oppositional consciousness in the postmodern world. *Genders* 10 (Spring): 1–24.

Sullivan, S. (2014). *Good White People: The Problem with Middle-Class White Anti-Racism*. Albany, NY: State University of New York Press.

6

Building Trust and Negotiating Conflict When Teaching Race

Pamela E. Barnett

When emerging white nationalist leader Derek Black enrolled in Florida's New College, he kept his identity and his beliefs to himself for the first year. For one, he quickly realized that most fellow students would not be sympathetic to his argument that immigration was leading to a "white genocide." He was right. When he was outed by a fellow student, the New College student community engaged in an enraged Facebook thread. Some students with whom he had socialized felt betrayed; many called on the community to shun him. But a handful of students saw an opportunity to influence him through engagement. One student posted the question: "Who's clever enough to think of something we can do to change this guy's mind?" (Saslow, 2016). The answer: a Shabbat dinner invitation.

Derek had been collegial with an Orthodox Jewish student in his residence hall, and in the fall of 2011, after months of alienation, he accepted the invitation to join a diverse group of students for the dinner. He became a regular guest, and for a few months no one addressed the elephant in the room. But with time and trust people began to ask him about his beliefs, which he defended, including his belief that it would be better if each race lived

Teaching Race: How to Help Students Unmask and Challenge Racism, First Edition.
Stephen D. Brookfield and Associates.
© 2019 John Wiley & Sons, Inc. Published 2019 by John Wiley & Sons, Inc.

separately, "in its own homeland." The dialogue continued, with Derek straddling two different communities, occasionally joining his father to produce a weekly white nationalist radio program. But he liked his new friends and found himself increasingly unsettled by the questions and perspectives they shared. He was also scholarly and aspired to base his beliefs on "facts." He was affected by research on structural causes of racial achievement gaps, the scientifically verified health impacts of discrimination, and bias in the media. He read about white privilege.

By 2013 his views had changed significantly, and he sent a letter to the Southern Poverty Law Center disavowing white nationalism and inviting the organization to publish his letter. His statement bespoke an ideological and personal transformation: "The things I have said, as well as my actions, have been harmful to people of color, people of Jewish descent, activists striving for opportunity and fairness for all. I am sorry for the damage done" (Black, 2016). His defection led to outrage on Stormfront, a prominent white nationalist website founded by his father, and painful conflict with his family.

After Donald Trump's election to the presidency, Derek was again moved to speak publically in a letter to the *New York Times*. He expressed concern about Trump's appeal to racism and also addressed a question he was uniquely equipped to answer: How can we change racist or racially biased hearts and minds? Derek offered that such change would require "person-to-person interactions" and a "lot of honest listening on both sides." He credited his newly democratic and antiracist commitments to "diverse people," who included him in conversations rather than "ostraciz[ing] him" (Black, 2016).

Derek's explanation for his new knowledge and personal growth echoes research on the impact of diversity experiences on students in higher education. Students develop both cognitive and social skills through engagement with diverse peers (Antonio et al., 2004; Astin, 1993; Chang, Astin, and Kim, 2004; Gurin et al., 2002; Hurtado, 2001; Hu and Kuh, 2003.) Students who engage in structured intergroup dialogue sessions have been found to gain critical self-reflection and perspective-taking (Gurin, Nagda, and Lopez, 2004; Nagda, 2006; Nagda and Zuniga, 2003). Both the University of Michigan's model of intergroup dialogue and Charles Rojzman's Transformational Social Therapy prioritize dialogue and narrative for addressing the cognitive, but also the affective, dimensions of teaching race (Dorman, 2017).

This chapter provides strategies for meeting a key cognitive learning goal: the ability to recognize and apply the concept of structural racism to analyses of social inequality and to lived experience. This cognitive goal is tied to an affective, or so-called human dimension, goal for students to better understand themselves, others, and their relationships to others within pervasive systems of structural inequality (Fink, 2003). As a teacher of race, I aspire for this affective development to influence students to recognize commonality with, feel empathy for, and collaborate with peers from diverse backgrounds. These cognitive and human dimension goals are met through engagement with scholarship, but also, critically, through sustained and meaningful engagement with diverse others. The strategies shared here are grounded in dialogue and narrative, which are well suited to teach these twin goals in relationship to each other.

I first became aware of Derek Black's story from colleagues who posted it on Facebook with celebratory announcements about the value of liberal-arts education. Higher education is a ripe arena for such learning and development, but there is nothing inherent in our context to produce such outcomes. Indeed, some pedagogical practices are barriers. True engagement on race (whether through the lenses of biology or sociology, or the lenses of literature or psychology) is hard to come by. Students often avoid the "contentious and difficult" (Keith, 2010, p. 2), and students are not unique in their reticence to speak honestly about race and avoid potential conflict (Dalton, 1995). Students may avoid asking questions or making statements for fear of offending others or being negatively judged or ostracized.

Faculty can promote this avoidant behavior by lecturing for the majority of a class period focused on racial content, or by correcting or minimizing student contributions that are uncomfortable or even offensive. This chapter assumes the productive power of honesty, well-managed conflict, and reflective questioning. This chapter assumes that there is less cognitive and affective learning in classrooms that requires students to censor their potentially racially biased questions or beliefs, or their anger and frustration about racial discrimination. As teachers of race within higher education, we are in a profound position to engage students who are not "in the choir": Students who may be on one far end of the continuum (like Derek) as well as students who are less toxically bound, but still fettered by all the biases, fears, and frustrations they have inhaled from American culture. This chapter offers specific exercises for creating trust and managing conflict, some of the very conditions for honest dialogue that helped change Derek Black's mind and life.

Techniques for Building Trust

Why should students trust you? Chances are that their experience of at least some teachers has been in the form of authorities, avoiders, or correctors when it comes to discussions of race. When you ask students to openly engage this historically, socially, and emotionally significant topic, you should do so knowing they are likely eager to "say the right thing" in front of you and other students until they know you better. Students of different racial identities will fear being publicly shamed, humiliated, or embarrassed. White students will shut down and stay quiet so as not to be called racist, and students of color will be weary, and wary, of being asked to speak for their race. They will also have seen discussions intended to challenge racism actually worsen the situation by leaving students resentful and angry with their peers' refusal to listen seriously. In this situation teachers need to be especially mindful of working in a way that builds trust and to feel prepared to find themselves in highly conflictual discussions.

The Good Doctor

Students need to know they are in good hands. Will you listen to them, respect them, care about them, and treat them fairly? Will you lead difficult conversations competently? Charles Rojzman, founder of Transformational Social Therapy, teaches that all facilitators of diverse groups must represent themselves first as "the good doctor," communicating competence and instilling trust (Rojzman, 1999). Carefully plan how you will introduce yourself on the first day of an entire class or an individual lesson on race to reassure them on these points. This is also the time to address your racial identity. For example, students may be afraid of triggering or offending you as a person of color, or having their experiences misunderstood by you as a white professor. Reflect on what your social identity might signal to different students and be prepared to discuss it with authenticity and even vulnerability. In my first year as a white professor of English and African American Studies at the University of South Carolina I lacked the courage and expertise to address my whiteness honestly. I knew none of us was color blind, but had convinced myself that if I communicated warmth, accessibility, and fairness that students' racial concerns would magically recede. To this day I am grateful to a black student who took the risk of confronting me in a poem he submitted along with his first essay. It read:

It is the first day of AFRO 398 and who do I see?
A short, black-haired white lady looking at me.
Why is she here? What is her story?
I didn't think whites cared about our history.
The answer to these questions I do not know,
So I will sit back, watch, and go with the flow.

I often recite this poem on the first day, telling the story of my original reluctance to name my whiteness and how this student challenged me to be honest. I also share that he taught me to recognize and have empathy for my students' feelings, which could include confusion, fear, anger, and distrust. I explicitly name and allow negative emotion and then tell some of my story, commitments, and experience as a teacher of race. I intend to inspire confidence as their guide, in part by naming my vulnerability and modeling capacity for growth in this area. Each instructor who teaches race has his or her own authentic story. Tell it.

When teaching race, it is essential to convey your experience and expertise to teach material that is often difficult. I offer that after years of practice, I have strategies for facilitating lively, interactive, and even transformative classes on race. I think it is worth explicitly articulating that you have rich experience building a classroom that is challenging but nonviolent, a classroom that is sometimes uncomfortable but characterized by trust and goodwill. You can reassure them that they don't have to say anything that they don't want to say, but that you believe they will gain courage after engaging in your intentional methods for building trust and confronting fears. It is essential that we communicate our ability to give students the benefit of the doubt as they work through difficult material, and to be kind, calm, and generous guides in difficult conversations.

Once teachers have initiated the relationship to ask for students' trust, they should give students time to respond and have empathy when they do not. The fears can be quite deep. After setting the stage for students to trust you as the teacher, I recommend that instructors turn to a series of exercises for building trust in the group. I use the four that follow, sometimes in sequence, sometimes in isolation, depending on the nature of the material and my particular learning goals for the class.

Naming and Narrating: My Favorite Icebreaker for a Class on Race

In order to build classroom community, students should start getting to know each other as human beings as soon as possible. My favorite icebreaker for a race-based class is based on a two-page vignette from Sandra Cisneros's (1987) *The House on Mango Street*.

The chapter "My Name" models a reflection on names that entails family history, ethnicity, and even fantasies of self-definition or transformation. The narrator Esperanza reflects: "In English my name means hope. In Spanish it means too many letters. It means sadness, it means waiting...It was my great-grandmother's name and now it is mine" (p. 10). She remarks that at school people "say [her] name funny, as if the syllables were made out of tin and hurt the roof of your mouth" but that her name is made of a "softer something" when voiced in Spanish (p. 11). Still, she says: "I would like to baptize myself under a new name, a name more like the real me" (p. 11).

I ask students to read "My Name" and to use it as inspiration to craft and share their own reflections or relevant stories on their names. It is a low-risk exercise and students will share as much or as little personal information as they wish. But inevitably quite a few students will share personal information that will make them less mysterious and more accessible to class members. I always participate in the exercise as well, in an effort to continue to humanize me as their teacher and to reduce fear.

Trust in interpersonal relationships is built as people take the risk of expressing authenticity and vulnerability (Cook et al., 2005; Holmes and Remplel, 1989) and also as they successfully engage in collaborative experiences and repeated interactions with an immediate circle of collaborators (Marschall and Stolle, 2004). I believe it follows that if students in an interracial classroom gain "personalized trust" and collaborate with each other, those students are more likely to have the "generalized trust" necessary for citizenship and collaboration in diverse neighborhoods, diverse workplaces, and ultimately a diverse democracy (Marschall and Stolle, 2004). It is worth being aware that personalized and generalized trust varies by social identity. In short, "[w]ealthy people tend to be more trusting than poor people; white people tend to be more trusting than minorities, and college graduates tend to be more trusting than people who are less educated" (Tablante and Fiske, 2015, p. 186). This icebreaker begins the gradually escalating trust process that you will facilitate for the group, providing conditions for authenticity and self-revelation. Aspire for all students to gain this level of comfort, while expecting differences in how, when, and if students relax into vulnerability.

Articulating Hopes and Fears: Three Feedback Formats

I advocate (Barnett, 2011) scaffolding students' learning with less challenging tasks at the outset to build both skill and confidence for more demanding intellectual, psychological, and social exercises. For example, building trust might take the form of "asking students to reveal relatively neutral information about the self, gradually asking for more revelation on more difficult, potentially controversial questions" (p. 677). The Articulating Hopes and Fears exercise escalates the risk by asking students to reflect on, and potentially express, the hope and vulnerability they feel as they anticipate discussing race in a particular class, with particular people. I encourage students to write as freely as possible, without self-censoring, on the two questions that follow. I am always careful to introduce the exercise by communicating that no one will be called on, expected to speak up, or judged negatively for not sharing.

1. How do you *hope* we will interact and discuss with each other in a class that teaches about race? What do you *hope* to learn or gain?
2. What *fears* do you have about discussing race with the people in this room (including teacher and fellow students)?

After approximately 15 minutes of freewriting, I ask them to share their hopes and fears in one of three formats: (1) a large group discussion, (2) a Gallery Walk, or (3) through interactive presentation software with survey capability. In my experience, several students will initiate and take the risk of sharing in a *large group discussion*. If you choose this feedback format, write their hopes and fears on the board as they speak, using students' own words as much as possible. If students play it too safe, be prepared to add some of your own hopes and fears, or to mention hopes and fears that you've heard expressed by students in the past. I try to model the level of disclosure and naming with contributions such as the following: "I hope that we won't be too politically correct," "I fear that I might say something biased," "I fear that everyone's going to look to me for the so-called black or Latino or Asian point of view." An advantage of the large group discussion is that students get to connect vulnerable statements to particular individuals, creating bonds of trust between a set of the most involved individuals.

When students share their hopes and fears through a *Gallery Walk* I distribute Post-it notes of one color and ask students to write just one hope or one fear on each note. They can have as many Post-it notes as they want. I collect and shuffle them to protect anonymity and then hang them about the room for students to view and contemplate. The advantage of this method of sharing is that students are likely to see a significant number of common hopes and fears. This can make them feel less alone with their own desires and concerns. This method also enables students and you, the instructor, to get a good read of the room; that is, what the prevailing hopes and fears to be managed are.

You can achieve similar outcomes by collecting and sharing students' hopes and fears with interactive presentation technology that has survey capability, such as Poll Everywhere, Mentimeter, Nearpod, or UMU. These software applications can be used with cell phones and allow students to respond with short answers to questions in a yes-no, multiple-choice, Likert-scale, or open-ended format. I advise that students engage in the Hopes and Fears freewrite before being polled so that they can see their own ideas reflected in the responses of others or in the survey items you provide. You can have students send short answers to each prompt, which will be collected and presented by the software. You might also invite students to weigh in anonymously on a set of Likert-scale items (*strongly agree* to *strongly disagree*) such as the following:

I have lots of experience talking about race in an interracial group.

I have minimal experience talking about race in an interracial group.

I think America would be better if people from different races felt more comfortable with each other.

I can learn from people in this class who have different experiences from me because of race.

Sometimes I don't say what I am thinking about race because I am afraid I will offend someone.

Sometimes I don't say what I am thinking about race because I am afraid of being misunderstood.

I am nervous about talking honestly about race in this class.

I think it is better not to talk about race because there might be conflict.

I would be very upset if someone said my comment was prejudiced (or biased or racist).

I would be very upset if someone said my comment was irrational or overly sensitive.

Instructors can set up the presentation to reveal histograms of answers on yes-no and Likert-scale items. They can also reveal the short answers after all answers are in and keyboards are silent, thus protecting students' identities. As with the Gallery Walk, the collected anonymous responses will very likely name some common hopes and fears, reassuring students that they are not alone and providing a public airing of the emotional tenor of the classroom.

Of course, a disadvantage to this format is that not all students will have cell phones.

Any of these three formats for naming hopes and fears can be productively followed up by small groups of students, in which they talk about what surprised them in the responses, what resonated with them, and what they agreed or disagreed with and why. Small groups are likely to be lively and honest after this exercise that begins with individual reflection and is followed by large-group sharing.

Addressing Hopes and Fears with Ground Rules

Scholars of teaching and learning have recommended collaboratively establishing discussion ground rules, often with student input (Brookfield, 2005; Copp and Kleinman, 2008; Warren, 2005). Community practitioners of the University of Michigan intergroup dialogue model also establish ground rules for communication (DeTurk, 2006). This step in the process can build on the scaffold provided by the previously described Hopes and Fears exercise. It begins by inviting students to draft rules of engagement and communication that explicitly address how to realize the expressed hopes and how to minimize the expressed fears. For example:

Hope: That people will connect the course material to their personal experiences. → *Ground rule:* We will connect course material to shared personal experiences.

Hope: We will listen to each other and feel heard by each other. → *Ground rule:* We will listen attentively and reflect back what we hear said.

Fear: Being judged or shunned by people outside of class based on something said inside class → *Ground rule:* We will keep the confidence of all class members.

Fear: Being misunderstood. → *Ground rule:* We will give and take opportunities to clarify or amend comments.

Telling Our Stories in Relation to White Privilege

What might the next landing on the scaffold look like in classroom practice? How can we escalate the risk to teach structural racism and the way that it is manifest in socially determined advantages or disadvantages? This cognitive goal is well met by close reading of Peggy McIntosh's (1988) "White Privilege: Unpacking the Invisible Knapsack". I ask students to brainstorm independently about other privileges that accrue to whiteness and then apply the concept by reflecting on specific experiences in which they had one of the privileges on the list or did not.

Once they have identified a specific experience of privilege or lack of privilege, I ask them to fully describe that experience using the sentence starter "I remember" for every detail they can summon about that experience. Students essentially write a prose poem rich with details about where they were, what happened, what was said, who was involved, what they felt, and what they thought. This requires students to apply the concept directly to their own experiences, so that as they share and listen to others' experiences it takes on the flesh, bones, and blood of racialized experiences. These prose poems entail risk and require vulnerability that can lead to greater trust and cooperation within the class.

The exercise is not without complication, as some white students will resist the idea that they have white privilege. There are both cognitive and affective dimensions to this resistance. The cognitive objection often takes the form of legitimately noting that other categories of identity may undercut some of their privilege. A working-class white student does not have the identical experience of white privilege as an upper-class white student does. A white gay male does not have the exact experience of white privilege enjoyed by a straight white male. White students who identify with their ethnicity or relatively recent stories of immigration are likely to cite their ancestors' experiences of discrimination.

These objections offer valuable teachable moments, as they provide some stake in learning about the concept of intersectionality.

I acknowledge the power of their insights and encourage them to tie these to course readings on intersectionality. My goal is not to shut down this line of argument, but to direct students to focus on racial privilege or disadvantage first. They must explore white privilege fully. They are then free to consider how other aspects of identity (gender, class, ethnicity, ability) either compound or diminish their experience of privilege or disadvantage.

The affective dimension of this resistance may be linked to white guilt. I address this feeling directly when setting up the exercise by reminding students that the concept describes a broad social experience, not only their individual experiences. No matter where they fall on the continuum, students are the recipients of and subordinates to this system of privilege and disadvantage. Rather than feel guilty, they might feel indignant and resistant, willing to make common cause to dismantle these structural inequalities.

Strategies for Responding to Classroom Conflicts

After the white nationalist demonstration and death of an antiracist counterprotester in Charlottesville, Donald Trump suggested that removing a statue of Robert E. Lee was the top of a slippery slope that could lead to the removal of monuments to George Washington and Thomas Jefferson, founding fathers and enslavers both. Many scholars and commentators argued that Trump's was a false equivalence that failed to recognize crucial historical differences. These American figures certainly enslaved people, but their legacy was more complicated in that they founded the nation, whereas the Confederates sought to dismantle it. Trump's suggestion was dismissed in many circles: Of course removing monuments to Washington and Jefferson did not logically follow from the decision to remove monuments to the Confederacy!

But for some in my social circle, Trump was articulating a real and welcome possibility. In sometimes heated arguments, friends and colleagues asked why enslavers should be so valorized. They challenged those of us who suggested that contextualizing plaques

telling a fuller story about these founding fathers would be appropriate and sufficient. The conflicts I have participated in on this
topic of memorialization have not fallen along strictly racial lines,
but they have included a variety of perspectives informed by racial
identities. In one disagreement, a Latina colleague offered yet
another way to address these monuments to white men who have
historical significance but have also done harm: Some South
American artists had been commissioned to dismantle and remake
statues to dictators, preserving these historical objects but commenting on them visually.

These conflicts have not changed my mind about the Jefferson
Memorial and Washington Monument, but they have made me
work harder to understand and articulate where I stand. I am less
certain of my initial thoughts and more curious about alternate
perspectives as I consider other memorials close to home: the statue
of Frank Rizzo near Philadelphia's City Hall and Princeton's
Woodrow Wilson School. Collectively we are doing the uncomfortable work of understanding what America is and how it has and
should represent its history. The section below offers strategies for
responding to conflicts like these that are often at the heart of
powerful learning experiences about race.

Using the Lens of Structural Racism to Depersonalize Comments and Conflict

Twenty years ago Bonilla-Silva (1997) famously critiqued prevailing "ideological" definitions of racism as too focused on individual
beliefs and ideas and failing to address the larger "racialized social
system" that "racism is only part of" (p. 467). The individualist
focus persists in college classrooms, particularly in predominantly
white institutions, where students are quick to claim so-called
color blindness and routinely express antiracist beliefs and values.
Individual commitments can certainly be mobilized for positive
change, but alone they are insufficient for dismantling the normalized social structures that reinforce racial inequity at every level of
social life. I assign Bonilla-Silva's foundational essay and share a

concise definition of structural racism from the Aspen Institute (n.d.) that prepares them to read it:

> A system in which public policies, institutional prac-
> tices, cultural representations, and other norms work
> in various, often reinforcing ways to perpetuate racial
> group inequity. It identifies dimensions of our history
> and culture that have allowed privileges associated with
> "whiteness" and disadvantages associated with "color"
> to endure and adapt over time. Structural racism is
> not something that a few people or institutions choose
> to practice. Instead it has been a feature of the social,
> economic and political systems in which we all exist.

It can be especially helpful to linger on the final sentences of this definition, which asserts that structural racism transcends specific individuals or institutions. Students should be reminded that whatever bias and racism exists in their particular classroom, they came from systems much larger and more powerful that exist outside it. A class goal is to fully understand and recognize structural racism in the systems in which we all exist.

This introductory academic contextualization prepares us to depersonalize conflict-inducing comments that emerge through open, honest discussion. Any idea or belief students put forward can be examined as a product of pervasive racialized social structures that we must understand and work to dismantle. Zuniga, Nagda, and Sevig (2002) connect the dots between the structural nature of racism and the conflict that can emerge among individuals in a group as follows: "Gradually [students] may be able to understand that the tensions and misunderstandings surfacing between members of the social identity groups do not happen in a vacuum randomly but are a result of historical and institutional dynamics of privilege and oppression" (p. 9). These historical and institutional dynamics frame the socially constructed norms and ideologies that guide their (often unconscious) beliefs.

Our classroom practice must be informed by this connection between the macro- and microlevel experiences of race, and also *enact its truth.* We must take every opportunity to depersonalize expressions of bias, or thinly veiled, implicit beliefs about racial supremacy or inferiority. Warren (2005) recommends that instructors reorient students toward issues, not individuals, when discussions get too heated, with students attacking or on the defensive, rather than listening and learning. We can reorient toward issues by asking questions that situate students' comments about race within broader social systems.

The list of questions that follows will provide students with metacognitive distance for critical thinking, a release valve for escalating conflict, and guidance on applying the concept of structural racism to their own comments. Teachers of race might create a handout with these and other questions to distribute to the class or post on a course management site to be referred to throughout the semester. Students should be encouraged to take responsibility for asking these questions of themselves (when preparing for class or reflecting individually), of each other (when in pairs or small groups), or of the entire class during discussions.

Interrogating Knowledge and Beliefs About Race

Is the comment based on facts (knowledge) or on personal and/or cultural convictions (beliefs)? How do you know?

Where did you learn this knowledge or belief?

Where does your knowledge or belief originate?

What social systems or factors reinforce or challenge this knowledge or belief?

What economic systems or factors reinforce or challenge this knowledge or belief?

What political systems or policies reinforce or challenge this knowledge or belief?

What cultural representations reinforce or challenge this knowledge or belief?

How is this knowledge or belief shared? By who or what?

What interests are served by this knowledge or belief?

What structure, policy, or condition is challenged if we believe this?

What structure, policy, or condition is challenged or undermined if we reject it?

What social identities would be more likely to believe this? Why? (Consider intersectional identities, including race, class, gender, sexuality, etc.)

What social identities would be more likely to reject this? Why? (Again, consider intersectional identities.)

What evidence should we consult to confirm or question this knowledge or belief?

This handout is good complement to assigning *conversational roles*, a structured discussion method that gives students specific responsibilities for advancing and managing discussions (Brookfield and Preskill, 2005). Two of the conversational roles in this method are particularly focused on listening for and responding to biased, judgmental, or even offensive, comments.

Detectives: Detectives listen carefully for unacknowledged, unchecked, and unchallenged biases that seem to be emerging in the conversation. As they hear these biases, they bring them to the group's attention. They assume particular responsibility for alerting group members to concerns of race, class, and gender. They listen for cultural blindness, gender insensitivity, and comments that ignore variables of power and class.

Umpires: These people listen for judgmental comments that sound offensive, insulting, and demeaning, and that contradict ground rules for discussion generated by group members. (p. 114)

These are highly demanding roles for students, and likely raise (legitimate) fears about being judged negatively or disliked for confronting bias (Czopp, Monteith, and Mark, 2006). Students will likely struggle with exactly how to phrase a pointed critique of a fellow student. These reflective questions give unpracticed students a scaffold for intervening productively in difficult moments in the discussion. One of my goals as a teacher of race is for students to internalize these types of questions so they can be mobilized against bias or racism in other formal and informal contexts. They promote dialogue, reflection, and learning in a way that correction and censure do not.

Not Preaching to the Choir

Derek Black is the godson of David Duke, but he is also a graduate student in history who has studied Arabic to better understand the more advanced Islamic culture of the early Middle Ages. As a young man he campaigned for anti-immigration legislation, but he has reconsidered that stance after studying research demonstrating the social and economic benefits of diversity. He has traveled to Europe and South America, and joined a couch-surfing online community, opening his home to strangers (Saslow, 2016). The trust and openness he began to develop in college has affected his adult life and also his deepest convictions. In his letter to the *New York Times*, he called on Americans to embrace, rather than reject, "multiculturalism...It is the choice of embracing or rejecting our own people" (Black, 2016).

Teachers of race are drawn to the democratic promise of the work, manifest in this narrative of a life-changing college experience. Through our intentional facilitation of engagement with relevant scholarship and diverse fellow classmates, students can gain understanding of the systemic ways racial inequality is reproduced and gain empathy for fellow citizens. Students who develop along these cognitive and human-dimension lines are better prepared for citizenship and the work of making common cause for racial equity.

We value pluralism, and the variety of experiences, perspectives, and worldviews represented in our classrooms are ideally microcosms of our diverse democracy. Yet the very variety we value often manifests in comments that trigger strongly antagonistic reactions in teachers or students. Teachers are people too, and students can offend, anger, or hurt us. From years as a teacher of race and as a faculty developer, I know that instructors may be tempted to use their authority or power to shame, induce guilt in, or silence a student who triggers such negative emotions. Teachers also struggle with their responsibility to protect students from hate speech and harassment. For years I co-facilitated a faculty learning community on teaching race and diversity at Temple University with Tchet Dereic Dorman and Donna Marie Peters, and several colleagues noted how very hard it is to determine, in the moment, if a triggering statement is introducing healthy, challenging conflict or perpetrating violence. Has the student crossed a line into hate speech, or is the contribution or question adding productively to the profound discomfort that can lead to true learning?

There is no simple rubric for making these determinations, and a reflective community can be a lifeline for teachers of race who need to process such incidents and engage such questions. Teachers dealing with racial issues must be prepared to make these determinations during every class period and to resist the impulse to immediately avoid or shut down the conflicts that emerge. They must also resist the impulse to lecture away the messiness or to correct the ill-informed or troubling student too forcefully before quickly moving onto other topics.

Years ago I earned a certificate in diversity leadership, which was based on the theory and practice of Charles Rojzman's (1999) Transformational Social Therapy. One day he instructed that the leader of any diversity engagement must "love every person in the room" and that meant the leader "could not fear anyone in the room." Being "the good doctor" that students can trust to lead them through a challenging but transformative experience demands emotional self-regulation. We have to stay in our professional role and have the presence of mind to ask students questions that de-personalize the interaction and teach the concept of structural racism. We must be truly learning centered. Students' less-considered, uninformed, or prejudiced ideas about race may feel more threatening, but are akin to all kinds of learning that needs to be interrogated and rethought.

It is less demanding to teach students who are all in the choir, self-identifying as antiracist and earnestly working toward greater awareness and sensitivity of racial inequality. But there is missed opportunity, and even danger, in too much harmony. Indeed, we must create enough trust so as to invite some of the very ideas we see as most undermining to democracy and human connection. If we do not put these ideas to the test in a diverse, trusting community, those ideas remain normalized in the social, economic, and political systems that reproduce them. As the American polity is increasingly polarized, the echo chamber is a truer danger to our democracy than an open forum in which uncomfortable, uninterrogated, or even offensive, hurtful comments are exposed and debated.

References

Antonio, A., Change, M., Hakuta, K. et al. (2004). Effects of racial diversity on complex thinking in college students. *Psychological Science* 15 (8): 507–510.

Aspen Institute (n.d.). Glossary for understanding the dismantling structural racism/promoting racial equity analysis. https://assets.aspeninstitute.org/content/uploads/files/content/docs/rcc/RCC-Structural-Racism-Glossary.pdf (accessed 6 September 2017).

Astin, A. (1993). Diversity and multiculturalism on campus: How are students affected? *Change* 25 (2): 44–49.

Barnett, P. (2011). Discussions across difference: Addressing the affective dimensions of teaching diverse students about diversity. *Teaching in Higher Education* 16 (6): 669–679.

Black, D. (2016). Why I left white nationalism. *New York Times* (16 November). www.nytimes.com/2016/11/26/opinion/sunday/why-i-left-white-nationalism.html?_r=0 (accessed 6 September 2017).

Bonilla-Silva, E. (1997). Rethinking racism: Toward a structural interpretation. *American Sociological Review* 62 (3): 465–480.

Brookfield, S. (2005). *The Power of Critical Theory: Liberating Adult Learning and Teaching.* San Francisco, CA: Jossey-Bass.

Brookfield, S. and Preskill, S. (2005). *Discussion as a Way of Teaching: Tools and Techniques for Democratic Classrooms.* San Francisco, CA: Jossey-Bass.

Chang, M., Astin, A., and Kim, D. (2004). Cross-racial interaction among undergraduates: Some consequences, causes, and patterns. *Research in Higher Education* 45 (5): 529–553.

Cisneros, S. (1987). *The House on Mango Street.* Bloomington, IN: Third Woman Press.

Cook, K., Yamagashi, T., Cheshire, C. et al. (2005). Trust building via risk taking: A cross-societal experiment. *Social Psychology Quarterly* 68 (2): 121–142.

Copp, M. and Kleinman, S. (2008). Practicing what we teach: Feminist strategies for teaching about sexism. *Feminist Teacher* 18 (2): 101–124.

Czopp, A., Monteith, M., and Mark, A. (2006). Standing up for a change: Reducing bias through interpersonal confrontation. *Journal of Personality and Social Psychology* 90 (5): 784–803.

Dalton, H.L. (1995). *Racial Healing: The Fear Between Blacks & Whites.* New York, NY: Doubleday.

DeTurk, S. (2006). The power of dialogue: Consequences of intergroup dialogue and their implications for agency and alliance building. *Communication Quarterly* 54 (1): 33–51.

Dorman, T. (2017). An Afrocentric critique of race dialogues: The application of theory and practice in Africology. PhD dissertation. Temple University.

Fink, D. (2003). *Creating Significant Learning Experiences: An Integrated Approach to Designing College Courses.* San Francisco, CA: Jossey-Bass.

Gurin, P., Dey, E., Hurtado, S. et al. (2002). Diversity in higher education: Theory and impact on student outcomes. *Harvard Educational Review* 72 (3): 330–366.

Gurin, P., Nagda, B., and Lopez, G. (2004). The benefits of diversity in education for democratic citizenship. *Journal of Social Issues* 60 (1): 17–34.

Holmes, J. and Remplel, J. (1989). Trust in close relationships. In: *Close Relationships* (ed. C. Hendrick). Thousand Oaks, CA: Sage.

Hu, S. and Kuh, G. (2003). Diversity experiences and college student learning and personal development. *Journal of College Student Development* 44 (3): 320–334.

Hurtado, S. (2001). Linking diversity and educational purpose: How diversity affects the classroom environment and student development. In: *Diversity*

Challenged: Evidence on the Impact of Affirmative Action (ed. G. Orfield and M. Kurleander). Cambridge, MA: Harvard Education Publishing Group.

Keith, N. (2010). Getting beyond anaemic love: From the pedagogy of cordial relations to a pedagogy for difference. *Journal of Curriculum Studies* 42 (4): 539–572.

Marschall, M. and Stolle, D. (2004). Race and the city: Neighborhood context and the development of generalized trust. *Political Behavior* 26 (2): 125–153.

McIntosh, P. (1988). White privilege: Unpacking the invisible knapsack. *Peace and Freedom Magazine* (July/August): 10–12.

Nagda, B. (2006). Breaking barriers, crossing borders, building bridges: Communication processes in intergroup dialogues. *Journal of Social Issues* 62 (3): 553–576.

Nagda, B and Zuniga, X. (2003). Fostering meaningful racial engagement through intergroup dialogues. *Group Processes & Intergroup Relations* 6 (1): 111–128.

Rojzman, C. (1999). *How to Live Together: A New Way of Dealing with Racism and Violence*. St. Kilda, West Australia: Acland.

Saslow, E. (2016). The white flight of Derek Black. *Washington Post* (15 October). www.washingtonpost.com/national/the-white-flight-of-derek-black/2016/10/15/ed5f906a-8f3b-11e6-a6a3-d50061aa9fae_story.html?utm_term=.71493a0a358f (accessed 6 September 2017).

Tablante, C. and Fiske, S. (2015). Teaching social class. *Teaching of Psychology* 42 (2): 184–190.

Warren, L. (2005). Strategic action in hot moments. In: *Teaching Inclusively: Resources for Course, Department and Institutional Change in Higher Education* (ed. M. Ouellet), 620–630. Stillwater, OK: New Forums.

Zuniga, X., Nagda, B., and Sevig, T. (2002). Intergroup dialogues: An educational model for cultivating engagement across differences. *Equity and Excellence in Education* 35 (1): 7–17.

7

Creating the Conditions for Racial Dialogues

Lisa R. Merriweather, Talmadge C. Guy, and Elaine Manglitz

When preparing to lead a class, meeting, workshop, or consultation relating to race, teachers need to create the conditions for racial dialogue by thinking about how to deal with the possibility of conflict that produces resistance, silence, or backlash ahead of time. For example, during a workshop on constructing cross-racial dialogues, the three of us broached the topic of the constructed nature of race and introduced the topic of white privilege as an analytic tool for understanding how cross-racial interactions (e.g. conversations, replies, explanations) are set by structural and systemic power. Each of us offered a story to illustrate how white privilege has operated in our practice, and we asked the small groups of attendees to think about what was challenging in our stories, what was positive, and what issues they unearthed. They were then invited to share stories of their own before we debriefed the activity. During debriefing, it became clear that attendees were reticent to speak. Finally, a white female unknowingly offered a comment that illustrated what we sought to highlight: how white privilege influences cross-racial dialogues.

The impact of structural and systemic power is not always apparent to learners, who attribute the ensuing interactions to

Teaching Race: How to Help Students Unmask and Challenge Racism, First Edition.
Stephen D. Brookfield and Associates.
© 2019 John Wiley & Sons, Inc. Published 2019 by John Wiley & Sons, Inc.

individual idiosyncrasies, personalities, and personal experiences. But structural and systemic power determines what is allowable speech and who is allowed to say it. White privilege often asserts itself as the arbiter. That is, those who have white privilege feel emboldened to speak more freely than others more often. A black male quickly recognized this and sought to challenge the comment being made by the white female. The ensuing dialogue created an uncomfortable tension in the room and resulted in the white female feeling attacked and the black male feeling dismissed and misunderstood. The remaining attendees chose a side or sat on the sideline.

In another instance Elaine was asked to lead a campus conversation on diversity. The meeting included campus and senior administrators who were responsible for managing major organizational divisions of the college. When she brought up privilege and exclusion as topics, the conversation was summarily shut down by one of the administrators. Lacking the ability to control the agenda for such a meeting, the attempt to facilitate a campus conversation about diversity and inclusion met with resistance and ultimately failed. Afterward, the organizers and Elaine talked about what could have been done differently and determined that the topic of white privilege could have been introduced before the group was expected to delve into a discussion of it. An inaccurate assumption had been made that structural racism and privilege were somewhat understood by participants, who were thought to be starting from the same place in the discussion. Our stories demonstrate that adult educators must prepare for the possibilities of resistance, silence, backlash, privilege, and exclusion in cross-racial dialogues.

It is against this backdrop that we try to be pedagogically innovative and strategic, particularly in mixed-race settings in which individuals are reluctant to openly express their fears, anxieties, beliefs, or assumptions about race, to pose questions about race relations or the experience of racially different groups, and to admit racial bias tends to be unrecognized because it now manifests less as explicit discriminatory actions and more as covert, seemingly nonracial actions. For instance, white Americans are pushed to acknowledge that we do not live in a meritocratic society and that they may be privileged due to having a white racialized identity when talking about experiences related to their own race that are materially and symbolically different from those of minority groups. For educators dedicated to racial justice in adult educational contexts, color blindness, unrecognized racial bias, and unacknowledged white privilege pose serious problems in creating constructive and generative cross-racial dialogue.

As we have previously discussed (Manglitz, Guy, and Merriweather, 2014), creating the conditions for constructive dialogues about race, racism, diversity, and inclusion is fraught with challenges and pitfalls. In this chapter we offer strategies for creating conditions for learners to examine and dialogue about racialized experiences. Educators need more than just tools ready to pull out of the toolbox to build their capacity for facilitating racial dialogues; they also need to continually develop their sensitivities, timing, and ability to be reflective before, during, and after interactions (Schön, 1983). Our focus in this chapter is on pedagogical strategies and tools that require the educator to be proactive as well as reactive, structured yet flexible, and vulnerable as well as guarded. These strategies include researching your students, anticipating resistance, balancing safety with risk, and building racial self-awareness.

Researching Your Students

Understanding who is in your class or group as you enter into discussion can help you know how far you can take the group in terms of challenging participants to address their assumptions and respond authentically to the experiences of other members. This process is always developmental and contingent on the length of instruction time: A semester is a very different block of time from a two-hour workshop. Regardless, the importance of being aware of where learners are in terms of understanding their racialized identities remains the same.

Lisa recalls the experience of teaching an adult-learning course online and reading these statements posted in the Critical Race Theory forum:

> Being in the military, where race discrimination is not tolerated, I've been liberated from much of the controversy still plaguing the private and public sectors...I can think of no other career path where race has been more effectively eliminated as a discriminator for performance or potential.

Lisa challenged the notion that the military and military education were race neutral by responding:

> What I am hearing is that the armed forces has a kind of color-blind mentality in which race is not only not seen but is not a factor...The problem with color-blind philosophy is that it ignores reality. CRT says that racism is endemic to our society and unless the organization is not only functioning outside of society (which you suggest the military does) and all of its members have never participated in society, then the organization will inevitably be affected by it...to ignore its existence becomes another way of reinforcing it.

In retrospect, Lisa acknowledges the opportunity she lost to honor this Marine's experiences and to recognize his identity as a white soldier. Her initial response probably left the student feeling attacked and isolated. Lisa was reminded that not everyone agrees that race matters and worldviews are rooted in personal experiences. While racial dialogue should challenge positionality, privilege, and truth claims, such challenges must occur through relationships built through an ever-evolving process of attaining knowledge and making connections with the other.

After that initial terse exchange, Lisa began asking about her student's military experiences and role on campus as an educator for those affiliated with the military. She shared that her brother was a former marine, invoking the spirit of *Semper Fi*. She told him that she talked with her brother about color blindness in the military and acknowledged that he too felt that the Corps superseded race, gender, and class, but that he also felt that organizational systems such as the military are fraught with structural inequity. That created a point of connection that opened the door to the possibility that racial bias and white privilege may operate in her student's social world. He began to connect to the material and Lisa through the experience of a fellow soldier.

This story illustrates that relationality is required for the facilitation of more effective racial dialogue. To create the conditions for relationality, strategies for listening to and connecting with learners are needed. By listening to what is said and not said, and who is speaking and silent, instructors can learn more about their learners. Getting to know the learner may be as simple as asking participants to introduce themselves, answer a questionnaire, or respond throughout the session to prompts. Brookfield's (2017) critical incident questionnaire can be modified for quick, in-the-moment feedback to check for understanding, gauge learners' emotional barometers, and obtain useful information. Technology such as Twitter and clickers can also help us gain a firmer understanding of who learners are, where they are in their racial journey, and how they are connecting to the material. Activities such as a *privilege walk*, in which learners respond to prompts related to multiple identities and social positions, can be an initial way to learn about the learners in a particular setting. Through these kinds of activities, learners also learn about each other and start to see unexpected commonalities and differences.

The implications for knowing about the participants are vast. It could mean the difference between a defensive, combative learner and an engaged, responsive one; a learner who helps usher the dialogue to deeper depths as opposed to one who drives it into a brick wall of anxiety and anger. Dialogues are more apt to be generative when learners are receptive and responsive, as opposed to reactive. Facilitators who have invested time in knowing the learners in a particular setting better understand how far they can take the group and have a sense of how quickly they can get there. Remembering that the process of creating the conditions for racial dialogue is developmental reminds us of the import of scaffolding the experience, regardless of how long or short the time available for learning. The focus must be on the process not just the product. Being realistic in our expectations and flexible with the process improves the chances for richer racial dialogues.

Anticipating Resistance

Racial dialogues by nature are complex, with multiple moving parts. These parts include learners' and educators' racial identities, development, experiences, and assumptions; the context of the learning environment; and the broader social climate, all of which inform the interactions in the learning space as well as the understanding of the specific content of the lesson. Resistance is a commonplace reaction that emanates from the confluence of those moving parts, and it comes in multiple forms. Sometimes it is active and overt, as when students declare there is no need to talk about race because racism is dead or when they complain of race fatigue and of being forced constantly to focus on what they see as a nonissue pushed by a politically correct liberal elite. Sometimes resistance appears as silence and noncompliance: After all, the easiest way to sabotage a discussion on race is simply by no one speaking! At other times it appears when the discussion topic is hijacked for the purpose of avoiding and detracting from the intended focus.

Resistance can be triggered by any number of factors. For example, contemporary events are often hot-button topics that can be polarizing and can unveil how one understands race. Tal noticed how contemporary events and racialized identity combined to influence talk space. He observed how talking about Islamophobia became different after 9/11. He was aware of how conversations regarding Native American rights had new meaning in the midst of the Standing Rock Sioux standing their ground in protest of government abuse of their land. And he perceived how the tenor of discussions on whether black lives really mattered was visibly altered as videos of black men being killed by police and depictions of Colin Kaepernick taking a knee on the national stage consumed the popular imagination. In an information age, learners are constantly receiving data that reveals, reinforces, or alters something about their racial identities, which in turn impact how they understand an event. Being attentive to how learners talk and feel about events can reveal aspects of learners' racialized identities, concerns, and challenges. Educators who understand issues and situations occurring in contemporary society in meaningful ways are better poised to anticipate resistance in racial dialogues, to help learners discover more about themselves, and to reinforce the lesson being taught through the racial dialogue.

When contemporary events are discussed, educational norms that urge everyone to speak freely and to share experiences often unknowingly breeds resistance by supporting white privilege. Experiences are how learners connect their previous knowledge to the new material they hope to acquire, so it is natural to invite everyone to share experiences. The problem lies in how systemic power results in some learners automatically feeling empowered to speak while others feel shut down in the discussion. Facilitators who work from the premise that everyone can speak freely often reinscribe structural inequities created in the outside world. The truth is that in civil society everyone does not feel empowered to speak. Because of this, educators need to attend to the flow of conversation to ensure a more equitable sharing of talk space and promote understandings through analysis of experience. We found that by organizing the classroom interaction and dynamic in a way that creates space for diverse voices we set a tone for class participants to question their prior understandings of racial interaction.

One activity that Lisa facilitates is based on Derrick Bell's short story The Space Traders, which appeared in his classic *Faces at the Bottom of the Well* (Bell, 1992). In this story, extraterrestrials offer the United States unlimited resources if the nation hands over all black people to the aliens. In Lisa's adaptation of this story, learners assume the positionalities of persons different from themselves (for example, a white heterosexual male assumes the positionality of a lesbian Latina). Each student responds to a series of questions and discusses in small groups the impact trading would have on them materially and psychologically. This allows people to discuss difference and its significance within the context of adult education and our society.

Facilitators can raise issues in a nonconfrontational way about blind spots, assumptions, and factual errors and can gently nudge learners out of their comfort zones. For instance, in one group with two white females and two African American females, the discussion was deep and insightful when discussing trades related to class or gender, but when the discussion turned to race, it was shallow. The white females could not see how trading identities with an African American female would have much impact because of their shared female identity.

The African American women in the group in turn shared the role race played in their lived experience of being female. Race was additive in a way the white women's white privilege did not recognize. As a facilitator, illuminating this blind spot was critical to moving to a richer discussion of race. Lisa asked direct questions about what was different about the lived experience of being African American; for example, the last time they had been followed around a department store. White privilege, however, triggered white women's resistance to engaging in a discussion about race because they viewed sexism as the most significant cause of the oppression and discrimination women as a whole face. Because the activity was designed to allow everyone to speak and structured to encourage individuals to challenge each other's view, Lisa was able to probe some taken-for-granted assumptions about how race differentially impacts people's lived experiences.

Balancing Safety and Necessary Risk

Creating an atmosphere that promotes safety and encourages learners to take risks is another strategy useful for facilitating dialogues about race. Jane Vella (2002) introduces safety as one of 12 necessary principles of facilitating adult learning. Safety involves feeling welcomed, trusting the competency of the educator, and feeling that there is space for learner expression and autonomy and the freedom from being judged. Vella also stresses appreciating the politics present in a group, posing problems, being holistic and centered on the learner, requiring involvement, and always being as prepared as possible. We embrace and adapt these principles through promoting a strategic use of politicized talk, posing messy problems, creating uncomfortable safe spaces, and insisting on active involvement during racial dialogues.

To create the conditions for effective racial dialogues, educators cannot undervalue the import of understanding that every action in teaching (e.g. selecting materials, calling on students) is a political act. Educators therefore must be purposive in explicating for students the ways in which their teaching is politicized. The intent is to remove the illusion that what teachers do is neutral. This models for the learners that they too operate from politicized positions. For example, at the start of a class called Equity and Social Justice in Adult Education, Lisa introduced the texts – Fanon's *Wretched of the Earth* (2005) and Freire's *Pedagogy of the Oppressed* (2000) – as being anything but politically neutral. She acknowledged that each was intentionally selected as a critique of the very educational systems that employ us and that they were being offered as counternarratives to the normalized discourse that positions racial bias as a minor consideration in adult learning. From the beginning, speech acts and decisions are framed as political and acknowledged politicized talk is introduced and welcomed. Politicized talk is always risky but is sometimes necessary to move the needle in classroom discussions. Discussions that languish within political correctness often result in students not posing questions to themselves or others regarding the assumptions informing how they hear, respond, and interpret narratives during racial dialogues.

This is part and parcel of Vella's (2002) injunction that educators pose problems that invite the whole person to the learning environment. In one of Tal's classes this was achieved through an exercise called Diversity Profile, which balanced safety with risk. This activity begins with the teacher listing a variety of positions, agencies, services, and organizations with whom most people interact, or are at least aware of. Examples include engineer, house cleaner, ex-con, neighbor, supervisor, minister/priest/rabbi/imam, and so on.

The exercise asks the learners to present a visual depiction of the race, gender, and ethnicity of a doctor, a minister, an ex-con, a neighbor. After students have done this, the responses are reviewed and a diversity profile is developed. The class is instructed to look for patterns among the responses. For instance, are most of the engineers white males, the house cleaners Latinas, and the ex-convicts black men? Do most of their Facebook friends and neighbors look like them or are there a variety of profiles? The exercise concludes with Tal asking what this says about students' experience with people of different backgrounds and what they know about those outside their milieu. This exercise helps personalize the discussion and highlights how the personal connects to the political in a way that is not threatening but does risk revealing aspects of self of which learners may not be aware.

Our intent as educators who engage racial dialogues is to move beyond the simplistic problems that cater to technical rationality and instead pose problems to students that are messy and dwell within Schön's (1983) swamp. We acknowledge that answers to these problems are never easy but are complex and varied, as are the learners who grapple with them. To illustrate this, Tal highlights an example from practice that seeks to disrupt the notion of race being biologically/genetically determined. The intent is to highlight its social construction. This is hard to grasp for many students, because on the surface race presents itself as simple and uncomplicated. People presume it is easy to identify race based on physical characteristics such as skin color, hair texture, and the shape of eyes, noses, or lips. Yet biological research has demonstrated there is no genetic basis for racial type. Posing race as a messy and complicated construct disrupts how individuals have come to understand their world and their relationship to it.

An activity Tal employs to challenge the myth of race is a short 20-question quiz called the Race Literacy Quiz (http://www. newsreel.org/guides/race/quiz.htm). Questions in this quiz range from facts about human and animal genetics and biology to historical, sociological, and economic questions about human groups in their communities and as objects of social policy. Once learners have completed the quiz, Tal invites reactions to it. Learners are often struck by how little they know. Tal then asks how this can be, when they are among the most highly educated persons in the world? This question adds emphasis to the point that many people are ignorant about race and its meaning. He follows this by inquiring how formal schooling, family and community socialization, and popular culture work to convey incorrect understandings about the nature of race, racial categories, and racism. This creates an opportunity to broach the idea of race as a social construction. The activity concludes by getting students to explore the sources of our information about race, such as our first experience of race and racial differences. What can we remember about what we thought and how we felt? The answers to these questions and the ensuing discussion highlight how race is constructed through social interactions, not biological processes.

To be maximally effective, learners should be fully present and engaged, which in this instance equates to being willing to risk being honest in revealing how they answered their quizzes. Learners and educators alike who feel unable to be true to themselves will never fully engage and participate in racial dialogues. An immersion of one's whole self and granting the latitude for others to do the same provides the foundation for meaningful dialogues on race.

Educators can model this immersion by sharing their own experiences with the activity. For instance, after taking the Race Literacy Quiz Tal mentions that he missed several the first time he took it and that in the almost 20 years of using this instrument with literally hundreds of students he can only think of only one time a student answered even half the questions correctly.

Attending to safety frees learners to learn without the fear of what others may think about where they are in their racial identity development. This highlights a critical aspect of racial dialogues: They are uncomfortable, but this discomfort should not be feared. If individuals never feel angst or discomfort, one of two things has happened. Either educators are not keeping it real, meaning the ugliness of race and racism have been prettied up like the proverbial pig with lipstick and the cutting rawness inevitable in such challenging conversations has been softened, or safety has not been achieved and learners are unwilling to trust the process, become vulnerable, and risk diving into the deep end. The shallow end is safe but requires little investment from the learner or educator.

As educators we should seek to create safely uncomfortable spaces of learning: spaces that engender risk and vulnerability. The rhetoric of safe spaces has been erroneously paired with uncritical spaces that feel good and fail to challenge and question. As Arao and Clemens (2013) concluded, safety as it is commonly understood is antithetical to social justice. This is why they advocate for brave spaces that invite provocation, risk, and difficulty. Brave spaces are emotional and embodied as well as cognitive and provide fertile ground for growth and exploration. The linguistic play on *safe* and *brave* helps us rethink strategies, such as establishing ground rules, for facilitating racial conversations. For instance, agreeing to disagree can lead to prematurely ended dialogues that lack conflict and discomfort. Instead, Arao and Clemens (2013) suggest controversy with civility (that) frames conflict not as something to be avoided but as a natural outcome in a diverse group. Moreover, it emphasizes the importance of continued engagement through conflict (p. 144).

In Lisa's classes she stresses healthy debate, de-emphasizes reaching consensus, and requires strict confidentiality. She designates one or two learners to serve as devil's advocates who have the job of highlighting controversial and politically incorrect points. Learners who fear that something unflattering they say will be shared outside of the classroom and thus out of context are less likely to feel safe enough to take risks. So a ground rule is that learners agree to keep confidential who said what during the discussion. While it is okay to talk about the discussion, because continued processing is often necessary to more fully grasp the topic, it is not okay to link the conversation to an individual person by using a name or other identifiable information. Another rule worth noting is that learners are given permission to feel – to step out of their cognitive selves – and are explicitly given permission to be angry, to cry, and to shout. They are encouraged to use *I* statements when responding in the discussion, which helps to avoid casting aspersions and punishing learners who took the risk of sharing.

When people with diverse backgrounds, characteristics, and ideas engage in racial dialogue, the narratives produced can be conflictual, tense, emotional, inaccurate, distasteful, shocking, and if not negotiated strategically, counterproductive. Reframing racial dialogues as controversy with civility alerts learners to these possibilities and therefore may position them to take the risk of being uncomfortable. The fishbowl technique is a tool Elaine finds useful for engaging challenging topics. This tool structures group process such that some learners are active participants in a discussion while others are observers who engage in active listening. Learners rotate through the roles, ensuring that all learners participate in the discussion. Engaging some learners to observe and comment on the active, dialogical process is helpful, as it surfaces not just what everyone is saying but how it is being discussed. It can promote greater civility in the midst of controversial discussions. Using this fishbowl technique engages learners' awareness at different levels and offers a chance to participate in more uncomfortable discussions.

Learners cannot have the choice of opting out of racial discussions and must commit to fully immersing themselves in the dialogue. Kendall (2013) notes that optimal learning happens when students acknowledge the presence of systemically granted privileges, an acknowledgement that will undoubtedly emerge during conversations about race, and make the decision to proceed anyway. The commitment to proceed represents a readiness to be challenged, to experience cognitive dissonance, and – for some – to give up privilege. Some online learning management systems allow instructors to create discussion forums that permit anonymous postings. We encourage learners to journal in those forums with the option of posting anonymously but honestly in the hope of providing additional opportunities to engage, take risks, and receive critical feedback.

Storytelling in its varied forms (personal, video, and pictures) has the capacity to involve learners in racial dialogue. We have found documentaries such as *The Power of an Illusion* (California Newsreel, 2003) to be compelling. The complete series consists of three one-hour segments that speak to how race is socially constructed in modern society while exploring race as a heritable characteristic, the historical and sociological development of race, and the impact of race on development of policy and institutional arrangements that secured the system of white-skin privilege. Each segment addresses a range of issues that can become the foci of discussions.

For example, the third segment in the series – "The House We Live In" – is particularly instructive. Tal and a colleague showed this segment in a workshop on racism. During the ensuing discussion, one student, a former banker, declared that in all his years as a loan officer, he never encountered an overt act of discrimination based on skin color. What the segment reveals is how the banking system, with government oversight, never explicitly used race as a means test for granting a loan. But zip codes were used, and these often reflected patterns of residential segregation. In effect, banks engaged in racist practices as a result of approving loans at disproportionately higher rates for individuals who resided in favored zip codes. Highlighting this point created an opportunity for controversy with civility and led to a serious pause and act of reflection on the part of this former bank executive.

Building Racial Self-awareness

Creating the conditions for effective racial dialogue certainly entails a knowledge of strategies such as those previously described. But as Sue (2015) states, people with poorly developed racial consciousness and identities will inevitably mismanage racial dialogues irrespective of how many tools they have in their facilitation toolbox. To decrease the incidence of mismanagement, educators must also work to build their own racial self-awareness.

Over the years we have collaborated with each other on several projects and relied on each other to further develop our racial consciousness. As educators, the three of us represent a wide range of intersectionalities (race, gender, age) that can, if not examined, result in unproductive collaborative working situations. Because we start at different places of racial self-awareness, we understand race differently. In our discussions, we have the advantage of being longtime colleagues and friends. We begin every work session by catching up on each other's personal lives, which engenders intimacy that carries through when the conversation moves to race talk. The same support we offer to each other as we talk about challenges and joys in our personal lives is shown as we talk about racial bias, prejudice, and discrimination in our work. Being in a relationship with trusted peers is a tool on which we often rely. While it helps that we are friends and share a mutual professional and personal respect for each other, we also intentionally share our stories, attend to our emotions, and engage in reflection to ensure that we continually develop our own racial self-awareness.

In sharing experiences of racial bias, our purpose is to compare our experiences as a way of better highlighting how privilege, which we each possess, operates within different situations.

Our diverse positionalities afford us the opportunity to hear each other's stories from different perspectives. Our contrasting identities and social locators mean we can analyze the stories we tell for common and uncommon ground and expect honest, forthright responses in return. We intentionally plan meetings to allow adequate space for talking through tensions and elaborating on commonalities, and these discussions are at times quite emotional.

In racial dialogues it is always difficult to surpass or overcome the common pitfalls that all too often undermine the creation of meaningful exchange. This is even truer when an underdeveloped racial awareness is in place. Educators unaware of their own racial-identity development with low racial cognizance tend to favor cognitive approaches that deny and undermine the claims made on behalf of counternarratives told by the learners. These discursively grounded cognitive strategies – lecturing, reframing students' experiences through the instructor's eyes, subverting and deflecting students' efforts to introduce race as a topic – are frequently deployed in ways that shape or inhibit racial dialogue and help mask the educator's own discomfort and feelings of inadequacy. Yet racial dialogue proceeds in emotionally laden ways and ignoring this fact makes more inclusive and holistic learning difficult to achieve.

When emotions run high, racially unaware educators tense up, become anxious, and exhibit other visible physical reactions when listening to or explaining their own views on race, racism, or racial oppression. This decreases the teacher's ability to facilitate effective dialogue. Their own emotions result in defensiveness and an inability to listen and respond constructively. In such situations, creating the conditions to help participants make sense of these emotionally laden experiences is challenging. Understanding this default reaction increases educators' awareness of it and allows for a reaction more conducive to facilitating racial dialogue. In class Lisa finds that quiet time is as important as talk time. If a discussion triggers her, she pauses, collects her thoughts, and allows time for silence before returning in earnest to the conversation. After class, she talks and debriefs with other instructors who also facilitate racial dialogues about times when dialogues have not gone well due to the educator's own emotions or assumptions.

Sue (2015) encourages educators to become more aware of their cultural identities because of the detrimental impact a lack of awareness has on facilitation. He advocates reading broadly on the topic of race and engaging in honest dialogue with trusted peers who share their racialized identities and those that do not. Regularly reflecting on biases, perceptions, beliefs, and worldviews is a productive and necessary exercise that we suggest educators do privately, but we recommend that educators describe the process to their students to provide a model of how this happens. Raising one's racial consciousness reveals more readily the hidden assumptions guiding one's behaviors. Understanding how your own privilege has benefited you at the expense of others is humbling and sensitizes you to learners who struggle in dialogue because of their blinders of privilege. Those facilitating racial dialogues must practice what they teach and preach.

Creating workable conditions for meaningful racial dialogue often takes time; contexts must be set, the terms of dialogue must be identified, and the framework for telling stories must be created. To best appreciate the stories that other participants tell, the narrators must detail who they are in terms of their privilege and position. Lisa models this by detailing who she is early in the course. She shares her cultural autobiography or creates and shares an "I am…" or "I am from…" poem that highlights her positionalities and political positioning. This helps her build her own capacity to acknowledge and understand the challenges faced by her students as they work to recognize and confront inequality from their different social positions (Bell, 2010).

Without an awareness of one's racialized self and of racialized trigger points, educators may end up modeling behaviors that derail effective racial dialogue and allow a racialized hierarchy to remain unexamined and unchallenged. To combat this, we should strive to be open about our biases and the ways our backgrounds and experiences shape our behavioral reactions. We each tend to be autobiographical when we teach and to share personal stories related to the issues being highlighted in class. These stories reveal we are not superhuman, but everyday people with biases who do not always say or do the right thing. Denying our racialization and how that structures our understanding of raced people, events, and situations results in unconscious and unintended discrimination and prejudice in facilitation. Lisa's experience with the military student was an example of this. His racialization as a white male needed to be attended to as much as the racialization of Lisa's minority students; perhaps more, because students of color typically enter the classroom with more developed racialized identities.

Teachers who are not secure in their racialized identities will be hypersensitive to how they are perceived and will be more concerned with not appearing biased or racist than with ushering learners to a deeper understanding of race. Being authentic with learners requires vulnerability but also offers an opportunity for increasing trust. Journaling and documenting one's reactions and subsequent behavior in racial dialogues can help reveal the patterns of control exercised to avoid emotional discomfort and unveil racial biases. Identifying trigger points, areas of sensitivity, and unexamined prejudices can help build capacity to facilitate racial dialogue.

Final Do's and Don'ts

Creating the conditions for productive race talk is tough and emotionally exhausting work but also incredibly rewarding. To end our chapter, we draw on Sue's (2015) work to provide a list of actions to encourage and actions to avoid, which serve as an instructive summation for utilizing the four strategies and the various tools we have discussed.

Do	Don't
Acknowledge fear	Be silent
Experience the power of emotions	Allow learners to co-opt the dialogue
Take a risk	Be passive – emotionally or behaviorally
Model race talk	Ignore controversial statements
Stick to the topic of race	Become defensive
Be confrontational and challenging	Seek harmony at the expense of productive dialogue
Avoid superficial treatment	Highlight commonality while avoiding the acknowledgement of differences
Be forthright	Create arbitrary conditions for conversation that subvert meaningful dialogue
Clarify conversation	Terminate the discussion by ignoring, deflecting, or procrastinating
Honor the principle of reciprocity	Suggest certain conversation is inappropriate for the classroom and better suited for after class
Control the process	Police the content
Appreciate when learners take risks	Invalidate effort
Acknowledge feelings	Be dismissive of experiences

We live in an interesting time when issues rooted in race are so blatant they cannot be ignored but so translucent they are not clearly visible. We are approaching the apex of a new revolution with race and racism at the forefront and a populace still ill equipped to adequately handle the tumultuous nature of racial dialogues. The late Robert Kennedy said in a speech to the Senate in 1966:

A revolution is coming – a revolution which will be peaceful if we are wise enough; compassionate if we care enough; successful if we are fortunate enough – but a revolution which is coming whether we will it or not. We can affect its character; we cannot alter its inevitability.

(Kennedy, 1966)

As teachers we can affect the character. The questions are whether we will be wise enough, care enough, and be fortunate enough to learn how to create the conditions that help people engage in more effective racial dialogues. We hope we will.

References

Arao, B. and Clemens, K. (2013). From safe spaces to brave spaces: A new way to frame dialogue around diversity and social justice. In: *The Art of Effective Facilitation: Reflections from Social Justice Educators* (ed. L. Landreman), 130–150. Sterling, VA: Stylus.

Bell, D.A. (1992). *Faces at the Bottom of the Well: The Permanence of Racism*. New York, NY: Basic Books.

Bell, L.A. (2010). *Storytelling for Social Justice: Connecting Narrative and the Arts in Antiracist Teaching*. New York, NY: Routledge.

Brookfield, S.D. (2017). *Becoming a Critically Reflective Teacher* (2nd ed.). San Francisco, CA: Jossey-Bass.

California Newsreel. (2003). *Race: The Power of an Illusion*. DVD, 3 episodes, 56 min. each, www.newsreel.org/nav/title.asp?tc=CN0149 (accessed 1 June 2018).

Fanon, F. (2005). *The Wretched of the Earth* (trans. R. Philcox). New York, NY: Grove Press.

Freire, P. (2000). *Pedagogy of the Oppressed*, 30th Anniversary Edition. New York, NY: Continuum International.

Kendall, F.E. (2013). *Understanding White Privilege: Creating Pathways to Authentic Relationships Across Race*, 2nd ed. New York, NY: Routledge.

Kennedy, R.F. (1966). Wikiquote, Robert F. Kennedy (9 May), https://en.m.wikiquote.org/wiki/Robert_F._Kennedy (accessed 25 November 2017).

Manglitz, E., Guy, T., and Merriweather, L. (2014). Knowledge and emotions in cross-racial dialogues: Challenges and opportunities for adult educators committed to racial justice in educational settings. *Adult Learning* 25 (3): 111–118.

Schön, D. (1983). *The Reflective Practitioner: How Professionals Think in Action*. New York, NY: Basic Books.

Sue, D.W. (2015). *Race Talk and the Conspiracy of Silence: Understanding and Facilitating Difficult Dialogues on Race*. Hoboken, NJ: John Wiley & Sons, Inc.

Vella, J. (2002). *Learning to Listen, Learning to Teach: The Power of Dialogue in Educating Adults*. San Francisco, CA: Jossey-Bass.

8

Developing Working Alliances with Students

Consuelo E. Cavalieri, Bryana H. French, and
Salina M. Renninger

We start this chapter by naming our identities and positionality. We are three female counseling psychology faculty members from either working-class or working-poor upbringings. We identify as indigenous from the Kootenai Nation, black biracial descendants of enslaved Africans, and white Pennsylvania Dutch, respectively. All of us are from the United States/Turtle Island, and are, at the time of this publication, tenured faculty. As counseling psychologists, we work with graduate students who are training to become either master's or doctoral level mental health professionals. Collectively we teach diversity-designated courses and integrate issues of diversity and social justice into all of our courses. Our classes are composed of predominantly white, cisgender, heterosexual, class-privileged women. Thus, our starting point for introducing race into our work begins with forming working alliances with our students.

What Is a Working Alliance?

The term *working alliance* is used in psychotherapy literature to describe the process of building trust and rapport between a therapist and client. It is widely regarded as a necessary foundation of

Teaching Race: How to Help Students Unmask and Challenge Racism, First Edition.
Stephen D. Brookfield and Associates.
© 2019 John Wiley & Sons, Inc. Published 2019 by John Wiley & Sons, Inc.

therapeutic change and has been found to relate to improved outcomes across different therapeutic techniques and orientations (Wampold, 2001). Scholars have recently connected the notion of a working alliance to that of a teaching alliance in training students in the mental health fields (Estrada, 2015; Rogers, 2009). For us, the working alliance framework serves as a foundation for our social justice and multicultural pedagogies.

In building a working alliance with our students, we leverage our identities as sources of power and draw from decolonizing and critical pedagogies to disrupt traditional models of education (Grande, 2004). Through the use of storytelling and self-disclosure, we write ourselves into our teaching scripts as a way to illustrate the validity of indigenous, racialized, and marginalized voices. We ask students to reflect on their own socialization to become more aware of themselves as cultural beings, and the three of us use these strategies to model our own development and vulnerability. Furthermore, our assessment of how our working alliances are developing contributes to when and how we time the introduction of topics, the depth to which we explore them, and how we plan for subsequent class sessions.

Our pedagogical styles support and reinforce one another, socializing students to expect and accept that racial and indigenous justice will be part of their learning. Our doctoral students begin their program in the summer semester with Salina's Vocational and Organizational Psychology course, in which she lays a foundation for students to question and critique biased perspectives common to the field of career counseling. In the fall semester that follows, students take Bryana's Diversity Issues in Counseling Psychology course, during which they engage in self-reflection and explore positionality around race, gender, class, and sexuality. Finally, in the January term immediately after, students learn to critique and challenge the white supremacist and colonizing foundations of our field in Consuelo's Historical Foundations class. As a result, students' foundational learning as counseling psychologists in training begins with this rigorous, critical, and interpersonal pedagogy that helps shift their thinking and feelings about the field and their roles as professionals. In this chapter we each describe ways that we integrate the working alliance process into our teachings about race and racism. Each author provides a first-person account of teaching race in the classroom; we present our accounts in the curricular order in which students take each of our courses.

Sharing Power (Salina Renninger)

I am Salina Renninger, and many of my ancestors came from Germany in the late 1600s and settled in Pennsylvania. Their descendants are now known as the Pennsylvania Dutch. I was born and raised in Alaska, moved to Minnesota as a young adult, and have lived in Minnesota for over 30 years. I am white, and I understand that my ancestors immigrated to the United States and felt free to move across the country at whim, and that I am the beneficiary of unearned privilege due to whiteness.

As an educator, I want to consider my place in the world. If who I am and what I've experienced in life impacts how I understand information, isn't the same true for my students? I want students to recognize this and to understand that when we learn together, bringing knowledge into the classroom space through our own unique lenses, we are learning in relationship to each other. Our learning is inherently deeper, more complex, and more insightful than if we learn alone. This approach contradicts the expectations that many students bring to class: that I will talk and they will listen, that a slide on a screen is the right tool to direct their learning, and that all they need to do is read the slide, write down my words, and remember my wisdom. Helping students experience the benefit of relationship-based learning so they can challenge previously held notions of the role of the educator and how learning occurs is an essential aspect of my teaching.

Co-creating the Curriculum

In the early stages of a course, I strive to ensure that the students and I have shared goals. I might ask them to write down their hopes on notecards and share them with me. Or I may have them report out to the classroom so the group can identify shared goals. I will also name the goals I have identified for the course. Together, we can blend our ideas so that we have a shared agreement on where we are headed. As a white instructor, this attempt to co-create learning objectives and recognize that each student brings something to the classroom is an effort to neutralize (if this can really be possible) relational patterns based on power imbalances perpetuated in the colonized systems in which higher education is situated (Kumashiro, 2000).

Once goals are agreed upon, the next area of focus becomes how we get there. I distribute responsibility for the course when I ask students to choose topics for presentations and then have them "teach" the class. I often ask students to work in groups to share their own understanding of assigned readings and to be mindful of how limiting understanding to a single perspective can limit learning. Students are encouraged to consider multiple viewpoints and to try to perceive content and practice in new and unfamiliar ways. I want them to work together to deepen their understanding by bringing different outlooks to the course topics versus allowing status quo viewpoints to be dominant.

Students sometimes resist this approach and ask for more lecturing and PowerPoint presentations or just stay silent during class conversations. Depending on the situation, I might utilize classroom activities in which every student is required to speak or I might share what I observe (for example, "I'm noticing a lot of silence right now"). I try to be transparent in explaining my process: Why I'm sharing the role of teaching with the students and my belief that everyone has much to offer each other. My perspective is developmental: Over time, students should learn how to seek knowledge and create their own understanding, so as to apply these to the practice of being an independent counseling psychologist. At times this is a bumpy road to travel, as students pull for me to take greater responsibility for their own learning. In these moments I return to my own inner experience and conviction, coaching myself to be firm in my approach and trusting that my certainty in their abilities will be justified. When my self-doubt is strong, I seek the support of trusted colleagues such as Bryana and Consuelo.

During these conversations there are inevitably times when my personal perspectives are challenged by the convictions students bring to class. It is especially difficult when I have a strong emotional reaction in disagreeing with something a student says. These moments feel fraught with the potential for error. On the one hand I want to model openness to all ideas, but on the other hand some ideas are misguided or hurtful to others in the class. I must balance the commitment to openness with the need to demonstrate respectful disagreement. This is obviously complicated by the power differential between the students and me. Again, it helps me to remember that every exchange is part of the developmental *process* of the course and not something to get wrong or right. I try to focus on what I am feeling and thinking, and bring those disclosures into the conversation along with an invitation for others to do the same. If someone shares an idea that could be hurtful, such as when a student told the class her boss was hired due to affirmative action and that it was reverse discrimination, I remember to observe my internal reaction and share it with the class. In this instance I said something like, "I'm having a hard time with that statement. I want to respect your perspective, but I also believe there's more to discuss with that comment."

Establishing a quality relationship with each student and with the class as a whole is key to my process, but aspects of the learning environment make this difficult. After all, inequality is embedded in the educational system. White teachers are typically in charge, and they assess students and assign grades. There is no denying the power of this role. Students have some power, but it is less direct. They can disrupt classrooms, provide negative teaching evaluations, and mentally check out in class. All these behaviors shape the teacher's use of power in the classroom. There are also the structural inequities embedded in unexamined processes of the standard American classroom. These inequities may be subtle, unconscious, or unknown, yet they impact the classroom process and outcomes

(Shahjahan, 2015). Forming relationships with each student and providing opportunities for them to form them with each other can disrupt these embedded inequities. In establishing relationships, we see each person as bringing unique experiences to class and this challenges institutional asymmetries of power. This is why early in any course that I teach I share something personal about my identity within the context of the course.

Modeling Self-disclosure

In my Vocational Psychology course, I share my family's heritage as immigrants to the United States in the late 1600s and my current Pennsylvania Dutch identity. I explain that this cultural identity is linked to a strong work ethic and the valuing of education. I also note social class distinctions, and that historically many Pennsylvania Dutch worked blue-collar jobs. I tell them that my grandparents were poor, and that Pappy and Grammy made it to the fourth grade and the eighth grade, respectively. I describe how my generation found economic success through higher education or skilled trades, and say that we are a large extended family that has transitioned from poverty to economic comfort. I point out that because of white privilege and the history of racism in the United States, those with my white identity may assume that hard work will bring equal gain for all and fail to recognize their privilege of whiteness.

Students may squirm when this privilege is articulated. I purposely name these dynamics to allow others in the room to examine their own belief systems and their areas of resistance to ideas of oppression (DiAngelo, 2011), especially as it relates to our topic of vocational psychology. I point out the personal aspects of my heritage and the systemic aspects. Through explicit conversation about white privilege and the structures within which this privilege is afforded, students begin to see themselves in new ways: not just as individuals, but as beings in a larger system. I then encourage students to write their own heritage stories, reflect on the meaning of their heritages, and explain how they are situated in history and current times. Students are encouraged to share whatever part of their stories they wish to with the others in their small group. This forms a foundation for self-understanding and understanding how others might make sense of course content. Heritage stories help students begin to question concepts embedded within the field of US vocational psychology and career counseling (Duffy et al., 2016), such as meritocracy and upward ascension, and how these are rooted in the deep structures of white supremacist and Eurosettler colonial ideology.

My use of self-disclosure is often questioned. Students suggest it is unprofessional to share personal information and that as psychologists we are meant to remain objective. As one student asked, "Why should I care about your personal history?" I welcome such questions and perceive them to represent greater opportunities to demonstrate a relational approach to class management. When questioned, I might first ask what's troubling to the student about what is being discussed. This often leads to a conversation about boundaries and what is appropriate in the classroom. I attempt to be transparent about how disclosure is linked to learning objectives and remain receptive to any concerns expressed. This conversation is another opportunity to co-define curricular goals and pedagogic tasks. Ultimately, all that I do in teaching is meant to share power, promote success, and create community in the service of equity.

Using Self-reflection to Illuminate White Supremacy (Bryana French)

My name is Bryana French and I identify as a black biracial American woman whose mother is the descendant of enslaved Africans and whose father's ancestors are Europeans who immigrated to the United States in the 1600s. I was raised in Minneapolis and am a first-generation college graduate on one side of my family and the first doctor on either side. I was hired to teach diversity-related courses, so consequently students enter the class knowing we will spend 16 weeks discussing issues of race, racism, and intersectionality. When assessing their expectations the first day, they often express a hope to learn specific strategies for working with cultural differences and fear that they will be attacked, say the wrong thing, or feel guilty for their privileges. Because of these fears, I find that I need to set a tone that allows students to feel safe in being authentic yet also brave enough to take risks and be challenged. Relationship building is key to setting this tone.

Turning the Gaze on Ourselves

In teaching multicultural counseling, I take the approach that it is less about the "other" and more about ourselves. Students often enter the classroom wanting a how-to manual for counseling specific racial or ethnic groups. I encourage them to resist this desire and instead turn the gaze back on themselves. I ask the question, "What would you say if someone asked you what culturally competent therapy looked like with white people?" They usually stare back quizzically. I remark that the question would be hard to answer given the breadth of diversity among white people, so why would they assume that there is a specific how-to way of doing therapy with the equally complex and varied group of people of color?

Instead, I ask them to learn the history and power dynamics concerning the construction of race in the United States and its various identity groups. I ask them to reflect on their own relationship with race, their understanding of race and their own racial identity, and the ways that whiteness shows up in their daily lives and in our field. In my master's level course, we have small group discussions and self-reflective assignments that explore dominant US racial narratives and ways those play out in their own lives. We then explore the impact these narratives have on therapy, particularly the way in which therapists may inadvertently rely on racial narratives in their perception of clients. We watch videos of counseling sessions that show the ways in which a counselor's worldview and blind spots might impact the working relationship with a client, and students engage in role plays to practice having conversations about race, racism, and privilege in a session. I encourage them to introduce the topics of identity, culture, and privilege, owning their positionality in a session with a client as a way of modeling and setting the stage for therapeutic work to occur.

I find that without a sense of authenticity, students in our liberal blue state and metropolitan area with a culture of Minnesota niceness will too often say the politically correct thing without being true to their beliefs and attitudes. Many want to be perceived as good white people and allies (Sullivan, 2014), and thus don't acknowledge their areas for potential growth. I want them to engage in deep self-exploration of their socialization, to challenge their assumptions, and to observe the reactions and behaviors that manifest themselves. As budding therapists, their unconscious reactions and biases play a significant role in the work they do. An often-cited quote in the field is "Therapist, know thyself." Therapists, counselors, and psychologists have incredible power in the counseling relationship; part of that power includes influencing people's self-perceptions. If therapists aren't aware of their own biases, assumptions, triggers, and countertransference, then clients can be particularly harmed by the implicit and explicit messages communicated about worldviews, values, and identity (Sue and Sue, 2015).

Modeling Vulnerability

To facilitate student vulnerability, I have a practice of modeling my own. Students have explicitly expressed apprehension when seeing that I am their instructor for such a course: A black biracial woman, first-generation college graduate, and amputee is going to teach them about diversity and social justice? Blame, shame, and/or defensiveness kick in. Thus, I have found that an important aspect of co-constructed learning is modeling my own development as the instructor. My use of intentional self-disclosure is shared in the context of race, gender, ability status, and age. Given the culture of Minnesota Nice and the power dynamics of my being the professor, students are often reluctant to share what they think out of fear of being perceived as ignorant or racist. So I use self-disclosure as I model my own development and process of consciousness-raising.

I use myself as a tool by sharing examples of my biases and ways I have become more aware of them. I discuss times that I've microaggressed and have been a victim of microaggression. I do this to acknowledge that I, someone who is marginalized in various identities, also have biases, assumptions, and privilege that I need to acknowledge and work through.

My intent is to help them be reflective and honest about their attitudes, make unconscious biases more conscious, and normalize these attitudes as part of the insidious system of injustice. I often say, "Most of us don't come out of the womb with our fist in the air ready for the revolution. We have to get there and unlearn the pervasive systemic systems of oppression that we've been taught." I say this to encourage students to let their guard down and move out of blame and shame. I want them to be curious about where their attitudes and beliefs come from, and to contextualize how they have developed these in a broader system of oppression. In particular, I have learned to use examples of marginalized identities in order to introduce general notions of power, privilege, and oppression before talking specifically about race. Because our classes are predominantly composed of white women, starting with discussions of gender, sexism, and male privilege is validating and affirming. It then becomes easier to make the cognitive and emotionally empathic transition to acknowledging racism and white privilege.

The Positionality Dialogue

These strategies set a tone for a semester-long assignment and activity I use with doctoral students. Positionality Dialogue is modeled after an assignment in Robert Carter's (2003) Racial-Cultural Counseling Laboratory course. My intent is to facilitate a dialogue that helps students consider the complex notion of positionality. I want them to explore how their positionality impacts their understanding of the world, their work as therapists, and the actions they can take to transform the way they interact with their clients.

Students are asked to write and reflect on questions about their social identities and their membership in their identity groups, including (1) the influence of their group membership on their personal development, (2) how they've affirmed or rejected a part of their identity, and (3) the ways they experience privilege and power. This written reflection is completed before the discussion to allow students ample space and time to prepare to share, reflect, and be challenged on their experiences in the 45-minute process discussion.

The positionality dialogue is structured in a particular way. Each week one student shares his/her/their story of identity development as the rest of the students sit in a circle and listen. Then the student sharing the identity story receives feedback (sometimes quite challenging) designed to push them to deeper reflection. This provides the other students with a chance to facilitate conversations about oppression, privilege, group membership, and identity. A typical dynamic that often develops is students wanting to rush in to rescue the person who is sharing his/her/their vulnerability, so as to help them feel better and move out of discomfort. This parallels the process that happens with discussions about race in general, in which people want to save one who commits a microaggression, for example, thus inadvertently glossing over the painful experience of the microaggression's victim.

Because part of training for psychotherapy is helping students sit with challenging emotions and then exploring this experience with them, I push them to resist the urge to rescue and instead focus on listening to understand, asking inquisitive questions, observing the process, expressing empathy, and facilitating insight. At the end of the semester, students write a reflective paper about the positionality dialogue, explaining what they have learned about themselves and each other in the process and the way that writing and telling their identity development story will influence their work as future psychologists.

Participating in positionality dialogue not only fosters self-reflection but also gives students the opportunity to practice facilitating difficult conversations and to ask the kinds of personal and culturally related questions that would likely come up in a counseling session. The idea is to help students become comfortable with the uncomfortable, and to give them a space to practice hard conversations before they enter a counseling session. Students are afforded firsthand the opportunity to experience the utility of personally exploring our sociocultural identities and how powerful that can be for one's mental health and wellness.

Teaching in Tumultuous Times

My teaching style does not come without consequences, however. My identity as a young black female faculty member is often a place of difficulty for students who have challenged my pedagogy and authority. So while showing vulnerability and modeling development for my students may help relieve tension and build alliance, it also opens the door for greater scrutiny, which faculty with more privileged identities in terms of age, race, and gender may never experience. As I reflect on the significant examples of structural racism and violence that have occurred in 2017, I am rethinking my approach. I find that I am less patient and willing to offer space for multiple perspectives when those perspectives are detrimental to oppressed people. It is challenging, as a woman of color, to witness such significant political violence happening in our country while also holding emotional space to the classroom. Having the support of Consuelo and Salina has improved my teaching significantly, by allowing for comradery and radical understanding of the need to disrupt white supremacist ideologies and pedagogies.

Uncovering Historically Embedded Positionalities (Consuelo Cavalieri)

N'ini ktunaxa ¢ hu qakłik ma'is k̓asuquna'tił. I am a member of the Kootenai Tribe of Idaho, and in my grandmother's language I am named "mother of twins." At birth, I was given the name "Consuelo" and the path of being a consoler. I grew up in traditional Kootenai territory, less than two hours from the former Aryan Nations compound. By identification and affiliation I am an indigenous person with connections not only to my grandmother's people but also to Guam and Minnesota. With the support of my tribe, I was the first person to complete a bachelor's, master's, or doctorate degree. Entering the professorate was a dream interrupted by the reality of early struggles to meet the quantitative markers for teaching excellence.

Since I work at a teaching university, the negative messages I received about my teaching during my early years framed much of how I approached my practice. One day, a student came to class wearing a Washington Redskins shirt. I wanted to say something, but ultimately I worried too much about how I would be perceived to speak out. I knowingly silenced myself and passed up my opportunity to use that incident as a teaching moment. Furthermore, I recognized that my silence was a reaction, an internalization to keep me safe within the system. It was at this moment that I reached out to my coauthor Salina.

I remember plopping down in Salina's office sad – existentially sad – about the powerlessness I was feeling. This moment seemed to be a turning point in our working alliance. Of course Salina was a good and caring listener. Yet she went further. Salina asked a question not about how I could cope with the annoyance on my own but what we could do programmatically to address the issue. Later she included a statement regarding mascots on her syllabus. Up until that point our relationship had been primarily collegial. Afterwards it became a deeper working alliance, one focused on justice-centered psychology, training, and scholarship.

Before I discuss my teaching further, it is worth noting that I believe I would have found the strength within myself, as my Ktunaxa Nation ancestors have, to take the arrows sent my way without my coauthors. Yet, having them has assuredly helped me to have just a little more courage to venture into the *impolite* territory of naming race and colonialism in my classes, especially when I teach our Historical Foundations course.

Place-based Learning

If there is one thing I have learned about teaching a history of psychology course, it is that most of the students I come across dread it. This is partly because it is history and partly because I teach it in January, when there is already a collective dread in Minnesota. Yet the more students dread the course, the more opportunity I see for transformation. When I start my classes, I typically go around the class and ask students to share their candid perceptions about the history of psychology and what they are expecting out of this class. When they share unfavorable attitudes, I affirm students by letting them know that former students have felt similarly. When all students have had a chance to share, I begin discussing how my teaching strategy differs, starting with an emphasis on positionality.

My initial working-alliance strategy is to *recognize our position-alities* (Takacs, 2003). I begin by telling my history as the first child in my lineage for at least three generations to not be raised in an assimilationist boarding school. I tell them about my grand-mother's declaration of war on the United States and its impor-tance to Idaho's history. I tell stories of places important to my history so they will be oriented to *where* psychology's history is located (Leipzig, Germany). I show them how I honor the Dakota Peoples, on whose land we live and learn. I model a (hopefully) respectful relationship to place and name how my ancestral history comes into the classroom, thereby impacting our construction of knowledge.

Like Bryana, I set up the learning task of recognizing position-alities by asking students to sit in a circle. I prompt them to intro-duce their histories by asking them to tell our class where they are from and where their ancestors came from. Whiteness becomes a place-based whiteness, located in Germany or Ireland or Norway. Indigeneity becomes place based, whether it is indigeneity from North America or elsewhere in the world. Diaspora, too, has a story to tell. Occasionally students may not know where their families came from, or they know very little. This sets up an opportunity to discuss race in light of colonial erasure, not just for indigenous peoples but for immigrants who suppressed their sense of connection to their familial homelands when they migrated to Turtle Island. This introductory circle tends to elicit more relationship building than pushback. When students discuss their ancestors and their homes, they bring in their own context and stories. Most of all, they are learning about each other's rootedness.

Identifying Who's Omitted from History

While I include writing activities and videos in my teaching, a significant portion of the class is dedicated to *discussion circles*. For an assignment on constructing a narrative of psychology's history, I ask students to systematically take on one of four group roles: *discussion leader*, *passage master*, *context researcher*, and *omissions analyst*.

1. The discussion leader's task is to create questions that facilitate critical, past-minded understanding of the day's readings.
2. The passage master highlights passages for the group to analyze further.
3. The context researcher has the job of helping to recreate a sense of the historical period we are studying by bringing the group information on major political, social, artistic, legal, and popular events.
4. The omissions analyst is responsible for considering whose perspective has not been considered in the day's readings. In this role, students have written poems and letters to the editor, created songs, and developed plays and other creative avenues to recognize the people that academic psychology has silenced.

The discussion circles leave the classroom for approximately one hour to create their historical narratives of the development of the discipline of psychology. They have the language and under-standing from Bryana's Diversity Issues in Counseling Psychology course and the interpersonal comfort with owning their position-alities from the collective sequencing that the three of us foster as instructors. As they discuss the readings, I visit the different groups to listen to the construction of their understanding. The groups rely on each of the four roles identified above to construct their own narratives of psychology's history, with the omissions analyst being particularly powerful. By asking students to systematically consider omitted perspectives, I have observed them becoming more sensitized to who is *not* in the narrative.

In our whole-class discussions I ask them to turn from the texts to how race is enacted in the classroom. For example, prompts such as "So how is that working with your cohort?" or "How do you see this in our class?" may be all that is necessary to start a reflective discus-sion on the racial dynamics of the class. Then I work to recognize that I can hear, hold, and process white students' anxieties about how they might be viewed on racial issues, while also holding that there are usually students in the room who want more white people to take action on racial justice. When I hear quietness I want to know what underlies the quietness, and I recognize that other stu-dents in the class may form interpretations of what that silence means. Rather than name it, I try to probe so students can name it themselves. In working to draw out students, I might use subtle tech-niques such as walking closer to a student while I engage in several back-and-forth exchanges. I still look around the room so that the rest of the class knows that I am including them in the exchange. While I strive to bring warmth and empathy, I do ask questions that challenge students to explore what they think and feel.

Navigating Visceral Responses: *Dakota 38*

At the conclusion of my course I show the film *Dakota 38*, which tells of the hanging of 40 Dakota men ordered by Abraham Lincoln (Smooth Feather Productions, 2012). The film activates visceral responses to genocide, war, and execution, which teachers need to help students process before moving to verbal discussion. To navigate the visceral responses to the film, I begin by keeping the lights low after the credits roll. I let students know that we will take 10 minutes for them to sit or write as they take in the story. Then I ask for students to turn to a partner and share their reactions to the film. Finally, I begin to go around the room to hear peoples' responses regarding what they are processing.

For groups with a lot of members who vocalize their thoughts, I open the process up so anyone can speak. For groups with members who do a lot of internal processing, I go around the circle and ask to hear each person's response. Then I try to find a good, relational closing activity. For example, I have asked students to share what they would like to honor about each of the members of their discussion group and/or cohort. I consider the closing activity to be essential to promoting the healing that this work entails. Emancipating myself from race and the colonial system in which racism and racialization operates enables me to focus on being in good relationship with all of creation; in this instance, the students with whom I journey toward deeper relatedness and understanding.

Summary and Conclusion

Educating the next generation of mental health professionals in the work of dismantling the systemic entrenchment of racism, increasing racial literacy, and fostering respectful relationships calls upon educators to form effective working alliances with students and with each other. Our working alliances provide the foundation for all of us to increase our awareness of how race structures relationships, knowledge construction, and the provision of professional services (Sue and Sue, 2015). Our relationships to each other provide a supportive network to narrate our positionalities and to challenge our students to wrestle with how white privilege structures their lives and the lives of their clients. Thus, our working alliance is based on personal commitments and professional expectations, and located in our Catholic social teachings on human dignity and worth.

We recognize that when we discuss our positionalities, we take race from an abstract concept to the domain of our lived experiences (Takacs, 2003). We all become more aware of how it is alive in the classroom. We enrich our students' knowledge when we honor our own voices and those of our ancestors. We also show them that they, too, are knowledge makers. Making space for students to discuss their experiences of racism with the support of an instructor, as well as making space for students to discuss the systemic perpetuation of racism and racial privilege, enables us to bring that knowledge into the everyday moments in which we have a chance to stand for racial and indigenous justice.

The support and challenge we bring to students is a reflection of the support and challenge we share with each other. We build trust by checking in with each other frequently, especially when critical events happen locally or nationally. When the killing of Philando Castile at the hands of a local police officer occurred in Salina's community, she processed her reactions with Bryana and Consuelo and affirmed her commitment to active change. This felt risky, as white shame was powerful during this event. And when, in response to the demands of Concerned Student 1950 at the University of Missouri, Bryana co-wrote a statement on the difficulty of retaining faculty of color in predominantly white institutions (French, Adair, and Cokley, 2015), she leaned on the radical support of Consuelo and Salina when she was criticized for critiquing her former institution.

We strive to create an environment in which we affirm each other's contributions to the work. Yet at times, an awareness of the different roles we inhabit (assistant professor, associate professor, director of training) has inhibited some of our communication. For example, on some occasions we have been somewhat unaware of what each other's viewpoints are on training matters. Yet, even in such situations, we have reconnected and talked through what our different perspectives mean. We also recognize that due to our separate positionalities, some options for teaching are open to only one of us. For example, Consuelo has introduced indigenous ceremony into key classes. We also strive not to allow our working alliance to become an island within our unit or university. We engage our colleagues in dialogue and have been involved in teach-ins and faculty learning communities.

Our work challenges students to think and act differently. Stories such as that of Derek Black (Saslow, 2016) illuminate how relationships and the knowledge from our professions can be powerful tools in reforming even the most avowed white supremacists. When our students enter our classrooms, we expect them to take on our challenge. We do it by modeling and telling our stories. We use our strategies for scaffolding student-to-student relationship building so they can practice breaking through dominant norms of avoiding racial discourse and writing whiteness as our structural norm. When good relationships guide our teaching, good relationships become an important outcome.

References

Carter, R.T. (2003). Becoming racially and culturally competent: The Racial-Cultural Counseling Laboratory. *Journal of Multicultural Counseling and Development* 31 (1): 20–30.

DiAngelo, R. (2011). White fragility. *International Journal of Critical Pedagogy* 3 (3): 54–70.

Duffy, R.D., Blustein, D.L., Diemer, M.A. et al. (2016). The psychology of working theory. *Journal of Counseling Psychology* 63 (2): 127–148.

Estrada, F. (2015). The teaching alliance in multicultural counseling course education: A framework for examining and strengthening the student-instructor relationship. *International Journal of Advanced Counseling* 37: 233–247.

French, B.H., Adair, Z.R., and Cokley, K. (2015). As people of color formerly employed by Mizzou, we demand change. Huffington Post (17 November). www.huffingtonpost.com/bryana-h-french-phd/people-of-color-employed-mizzou-demand-change_b_8584756.html (accessed 1 June 2018).

Grande, S. (2004). *Red Pedagogy*. New York, NY: Rowman & Littlefield.

Hagarty, S. (dir.). (2012). Dakota 38 (documentary). Smooth Feather Productions, https://www.youtube.com/watch?v=1pX6FBSUyQI (accessed 1 June 2018).

Kumashiro, K. (2000). Toward a theory of anti-oppressive education. *Review of Educational Research* 70 (1): 25–53.

Rogers, D.T. (2009). The working alliance in teaching and learning: Theoretical clarity and research implications. *International Journal for the Scholarship of Teaching and Learning* 3 (2), Article 28. https://doi.org/ 10.20429/ijsotl.2009.030228 (accessed 1 June 2018).

Saslow, E. (2016). The white flight of Derek Black. *Washington Post* (15 October). https://www.washingtonpost.com/national/the-white-flight-of-derek-black/2016/10/15/ed5f906a-8f3b-11e6-a6a3-d50061aa9fae_story.html?utm_term=.71493a0a358f (accessed 6 September 2017).

Shahjahan, R. (2015). Being "lazy" and slowing down: Toward decolonizing time, our body, and pedagogy. *Educational Philosophy and Theory* 47 (5), 488–501.

Sue, D.W. and Sue, D. (2015). *Counseling the Culturally Diverse: Theory and Practice.* Hoboken, NJ: John Wiley & Sons, Inc.

Sullivan, S. (2014). *Good White People: The Problem with Middle-Class White Anti-Racism.* Albany, NY: State University of New York Press.

Takacs, D. (2003). How does your positionality bias your epistemology? *Thought & Action* 19 (1): 27–38.

Wampold, Bruce E. (2001). *The Great Psychotherapy Debate: Models, Methods, and Findings.* Mahwah, NJ: Erlbaum.

9

Forming Classroom Communities to Help Students Embrace Discomfort

Buffy Smith

In the aftermath of another police shooting of an unarmed black male, one white male student in my class remarked that he was upset about the shooting and said, "All lives matter." A black female student stated that she was offended by his comment and the white student defended his statement, arguing it was more inclusive than just saying "Black lives matter."

This exchange encapsulates how students' internalized differences in perspectives frame their emotionally charged comments toward each other. I guided the class in a lively discussion of the historical and contemporary treatment of blacks in the United States by the law enforcement community, making sure other students in the class were given the opportunity to express their perspectives on the topic. Although the first two students did not fully embrace each other's perspective, they did gain a deeper understanding of how to unpack the complexity and multiple meanings associated with the statements "All lives matter" versus "Black lives matter." In addition, the two students also discovered they were both passionate advocates for racial justice.

Teaching Race: How to Help Students Unmask and Challenge Racism, First Edition.
Stephen D. Brookfield and Associates.
© 2019 John Wiley & Sons, Inc. Published 2019 by John Wiley & Sons, Inc.

For the past 13 years I have taught a sociology course called Race and Ethnicity at a private Catholic university. The majority of my students identify as white and middle class. I am an openly gay black female who is a first-generation college student from a low-income background. In this chapter, I examine how my approach to teaching Race and Ethnicity has evolved over the years, and the fears, challenges, and joys I've experienced. I share some specific teaching strategies that have helped my students and I build strong relationships and a sense of community, thereby allowing us to become comfortable with our discomfort in talking about race. I focus particularly on how principles of culturally responsive teaching (Ladson-Billings, 1995a, 1995b) establish and sustain meaningful relationships with students regardless of their racial and ethnic backgrounds.

The Challenges of Teaching Race and Ethnicity in the Classroom

My first two years of teaching the Race and Ethnicity course were focused on becoming an expert in the field. I spent numerous hours prepping for each class lecture, and the teaching mode was mostly lecture with little discussion. I had the mind-set that I needed to be in control of the conversation and "teach" students the best way to think about different racial and ethnic groups. I also felt I needed to show my students that I was qualified and competent to teach the course and that as a result I should be taken seriously and given respect. As the first tenure-track black woman hired in my department I felt the pressure to prove to my colleagues and students that I was hired based on my merits and not as a result of affirmative action. Although I earned my PhD from the top sociology graduate program in the country, I truly believe affirmative action did influence my department's decision to hire me. I wish this was a unique situation, but this is a common experience for many faculty of color.

It was my intention to increase my students' awareness and consciousness of how the ideology of white supremacy impacts individuals and institutions. I was afraid that if I did not present the information from a position of authority and control, my white students would make offensive comments to me and to students of color. I felt a responsibility to the students of color in class to make sure their voices were not silenced and their lived experiences were affirmed and validated.

It was difficult teaching the course because I felt as if I were in battle mode every time I entered the classroom. When students made offensive or prejudiced remarks I would immediately respond and "correct" them. On the other hand, when students were silent during the class discussion I interpreted their silence as being evidence of the lack of importance they placed on issues related to people of color. The course was emotionally exhausting, and I felt alienated from my white students and colleagues because I did not believe that they truly understood the psychological and emotional tax paid by professors of color every day we teach race and ethnicity at predominately white institutions.

My frustration became even greater when I read the comments on my annual teaching evaluations. Students' comments referred to me as "having a chip on my shoulder" and accused me of "hating white males." Those comments and the low numerical scores on the teaching evaluations did not make me more excited to teach the course; they only reminded me that race would play a major role in my tenure decision. I wished for some words of encouragement from my department chair and would have valued being told that teaching the Race and Ethnicity course was difficult for all professors and to therefore not take the comments too seriously. Instead, I received the general advice that I should use the teaching resource guides from the American Sociological Association. I did review those resource guides, but none of them provided strategies for preparing oneself on an emotional level to teach topics that white students might interpret as creating a hostile classroom environment.

My colleagues constantly reinforced to me that "good teaching" was highly valued at my university. Evidence of good teaching was based on feedback from student evaluations and colleagues who observed my classroom. It was clear that the pathway to tenure would be paved largely by the approval and acceptance of white students' perceptions of my teaching. My new challenge became how to talk about white supremacy and keep white students comfortable enough to engage in the topic. Unfortunately, I did not have faculty development courses or faculty mentors to teach me how to work with white students who had fears and discomfort when talking about racial issues with students of color and me.

Building Community as a Means of Examining Racial Identity

During my third, fourth, and fifth years of teaching, I decided to spend more time in the first two weeks of classes doing more community building activities. I realized the key to helping students have open, honest, and meaningful conversations about race and ethnicity was first to foster a strong, united, and collective bond among them. Therefore, the first goal was to make sure that the students learned the names of their classmates and something interesting about each other. I would remind them to always say each other's names when referring to their classmates and to not simply say, "I agree with her." Students would go over their syllabus together in small groups and then report back to the larger groups, highlighting what they regarded as the most interesting or exciting parts of the syllabus.

I also shifted my language in the classroom. Because many of my white students had a narrow definition of the term *white supremacy* and associated it only with extreme terrorist groups, such as the KKK and other white nationalist organizations, I reduced my usage of the term. They were unable to see that they benefitted directly from white supremacy, so I started to use terms such as *power* and *individual and institutional privileges*. In addition, I realized that if I did not provide more time for class discussions on these important issues, I was not allowing students the opportunity to learn from each other and to break down racial/ ethnic myths and misunderstandings. I incorporated time for small-group discussions into each class period. As the time for group discussions increased, my fears regarding losing control over class conversations receded. I realized that when I became vulnerable with my students, we had more open and honest conversations with one another. I had to become comfortable with allowing students to ask questions I could not answer and to be okay giving the response, "I don't know, but let's explore that question together."

Although professors of color are held to different teaching standards and more likely to be perceived as incompetent by white students, I became aware that trying to be invulnerable in front of my students would not automatically increase my level of competency in their eyes. I started liberating myself from internalized racism and mental shackles regarding what professors of color should say or do to present themselves as competent professionals in front of white students in the classroom.

As I began to embrace this new mental freedom in the classroom, I became less attached to the comments and scores on students' evaluations. To my surprise, the actual scores did increase (I received mostly 4s and 5s on a scale of 1–5) and the comments became more positive. However, what I was most proud of was that many of my students stated that I created a "safe and welcoming" classroom environment. Mission accomplished: The majority of my students liked each other, the course, and me, and I was granted tenure and promoted to associate professor. What else could a professor want?

Well, as a newly liberated tenured professor of color I felt a strong sense of responsibility to challenge my students even more in the classroom. I became eager to find creative and innovative teaching strategies that would increase learners' sense of community with each other. The first thing I started doing was referring to my students as family. I used the Native Hawaiian word for family, *ohana* – which means no one gets left behind. I would refer to students as ohana throughout the class. I also reminded students that it was healthy for family members to talk about difficult topics. We didn't have to agree with each other's positions, but we had to actively and empathetically listen to each other's perspectives. If we could do that we would have respectful dialogue, which fosters increased racial and ethnic awareness, understanding, and healing.

As a full professor I still have teaching challenges now but they are no longer rooted in fear, but rather in a sense of responsibility to liberate people from the pathology of racism. I challenge myself before I teach a lesson to do the necessary research on each racial or ethnic group represented in the class to make sure I represent their history and cultural heritage correctly and with great honor and respect. I constantly emphasize the distinction between individual and institutional white privilege, prejudice, and discrimination in class discussions. I no longer give lectures, but structure the class in a seminar format with small- and large-group discussions. I assign students to discussion leadership teams, in which they are responsible for teaching the readings for the week to the class. We are all treated as co-teachers and learners in the classroom.

As students come into the class, they arrange their chairs in a large circle. We do an ohana check-in with one another. We celebrate achievements, such as getting a paid internship, and offer words of encouragement for members of our family that are experiencing challenges, such as the theft of a bike. The check-in time period is critical to fostering a strong ohana connection with each other. We also talk about stories in the news or on social media related to racial and ethnic issues (such as police shootings in communities of color) before we start our official lesson for the day. I have learned that taking time to do a check-in and discuss current topics enhances students' mastery of the content material and gives them a stronger sense of belonging to our ohana, which increases their attendance and enhances their academic performance in the course.

Helping Students Be Comfortable with Discomfort

After I recognized how internalized racism was impacting my teaching, it was much easier to assist my students on their journey of self-awareness regarding how racism has influenced their lives. Most of the white students (the numerical majority) and students of color who enroll in my Race and Ethnicity course have a genuine desire to increase their knowledge and understanding of different racial and ethnic groups, but they want to do it in a safe classroom environment. However, my students have different interpretations of what *safe* looks like.

Many students of color seek a classroom environment in which they can have their lived experiences welcomed, affirmed, and validated. They do not want their historical and contemporary experiences minimized, marginalized, or ignored. They want classmates and teachers to acknowledge their voices, silences, and presence in the classroom. They want to learn as their peers do and not be forced to become teachers on a topic that they may or may not have knowledge about; after all, they are not being paid to teach the course. They want to be able to blend in or stand out on their own terms, without reinforcing stereotypes or being perceived as an exceptional student of color. This is the safety they seek in all of their classrooms.

On the other hand, many white students say that they want a classroom environment in which they don't feel judged or shamed for historical or contemporary acts of racism that they did not personally commit. They want to avoid conflict, tension, and other forms of discomfort when talking about race and ethnicity. They want to have the freedom and space to make politically incorrect statements and not be condemned for them, even if other students find them offensive. They want to leave the classroom feeling good about themselves and their racial group, despite reading and discussing the systemic forms of oppression that whites as a collective have inflicted, and continue to inflict, on people of color. The unspoken expectation is that my job is to take care of their emotional needs and to not hold them accountable for the rewards and privileges they earned as a result of the legacy of white supremacy.

I believe this unspoken expectation is what students evaluate me on at the end of the semester, even though there is no specific question on the student evaluation forms related to creating a safe classroom environment. I do not promise my students a safe environment. In fact, I tell them explicitly that they will need to "become comfortable with being uncomfortable." I encourage them that we have to have honest and difficult conversations around racial and ethnic issues because that is the only way we will improve race relations in our nation and in our global community. Instead of creating a safe classroom, I say that I will work hard to create a welcoming learning space in which all lived experiences are validated and affirmed and all ideas/ideologies are respectfully challenged and debated.

An Opening Question

At the beginning of class, I often pose a general question to all students and allow them time to write their individual responses. Then I go around the class and ask each of them to read their responses. Students are not allowed to interrupt or comment on each other's responses. The goal is to allow all students an opportunity to express their points of view without interruption. After all the students have read their responses, I remind students that in order to find the big truth on an issue we must listen, value, and affirm everyone's lived truths. During the class session, I incorporate as many of my students' opening comments into our discussion as I can. I do this to reinforce that all perspectives have value in our collective pursuit of racial healing and justice.

Recognizing Different Levels of Learning Readiness

Students show up in class with different levels of racial awareness and preparedness for risk. In order to gauge what they need at a particular time, I need to establish strong relationships with them inside and outside of the classroom. For instance, I am often able to discern students' levels of exposure to issues of race and ethnicity through previous class discussions, written assignments, and my connections with them outside of the classroom via extended office hours and attending club and sports events. The language students use and their behaviors and attitudes demonstrate whether they have a higher-risk or lower-risk capacity for engagements with racial and ethnic topics. I push and pull students to different degrees as they develop their racial consciousness.

Students who start the class with a more nuanced and deeper understanding of racial and ethnic issues are more receptive to being challenged to fight their personal racial bias and prejudice, and recognize how they benefit from systemic forms of oppression. Students who enter class with limited knowledge and experience in discussing racial and ethnic topics from multiple viewpoints have a more difficult time seeing the distinction between individual and institutional racism. I have to constantly be mindful of the different lived experiences of my students when talking about the topics in the course. I have to discern which students I can push harder to critically examine how they benefit from systemic racism every day and to know when to be a little more patient with students struggling with new information that calls into question their understanding of how they were socialized to perceive racial groups. I am mindful of language, tone, delivery, and nonverbal behaviors as I prepare my lesson plans for the course. It is not enough to share the latest research on a topic and provide peer-reviewed empirical data; I also have to practice how I deliver the factual information to my students so that it is conveyed in a way that they can actually hear. My task as the teacher is not to change my students' mindsets but rather to provide them a pathway to explore multiple perspectives on topics.

Most of my white students are more comfortable focusing on racism at an individual rather than an institutional level because US culture promotes individualism and meritocracy. People in our society are socialized to attribute social rewards and disadvantages to individuals' work ethics, talents, and skills, rather than to their social locations in a stratified racial hierarchy. Therefore it becomes easier to explain racism as simply due to individuals who act on their racial prejudice and to believe that if we could just get rid of those people, racism would go away. The challenge is to help my students question the institutional policies and practices that provide structural advantages, privileges, and rewards for those who do or do not profess racial prejudice.

Principles of Culturally Responsive Teaching

The driving force behind my pedagogy is to make my classes culturally relevant to all my students. In order to achieve this goal, I incorporate three major components of culturally responsive teaching: (1) caring, (2) communication, and (3) curriculum development. Geneva Gay (2010), a leading scholar of culturally responsive teaching, defines this pedagogy as "using the cultural knowledge, prior experiences, frames of reference, and performance styles of ethnically diverse students to make learning encounters more relevant to and effective for them" (p. 31).

Caring

Care and empathy are the essential building blocks in creating a strong learning community. Students are more likely to engage in courageous conversations in an environment in which everyone is expected to present their arguments with authentic care and empathy for one another. I demonstrate my care for students through my friendly and warm interactions during class check-ins and by the way I correct them gently in the classroom. For example, when a white student claims that affirmative action is the vehicle that allows less qualified students of color to be admitted over more qualified white students, it is my responsibility to explain that affirmative action requires race to be taken into account as one of many factors to be considered among a pool of applicants deemed qualified. Instead of dismissing the comment or shaming the student, I help the entire class gain clarity about the law.

In addition, I have extended office hours and I follow up with students regarding significant events in their lives (e.g. mother's surgery, birth of a nephew, job interviews). Also, I share resources with them that will advance their academic and professional goals, such as graduate school information, research opportunities, and internships. When it does not violate confidentiality, I try to celebrate students' achievements – such as marriage engagements, admissions to graduate schools and law schools, and scholarships – with the entire ohana. I want students to feel cared for, not only by me but by other members of our family.

Communication

The second component of culturally responsive teaching is communication. As well as demonstrating through my actions that I care for students, I also verbalize to members of my ohana that I respect and love them. I tell my students that because I care about them I will not lower my academic standards. Scholars Boutte and Hill (2006) contend that connecting students' home cultures with their school culture and maintaining high standards leads to academic success. I hold my students to high academic standards and provide them the support they need to meet and exceed those standards. One crucial way in which I support students in achieving success in my course is providing them with frequent, quality feedback. I want to communicate to students that I am actively engaged in a conversation with them when I evaluate their work. I provide specific ways students can edit their sentences in order to strengthen their arguments, and written and verbal feedback to help deepen their knowledge and understanding of the complexity of racial and ethnic topics. Through my feedback, I communicate to students that I am more concerned with how they critically analyze structural racism than with whether or not they use the "right" terminology when discussing racial and ethnic topics.

Curriculum Development

The third component of culturally responsive teaching is curriculum development. I am mindful of selecting readings that reflect the viewpoints of diverse scholars. It is important that when we are learning about American Indians, we read articles written by scholars who identify as American Indians. It helps to validate and affirm the identity of students of color as emerging scholars when they can read research by scholars from their racial or ethnic groups. White students also appreciate the depth, beauty, and richness of racial and ethnic groups when they read research written by scholars of color.

In addition to reading culturally relevant articles and books, I create assignments that allow students to learn first about their family heritages and racial groups before comparing and contrasting their groups with different ones. Students compile cultural portfolios in which they reflect on how their families' legacies were influenced and/or impacted by issues such as colonization, genocide, enslavement, immigration, and other systemic forms of power and privilege embedded in our institutions. The research is clear that students will achieve success if teachers have high academic standards and the curriculum reflects the experiences and stories of the students in the classroom (Ambrose et al., 2010).

Empathic Practices of Culturally Responsive Teaching

The guiding principles of culturally responsive pedagogy frame many of my specific instructional practices. But, just as importantly, they situate who I am in the classroom and how I present my full, embodied self to students. Culturally responsive teaching is not a list of best practices that can be checked off as they are implanted into the class, but more about relationships, tone, and daily mercies.

Instructional Relationships

Acknowledging the primacy of genuine relationships is my platinum standard for how I interact with students and how I want students to interact with one another. I constantly scan my classroom to see if students are demonstrating their engagement in a class discussion through their body language. If I observe students with a uninterested facial expression or folded arms I intervene and have students pause and write for one minute about what they are feeling as it relates to the class discussion. I collect the responses and read them all aloud, and as a class we process how this discussion is causing some of our ohana members to feel certain emotions. This impromptu classroom climate check-in activity takes time away from covering content in the class but is necessary to keep students connected to each other and me. I am confident what I do not cover in class students will learn on their own if I provide them with the information. But if I allow a student to shut down completely, I might never get that student reconnected to our ohana and the learning process.

Using a Positive Tone

I try to maintain a positive tone. I use humor to help sustain positivity, but while using humor I am mindful not to reinforce stereotypes or be mean spirited. I usually talk about myself and my many weaknesses, or I tell jokes that my students refer to as corny (for the record, my jokes are hilarious!). Over the years, I have practiced my facial expressions in the mirror so as not to appear shocked or disturbed when students make prejudiced statements and/or stereotypical comments. If I tell students we can talk about anything as long as we do it with respect and care, I have to be prepared for some students to make statements that they are unaware are offensive. For example, some of my students will say *colored people* when they think they are saying *people of color*. I will correct students, but I do it in a caring and respectful way. I remind students that the two terms sound very similar and say that I know how easily one could make that mistake, but that the term *colored people* historically had a different meaning from the contemporary phrase we use today, *people of color*. Students usually express gratitude for the gentle correction.

Offering New Mercies

I offer new mercies every day to students and myself. *New mercies* refers to the intentional and unconditional acts of grace and forgiveness we offer to people who unknowingly make offensive comments. This practice is connected to being relational and setting a positive tone. If our ohana is going to be strong we have to show mercy toward one another, because we are human and we know we will inevitably say something that is going to be offensive to another person. I remind students that they are going to be on both ends of the situation. They will make offensive comments and be hurt by offensive comments. I tell them there is no way to avoid this situation because it is part of our human condition. However, we can practice how to respond to people who make offensive statements to us by offering them grace as we explain to them why the comment was offensive. Then we can let them know that we still want to have relationships with them and have truly forgiven them.

I share with students some offensive statements I have made about different groups because I did not know that these were offensive at the time I made them. I share the stories to remind myself and my students we are all works in progress, but also to teach that we will never become better human beings if we end relationships with people who make hurtful comments because of their lack of knowledge and their early socialization process. One cannot be an effective teacher of race and ethnicity courses without having patience, a sense of humor, and a capacity for grace and mercy.

Strategies for Discussing Whiteness and White Privilege

According to Ladson-Billings (1995b), culturally relevant pedagogy has three major goals: academic success, cultural competence, and sociopolitical consciousness. Academic success focuses on students' learning outcomes and classroom experiences. Cultural competence refers to students' understanding of their own cultures and the cultures of other people. Sociopolitical consciousness is the awareness of how larger power structures create social problems, such as racism and poverty. As a culturally responsive teacher, I try to achieve these goals every time I address difficult topics in my Race and Ethnicity course. In this section I demonstrate how I incorporate culturally responsive teaching when I discuss white privilege in the classroom.

Every semester, during our discussion about white privilege, many of my white students begin to feel tense and to mentally prepare themselves for what they perceive as a public shaming process. I am mindful of the anxiety that some of my students have regarding this topic, so I always start with scientific evidence that race is a social construct (not a biological reality) and that our concept of white racial identity is socially constructed just as other racial identities are (e.g. Asian and black). As a class we watch the film *Race: The Power of an Illusion* (California Newsreel, 2003) and discuss the film along with our readings.

Then we talk about the individual and institutional forms of discrimination that all white ethnic groups historically endured unless they were landowners who were white Anglo-Saxon Protestant (WASP). We discuss the readings that indicate that white ethnic groups oppressed other white ethnic groups. The concept of whiteness is valuable when constructing a racialized hierarchy that documents the oppression, exploitation, and genocide practiced on American Indians and enslaved Africans. Since whites were at the top of the racialized social hierarchy, they had more individual and institutional rewards, privileges, assets, and power. These rewards and privileges were passed down from generation to generation based exclusively on white skin color.

After providing a historical, political, and social context of the construction of whiteness, students complete Peggy McIntosh's (1988) "Unpacking the Invisible Knapsack" worksheet. As a homework assignment, I ask students to select the top three statements representing the most important privileges. Then I ask them to explain the social benefits and rewards associated with those privileges. At the next class session, students are placed in small groups and asked to share their top three examples of white privilege and the social rewards attached to each of these. Groups then select their top three examples and write them on the board, ranking them 1 to 3. After each small group has ranked its preferences we reconvene as a whole class and discuss which privileges were ranked the highest and the social rewards connected to these. I end the class period asking the students to reflect on the experience and to think about the purpose of doing this exercise, and I tell them I want them to share their responses in the next class session.

When the next class assembles, for two minutes I allow students to reflect on and write about the purpose of examining white privilege. After they finish writing I ask each of them to share his/her/their response with a partner. I then go around the class to get all the students' responses about the purpose of the assignment. Responses most commonly fall into two broad categories: (1) increasing consciousness about white people's unearned privileges, and (2) making white people feel bad about their unearned privilege.

Once I hear all the responses, I then ask them to talk with their partners for four to five minutes about the advantages of making people feel guilty. After this paired discussion, we talk about that question as an entire class. Some common responses are the following: Guilt can produce good results, guilt changes people's bad behaviors, guilt leads to social change. After students state all the benefits of guilt, I add that guilt produces mistrust, increases social distance, fosters resentment and bitterness, and is focused on short-term results.

I remind students that if our long-term goal is to increase understanding and healing among racial groups, it can never be achieved through shame and guilt. Neither whites nor people of color benefit from white guilt: It is counterproductive, a lose-lose situation. In fact, white guilt leads to whites feeling self-absorbed and focusing a lot of their time and energy on trying to prove to other people that they are not racists but good white people (Sullivan, 2014). When whites become more obsessed with proving they are not racist, they don't invest the intellectual, social, and economic capital that is necessary to remove systemic forms of racism and other inequities in our society. Therefore, the purpose of doing the white privilege exercise is to increase racial consciousness and critically examine how institutions provide systemic advantages, privileges, assets, opportunities, resources, and rewards to whites.

Once we discuss why white guilt is not the desired educational outcome of the exercise, our conversation quickly moves from the individual to the institutional. We talk about the myth of meritocracy and how that contributes to the illusion that people have earned their privileges by their own intellect and hard work ethic. When white students accept that their privileges are based on their skin color more than merit it is an awakening of their racial consciousness. They can now see clearly how privileges are reinforced, reproduced, and sustained by all of our institutions in society. Students become less concerned with being perceived as racists on an individual level and instead explore how everyone has a responsibility to do their part to eliminate institutional racism. We shift the conversation from white guilt to social responsibility. For example, as an able-bodied woman who can walk independently using both legs, I do not curse my legs every morning. Instead, I have to be cognizant of unjust policies and practices that do not afford everyone with the same amount of access due to their mobility issues. It is my social responsibility to make sure that the same world that is accessible to me is also accessible to everyone. We share other examples of how social responsibility requires all individuals, not just whites, to actively engage in fostering a more just and equitable world.

The white privilege exercise takes three class periods, partly because we spend so much time on providing the historical, political, and social context of the concept of whiteness and the privileges and power associated with that social construct. Students have an opportunity to work alone, in small groups, and then in larger groups, to reflect and process the knowledge and emotional experiences related to the assignment. Students practice their written and oral communication skills along with being actively engaged listeners. They have to read articles associated with the topic and they have to write a reflection paper on the articles. During their first exam they have to address an essay question that asks them to identify three examples of white privilege and to explain the social rewards for each social privilege they select. They are also asked to think like a policy maker and explore what social policy they would implement to expand the privileges whites currently enjoy to others. I grade the written assignments and essays exams for the white privilege lesson with the same high academic standard as the other assignments. I do not lower my expectation for this assignment just because it is more controversial and emotionally charged. I expect excellence from my students at all times, even when the topic might be difficult to discuss and process.

The white privilege assignment promotes the cultural competence of all my students, those of color and white alike. Students of color have to do the same exercise as their white peers. It becomes clear during the small- and large-group discussions that there is great overlap in which examples of white privilege are considered the most important. This exercise helps demonstrate that people of color are very immersed in white culture in the United States. This assignment and discussion also provides all students with a deeper understanding of the process of how white ethnic group identity was replaced with white racialized group identity. Many students are unaware of the historical oppression many white ethnic groups encountered at the hands of other white ethnic groups. This assignment is usually an enlightening experience for all students, regardless of their racial and ethnic backgrounds.

The reason the assignment and discussion about white privilege is so transformative is that it elevates the conversation from the individual level to the institutional level. In Freire's (2000) terms, it helps to raise the sociopolitical consciousness of students. During the discussion, we go beyond the surface understanding of white privilege to critique the notion of meritocracy and how that idea tries to legitimatize the privileges that white people enjoy. I do not allow my white students to wallow in guilt or shame; rather I push them to critically examine how written and unwritten institutional norms, values, and expectations reproduce and sustain the inequities in our society. I encourage all my students to become socially responsible leaders who must critically challenge unjust policies and practices that systematically impede the success and social progress of marginalized people. Culturally responsive teaching provides me with the tools I need to motivate my students to become socially conscious citizens actively working on creating a more just and equitable world.

References

Ambrose, S.A., Bridges, M.W., DiPietro, M. et al. (2010). *How Learning Works: Seven Research Based Principles for Smart Teaching*. San Francisco, CA: Jossey-Bass.

Boutte, G.S. and Hill, E.L. (2006). African American communities: Implications for culturally relevant teaching. *New Educator* 2 (4): 311–329.

California Newsreel (2003). *Race: The Power of an Illusion*. DVD, 3 episodes, 56 minutes each, www.newsreel.org/nav/title.asp?tc=CN0149 (accessed 1 June 2017).

Freire, P. (2000). *Pedagogy of the Oppressed*, 30th Anniversary Edition. New York, NY: Continuum International.

Gay, G. (2010). *Culturally Responsive Teaching: Theory, Research, and Practice*, 2nd ed. New York, NY: Teachers College Press.

Ladson-Billings, G. (1995a). But that's just good teaching! The case for culturally relevant pedagogy. *Theory Into Practice* 34 (3): 159–165.

Ladson-Billings, G. (1995b). Toward a theory of culturally relevant pedagogy. *American Educational Research Journal* 32 (3): 465–491.

McIntosh, P. (1988). White privilege: Unpacking the invisible knapsack. *Peace and Freedom Magazine* (July/August): 10–12.

Sullivan, S. (2014). *Good White People: The Problem with Middle-Class White Anti-Racism*. Albany, NY: State University of New York Press.

10

Adapting Discussion Methods to Teach Race

Stephen D. Brookfield

It was during my initial week of teaching in September 1970 when I first encountered racial dynamics in the classroom. During that first week a muttered racial insult (I never found out from whom) exploded into conflict, and before I knew it I had a fistfight on my hands. A white and a black student suddenly jumped up and started slugging each other, and the rest of the students started enthusiastically cheering on the combatants. I did what I could to intervene and managed to calm things down enough so that students took their seats. From that moment on I knew that racialized flashpoints could explode unexpectedly out of nowhere, and that discussions could go off in completely unanticipated directions.

When to Use Discussions in Teaching About Race

For many years I privileged discussion above all other instructional approaches. It would be my de facto starting point, my go-to methodology that I thought would establish my Freirian legitimacy and prove to the world my democratic commitment. Over time (with help from Freire and Myles Horton) I've recognized the simplistic mistake of assuming that anyone who uses discussion is dedicated to social justice and anyone who lectures is an authoritarian demagogue. Paterson's (1970) notion of counterfeit discussion – something that

Teaching Race: How to Help Students Unmask and Challenge Racism, First Edition.
Stephen D. Brookfield and Associates.
© 2019 John Wiley & Sons, Inc. Published 2019 by John Wiley & Sons, Inc.

looks like a genuinely open dialogue but in fact is being skillfully engineered to arrive at a predetermined endpoint – has been particularly helpful in this regard.

Just having people talk is not a sufficient condition for respectful dialogue. Far too many discussions are dominated by egomaniacs pushing agendas. When an open-ended discussion question is posed, it's easy for extroverts, those who are more knowledgeable about the topic, and those who need to hear their voices educating others to foreclose the discussion of multiple perspectives. Unless steps are taken to prevent this from happening, these kinds of individuals will respond quickly and forcefully to the question and set the agenda for how the discussion will proceed.

So if you use discussion to teach about race, you need to be clear about what you are hoping to achieve. In my own teaching, race-based discussions are designed to accomplish three things:

1. To introduce multiple perspectives on an event, topic, or issue that demonstrate the complexities of race and racism
2. To democratize participation to ensure that all students have an opportunity to contribute ideas and share experiences
3. To uncover and challenge the analytical frames for making sense of race that are embedded in white supremacy

If these objectives are to be realized, a number of conditions need to be in place. Discussion leaders will have to model the kind of open-minded readiness to consider alternative viewpoints and "inconvenient" information that they wish to encourage in students. There will have to be some agreement on the norms and ground rules that are in place to stop people from ducking difficult issues and retreating from honest testimony. Participants will also need some initial time to study the topic that's the focus of conversation. This can happen through preliminary reading, the viewing of films or videos, listening to lectures, TED talks and podcasts, and through sustained individual reflection or journaling. Although the speed of current events (such as a morning presidential tweet) or the suddenness of outbursts in class mean you don't always have the lead time you'd like, I do find that the discussions in which people delve most deeply into questions of identity, privilege, and oppression are usually preceded by some preparatory thinking or study.

In this chapter I present six discussion techniques that I have found to be well suited to exploring race and racism. I present them roughly in sequence, beginning with the simplest and moving through to the most complex.

TodaysMeet

TodaysMeet (https://todaysmeet.com) is an electronic tool for getting immediate and anonymous input from group members that can be used to structure discussion, check for understanding, and generate new questions. It is open access and doesn't require any subscription or membership. It is also extremely easy to use. I have found it to work well for a range of group sizes and contexts: from meetings and classes of 10 students right up to town hall meetings, conference keynotes, workshops, and classes of several hundred.

As people are filing into your session you go to the TodaysMeet website and create a page named specifically for the day's session. For example, if you're examining microaggressions it could be called www.todaysmeet.com/microaggressions. If you wish to explore white supremacy it could be www.todaysmeet.com/whitesupremacy. You ask participants to open their laptops, smart phones, or tablets and to log on to the page by creating identities for themselves. I urge them to use numbers, not words, in order to keep their identities totally anonymous. I explain that TodaysMeet works really well for anyone worried about saying the wrong thing or appearing racially naïve, because no comment can be traced back to any particular individual. Students can say whatever they wish to with no fear of being shamed or embarrassed by peers or the instructor.

I use TodaysMeet in two ways. The first is to create a general back channel of communication for people to pose questions, express disagreements, and make comments as they feel the need to. I check the TodaysMeet feed every 15 minutes or so to see if someone has raised important issues we're not addressing or pointed out things we're missing. Second, I often want to provide an opportunity for everyone to be heard in a very short space of time. So I will pose a question to group members and give them a minute to think of their responses and post them to the TodaysMeet feed. By the end of 60 seconds I have a screen filled with comments from the majority of group members, which can then be used to structure the day's discussion.

Here are some examples of TodaysMeet questions I've used at the start of a session:

- *What emotions or feelings are you experiencing as we go into today's discussion of race?* This question is designed to name the elements in the room – the fear of sounding racist, the fatigue of having another racial discussion, the anger at presumed political correctness, and so on – that might be preventing people from engaging with the topic. I can then acknowledge and address these at the outset.

- *What's an example of interest convergence as explained in critical race theory?* This question functions as an understanding check before moving into a fuller discussion. Depending on the quality of examples provided, I can judge the degree to which people are ready to move into conversation and whether I need to do a quick recap of the idea.

- *In terms of what we've talked about so far today, what's the question or issue that's most on your mind?* Because extroverts and students for whom English is their first language have a built-in advantage in spoken discussion, I use a question like this in the middle of class to provide students who are quieter, more introverted, and/or with English as a second language (ESL) the chance to determine where we might go next.

Although TodaysMeet is used mostly to prep participants for a discussion, it also sometimes takes on a discursive life of its own as people respond to each other's points in the TodaysMeet feed. In this regard it's interesting to note that if one person's post clearly crosses a line or boundary, others immediately call attention to that fact and critique the use of language. TodaysMeet can also be used when someone has made a particularly profound, or disturbing, comment and you want to make sure that the group probes this more deeply. In this case you would simply ask for a minute's pause and that people post what they are thinking about the comment.

Finally, TodaysMeet is a good way to debrief what's happened in small-group discussion. I try not to ask for small-group reports because these tend to run out of steam after the second or third group has given its report. I also feel that groups are sometimes more concerned with impressing me or their peers than with identifying contradictions, exploring differences, and raising issues. So as the small-group time is running out and just before the whole class reconvenes, I ask that each small group identify one or two questions that arose in its discussion and that it post these to the TodaysMeet feed. We then discuss as a whole group which of these we want to consider further.

Circle of Voices

Circle of Voices is a small-group discussion protocol that I use several times at the outset of my time with a group. It is designed to accomplish three specific things:

1. To give all of the people in the room a chance to participate by hearing their opinions spoken without anyone interrupting them.
2. To make sure that participants hear the widest range of perspectives on a topic before deciding what to focus on.
3. To socialize people early on into the idea that listening carefully to what others are saying is the most important habit to learn in discussion.

Circle of Voices begins with a period of mandatory silence. You pose a question to the group and ask the participants to stay quiet for two minutes as they write down some initial thoughts or responses to the question. Once the two minutes is up you call time and ask for groups of five to form.

Each group then engages in two distinct rounds of conversation. In the first round, each person shares for about 60 seconds what they were thinking about or wrote down during the initial two-minute period of silence. The ground rule here is that no interruptions are allowed. Even if extroverts want to jump in and support speakers by encouraging them or telling them why their comments are so great, they are not allowed to. Participants must listen quietly to each person's contribution. This no-interruptions rule is to ensure that everyone in the room hears his/her/their uninterrupted voice in the air at least once during the class session. The longer introverts stay silent, the harder it is for them to speak, so if you want to hear from everybody it's essential that you engineer an early opportunity for that to happen, even if only in a small group. The no-interruptions rule is also designed to stop an early consensus from emerging. Because everyone gives his/her/their response to the question, people hear all the perspectives that are held by group members.

Once all individuals have voiced their initial uninterrupted responses to the question, the second round of open conversation begins. Now anyone can speak in any order and interruptions are fine. However, a new ground rule regarding what people can talk about applies in this second round. Basically, participants can only comment on what another person said in the first round. Comments can include asking questions about someone's initial contribution, commenting on something that resonated, disagreeing with a comment, and indicating how a first-round contribution opened up a new line of thinking. But whatever comments are made in this open conversation, they have to link directly and explicitly to something someone said in the first round. This rule is designed to socialize students into acquiring the habits of careful listening and attentive responding. Knowing that you can only speak about what someone else said in the initial sharing forces you to listen closely to people's contributions.

Some race-based questions I typically ask during the Circle of Voices exercise are the following:

- *What images or actions come to your mind when you hear the term* racism? This would be a question I'd pose at the start of a session with people who probably haven't spent much time thinking about race. The idea would be to get a sense of where everyone is in his/her/their understanding. However, I have also used this question with relatively advanced groups composed of people experienced in discussing this issue.

- *What is the most important point for you in George Yancy's* "Letter to White America"? This kind of question would be used when members had studied specific material before the discussion. The responses help me understand how people are prioritizing elements of this content and provide a sense of which aspects resonate most with them.

- *What would be an example of white supremacy that you've witnessed or experienced in your everyday life?* This question is designed to delve deeply into participants' lives. I often use the *witnessed or experienced* phrasing because it gives group members the chance to decide how much they wish to reveal. Responding to the *witnessed* part allows people to put some limits on their personal disclosures; responding to the *experienced* prompt invites them into direct sharing.

Circle of Voices only takes 10 or 15 minutes to conduct, but it gets everyone involved early on and gives participants a sense of the different experiences and understandings people bring to the topic. As the circles are finishing up their discussions I ask all individuals to post one or two questions or issues that were raised in their discussions to the TodaysMeet page I've created for the session. These questions provide useful direction on how to frame the subsequent large-group discussion. Alternatively, you can ask students to nominate the questions they would most like to explore further in the next round of conversation.

Chalk Talk: A Visual Discussion

I'm a word person. I make lists, my PowerPoint slides typically consist of bullet points of words, and when I explain something I rarely use visuals or images. So as a teacher, one of the things I need to do is to ensure that I build in plenty of graphics, slides, and videos for those students who think more visually than me. The Chalk Talk exercise, developed by Hilton Smith of the Foxfire Fund (2009), is a great way to construct a visual representation of the different ways group members think about a topic. It also allows you to hear from a lot of people in a very short period of time. I mostly use it to unearth the concerns of a wide range of organizational members before building agendas for change. A Chalk Talk dialogue can be an excellent way to kick off an institution-wide meeting or workshop on how to combat racism or develop a more diverse, inclusive environment.

The process begins with the leader or teacher writing a question in the center of a large black- or whiteboard and circling it. (If you're in an online environment, the Zoom platform has a whiteboard function for this activity.) In auditoriums or large staff-development trainings I sometimes have to cover several walls with blank sheets of newsprint for groups of people to write on. Markers or chalk sticks are placed by the board, and once the question is posted, everyone is invited to come and stand by the board to participate in the activity. There is usually a group of nonparticipants whose skepticism or laziness means they'll refuse to get out of their seats. I advise going over and inviting them to move to the board.

As facilitator, you explain that people should write responses to the question on the board for about five minutes. While this is happening you should ask for silence so that people can think about the question and process the information going up on the board. Along with responding to the original question, people should be encouraged to post new questions as well as responses to what's going up on the board. I ask people to look for postings on different parts of the board that seem to connect in some way and then to draw a line connecting the relevant postings when they see connections and to write a brief remark along that line about why the two comments seem to be similar. I also ask that they follow the same process – draw a connecting line with a few words of explanation along the line – when they see two comments that appear to be contradictory or to represent significantly different responses.

Several people usually start writing immediately on different parts of the board. I also participate by drawing lines connecting comments, by writing questions, by adding my own thoughts, and so on. After five or six minutes there's often either a lull in posting or the board has become so full that there's no more space for people to write or draw anything else. I'll then announce that the silent part of the activity is over and that we can now stand back, view the whole board, and start looking for common clusters of responses. I'll point out the multiple handwriting styles, signifying that many people have posted. For me this is one of the biggest advantages of Chalk Talk: In five minutes or so you'll have secured input from the 60–70% of participants who will have posted a comment, drawn an image, or created a line connecting points together. If I had posed a question verbally to the whole group and asked them to respond verbally within the same five-minute period, I would have heard from maybe three or four people and felt compelled to earn my wages by responding in some way to each comment.

Figure 10.1 is a Chalk Talk I conducted using newsprint I posted on a wall during a workshop on teaching critical thinking. The question in the center of the dialogue is "What do you tell students that critical thinking looks, sounds, and feels like?"

Figure 10.2 presents two shots of one completed by a group of students on an old fashioned blackboard at the end of their

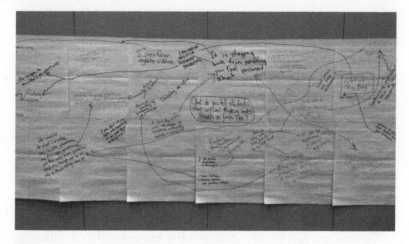

Figure 10.1 Chalk Talk dialogue on newsprint.

leadership program. The question is "How do you understand or practice leadership differently because of the program?"

The first couple of times I use Chalk Talk in a group I do the initial debrief by myself. I keep participants standing by the blackboard, as I look first for comments that have the most lines running to and from them. I explain that since these have generated the most dialogue, they probably represent issues for further discussion. But I also look for outliers: comments that stand alone with no lines. I point out that these could represent important blind spots or omissions, and that we need to look at them carefully. After the third or fourth time I've run a Chalk Talk in a group I change things up and ask students to start doing the debriefing. Standing by the board, they point out common themes, clusters of comments that get lots of attention, and outliers.

The final stage in this exercise is to invite the participants to use their laptops, smart phones, tablets, or other handheld devices to take pictures of the dialogue. I do this because I often run a Chalk Talk exercise at the outset of a new unit of study or as the first activity in a community dialogue. Photographing or videoing the board allows us to return to this dialogue over the coming weeks as we go deeper into the topic.

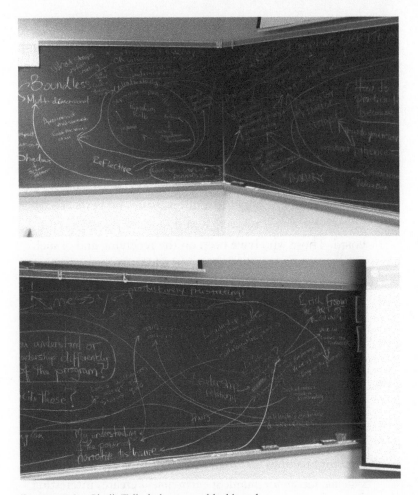

Figure 10.2   Chalk Talk dialogues on blackboard.

I end the exercise by reminding participants of why we've spent time on this activity. I point out that it has democratized the conversation by securing the participation of a lot of people in a short time, and that on the board no one's voice can be louder than anyone else's. I remind people that those who think and express themselves visually, as well as introverts and ESL participants, will have been served by the exercise. And I emphasize that the graphic mind map produced demonstrates that there are multiple perspectives, different experiences, and various interpretive frames being applied in the room. In race-based teaching, capturing these differences is crucial. As early as possible I want participants to stop universalizing their experiences of race and to realize that completely different, even contradictory, worlds are in the same room. Expressing this reality visually is very powerful.

Here are some questions I have used as the focus for Chalk Talk dialogues based around race:

- *When have you witnessed, experienced, or enacted a racial microaggression?* Using the terms *witnessed* and *experienced* offers participants two different frames for posting on the board. Those who have been on the receiving end of such an action can share how that felt, while others can talk about seeing microaggressions committed. The term *enacted* invites those with a degree of self-awareness to share about times they've committed these kinds of aggressions. This question has been very helpful in generating dialogues that clarify the subtle, slippery nature of such acts.
- *What does an antiracist environment look, sound, or feel like?* The phrase *look, sound, or feel like* is a common formulation for a Chalk Talk dialogue. It is designed to free up people's creativity by encouraging them to draw images that represent feelings and sounds. Substituting *privilege* or *systemic racism* for *antiracist environment* creates interesting variants of the question.

Although I typically use Chalk Talk early on as a way to communicate a sense of the different agendas and experiences surrounding race that group members hold, I have also used it in a more summative way. It's interesting to have the group respond to the same question you used in an opening session as its final activity. Comparing the two graphics presented can indicate how much a group has grown. For example, when I have used the question "What does an antiracist environment look, sound, or feel like?" to bookend a group's time together, some very clear differences

Adapting Discussion Methods to Teach Race   203

emerge. In the first visual dialogue there will be multiple comments about institutional conduct, personal behavior, and organizational policy. The emphasis is all on actions "out there" in the world. In the summative graphic the postings are usually focused much more inwardly, as people emphasize the importance of rooting out the racism in themselves as well as in others.

Circular Response

This exercise shares the circular seating format of Circle of Voices but is significantly more complex. I would never use this protocol early on in a group's history but instead hold it in reserve until we're past the midpoint of our allotted time together.

Circular Response was devised in the 1930s by Eduard Lindeman (Brookfield, 1987), a social-work educator in New York. When working with neighborhood and civic groups, Lindeman noticed two tendencies that quickly killed group discussion. First, people were so committed to articulating their agendas and proposals that they rarely heard what others were saying. Second, when groups met to discuss actions to address a specific problem facing them, there were so many ideas proposed early on that it was difficult for the group to focus on just one or two. Circular Response was designed to combat each of these tendencies by encouraging careful, active listening and by getting participants to drill down into one or two issues.

The process begins with the facilitator, or the group itself, posing a common question. People group themselves into circles of 10 to 12 members. They are silent until one person decides to start off the conversation by giving an initial response to the question posed. In this first round of conversation, people are asked to keep their comments to a maximum of two minutes and to not interrupt each other, no matter how enthusiastic they are about a comment or how much they want to ask questions.

After the first person has finished speaking, the person to his/her/their left goes next. After taking the time to process the initial speaker's comments silently, this person also takes two minutes to speak with no interruptions. However, whatever he/she/they says must build on, or respond to, the initial speaker's comments. This response does not have to be an endorsement or paraphrase of the opening contribution. The second speaker can raise a criticism, express a disagreement, extend the first comment in an unpredictable way, or simply say that he/she/they finds it difficult to come up with a response. In this last case, the person will say something about the source of the difficulty (maybe the first speaker used unfamiliar language or was talking about unfamiliar experiences).

The third speaker then has up to two minutes of uninterrupted time to build on or respond to the second speaker's comments, and the process continues around the circle until everyone has spoken. I advocate that the facilitator be a part of the group but not be the first to speak. It's important for teachers to show that sometimes they need time to think before speaking, that they too struggle to build on previous comments, and that they're striving to listen carefully.

During this first conversational phase, anxiety is usually high as people wait anxiously for their turns, hoping and praying that the people who speak before them say something they can make sense of and respond to. I notice people leaning in to follow what people do with their comments and how earlier contributions frame subsequent ones. Once everyone has spoken in the first round, the group moves into open conversation with no ground rules, time limits, or order of speech. People can introduce completely new topics, express support or disagreement, extend previous contributions, and raise questions about something someone said in the first round.

The design of Circular Response is intended to achieve two things. First, to do it well you have to listen carefully. After all, if you don't attend closely to the person before you then your opportunity to respond appropriately to his/her/their comments is significantly reduced. Paying careful attention to an unfamiliar perspective is particularly important when race is concerned, since people often bring such entrenched worldviews to this topic. The ground rule disallowing interruptions in the first round of talk means people have to attend to experiences, opinions, and stories very different from their own. Second, as the first round of discussion progresses, often one or two issues will seem to keep surfacing, albeit with different interpretive frames. So when people move into the open-discussion phase they're more primed to see complexities and contradictions. This is very helpful when considering the multilayered topic of race.

Some typical questions I have used for this protocol are:

- *What are the most powerful blinders to whites in seeing their own racism?* This is not a question I would start a program off with, so it fits well with the placing of Circular Response in the second half of a group's life together. By the time I introduce Circular Response the group has come to know each other fairly well, so it is more possible to present a potentially threatening or probing question such as this one than it would have been at earlier stages of the group's existence. The complexity of the question seems to suit the first round of the protocol, since people often wait and think about their responses to the previous speaker's comment on this topic.
- *What's the best way to open someone else's eyes to a different racial perspective?* I like to use action-oriented questions in Circular Response discussions, since these typically occur after people have spent a considerable time becoming acquainted with the building blocks of racial cognizance (white supremacy, white privilege, microaggressions, aversive racism, interest convergence, and so on). By then lots of stories have been shared and experiences analyzed. So when we get around to doing this protocol, people are usually ready to focus on taking action.
- *How should we respond when as a marginal, disenfranchised, or outlying member of a group we witness racism?* This question

is worded to focus on the times that people with little positional power or authority wish to take action but are either not used to having their voices taken seriously or know that they will suffer serious consequences for speaking up or protesting. The intent of the question is to move people into realizing the need for solidarity, alliances, and networking in any social-change effort. Although making an individual stand is important, I want people to shift their frames toward the crucial dynamic of collective mobilization. Organizations and institutions are far more likely to integrate antiracist policies, structures, and practices when people collectively commit to holding them accountable.

Bohmian Dialogue

The most complex of the discussion protocols I propose in this chapter is *Bohmian Dialogue*. Named after the theoretical physicist David Bohm (1996), this process builds on Bohm's attempt to create an open forum to explore intractable problems. The purpose is to build an organic conversation in which participants collectively create meaning by recognizing connections and commonalities and by building on each other's ideas as freely as possible. The activity is designed for large groups of around 40 people, but I have also used it with groups of 15, 20, and 25. Bohm recommends spending up to two hours in this dialogue, but it can also be used in 45-minute periods.

The first stage in a Bohmian Dialogue is for people to study some common resource. When an academic class is engaged in the process, you can ask students to read or view some pertinent material beforehand. Because I use this activity mostly in organizational or community settings in which I don't know who will show up, I usually begin the process with everybody together viewing some relevant video. One of my favorites is *A Conversation with My Black Son* (Gandbhir and Foster, 2015) from the Op-Docs section of the

New York Times, in which black parents recount how they prepare their sons to be pulled over and racially profiled by the police and the different ways in which they advise them to respond to this event. Another is the "What It Means to be American" excerpt from *The Color of Fear* documentary (Wah, 1994). Here a black man (Victor) expresses his pain, anger, and frustration in response to a white man (David) who has told him to stop obsessing on race and just be American. There are many other possible film and video resources suggested in other chapters in this book.

After the videos are over, the group arranges the chairs into one large circle and I explain how the process will work. I begin by stating what the conversation is for. I say that there are two primary reasons we're doing this. First, we want to understand the different experiences of race and racism that are in the room so that we can try to identify and develop possible points of common connection. Second, we want to build on the intersections we discover to explore steps we can take to combat racism. We are trying to develop some collective thinking about how we can best make common cause against white supremacy.

I remind people that these are both incredibly difficult projects, so if we are to have any hope of success we need to listen carefully and intently to each other and spend a lot of time processing the meanings others' contributions have for us. I predict that there'll be necessarily long periods of silence in the room as people digest and mull over what others have just said. I urge participants to try to be comfortable with the room being quiet and insist that this is an essential part of the process.

Then it's time to explain the specific ground rules that structure Bohmian Dialogue:

- There are no winners or losers, so don't try to overpower or diminish contributions you dislike or take issue with.
- This is not a debate, so try to refrain from creating binary alternatives ("He's racist but she's antiracist"; "That's moral but this is oppressive").

- Don't try to convince or persuade; the point is to understand and connect when we can.
- Only one person speaks at a time.
- Speak only when you have something to say or you have a response that's prompted by another person's remarks.
- Be comfortable with long silences.
- If it helps you to focus, feel free to close your eyes or look at the floor.
- Expect radically different opinions and perspectives but express them in just that way, as different takes on an issue.
- Focus on identifying common ground and how to build on it.

I also need to clarify my own role in the dialogue. I let people know that I'll be both a contributor and an umpire. If people start to get into a debate, try to convince or rebut each other, or declare another contribution to be wrong, my job is to step in and remind people of the point of the exercise. We are trying to understand the alterity of racial experience and to find points of common connection that can prompt action.

A quick side note here. There are many times when I have been highly confrontational and judgmental during organizational efforts. I have been known to insult chairs and committees publicly and to accuse them of racist manipulation. I welcome conflict, getting issues in the open, and trying to show up the idiocy of my enemies. But I engage in these actions in the context of organizing, not in the context of education. As Myles Horton (1990, 2003) helped clarify for me, there's a difference between organizing and educating. In the former case you want to outmaneuver those in power and mobilize people for collective action using propaganda and slogans. It often helps to dichotomize issues by framing them in terms of good guys and bad guys, oppressors and oppressed, moral and immoral conduct. And frequently you have to move quickly, as events dictate your actions. In contrast, in an educational process you want to complexify not simplify, to show diversity rather than privileging only one reality. That's what Bohmian Dialogue is all

about: helping people understand the multiple layers and complexities of race as a precursor to developing authentic common cause.
Some questions suited to this activity are:

- *What would it take for us to trust each other?* This question is
  suited to multiracial groups that include whites whom you
  feel are too quick to declare themselves allies, assuming
  that, having made this declaration, they will be welcomed
  and trusted by people of color.
- *What stops us from realizing our common potential?* This
  question works well with groups that are getting frustrated
  with their inability to progress as fast as they'd like in some
  kind of antiracist work. In groups of this kind it's easy for
  people to slip into race-based blaming and commit all kinds
  of unwitting microaggressions.
- *What do we most overlook or misunderstand about how racism
  works?* Here you're trying to challenge a group to go deeper
  into analyzing the workings of racism. I use this question
  if I feel that the group is slipping into an easy certainty of
  assuming that just by citing the clear existence of racism
  and the injuries it inflicts, people will be convinced to give
  up racist ideas and practices. My hope is that the deeper,
  visceral, emotionally sedimented nature of white supremacy
  will be revealed.
- *How do we build common cause?* This question is project
  focused and appeals to many people. It is hopeful and
  oriented to the future. Of course, once people start
  responding to it, the complexities of how people define
  common cause, let alone how it is realized, quickly come to
  the fore.

Appreciative Pause

This final activity is used as a coda to intensive discussions on race.
One of the behaviors most absent in discussions is that of people

giving appreciation for the contributions others have made to their learning. So, after a race-based discussion, particularly one that has been tense, fraught, and emotional (in other words, after pretty much every discussion about race!), I find it's helpful to practice the Appreciative Pause. This is a brief period during which *only* expressions of appreciation are allowed. Appreciations are publicly spoken (in small or large groups) for questions posed that suggested a whole new line of thinking, comments that clarified something that up to then was confusing, connections identified among ideas or contributions, and examples that increased understanding of a difficult concept. People also identify tonal contributions, referencing the honesty, supportiveness, and empathy demonstrated by peers.

Conclusion

I used to think that the longer I ran discussions, the less I would need to have ground rules or structure. The opposite has proven to be the case. I now rarely hold unstructured conversations on race because I realize that people's experiences, prejudices, and ideological assumptions quickly surface and effectively shut down communication. Instead, I lay out for participants the reasons why I'm moving into discussion, what it's designed to achieve, and how the specific protocol I'm using operates. Of course community and organizational groups sometimes rebel against my rationale and declare ground rules to be unnecessary. Students rarely do, but they can still sabotage protocols by misapplying them, skipping steps, or not following directions. The point I made in the opening chapter about the ontological reality of nothing ever working is very true when discussion protocols are concerned.

But I still believe that the protocols described in this chapter have a good chance of stopping conversations from prematurely spiraling out of control. Race evokes such strong feelings that egomaniacs will run riot trying to convert everyone else to their agendas unless something is in place to prevent this from happening. Alternately, people will be frozen in fear of saying the wrong thing and anxious about being called racist unless some activity deliberately invites participation in a way that feels comfortable. Clear protocols can encourage contributions, equalize participation, acknowledge different learning styles or expressive modes, and keep in check domineering members or confident extroverts. Applying protocols that surface and privilege unacknowledged and excluded perspectives and experiences can help keep people in conversation longer than would be the case if discussions were habitually unstructured.

References

Bohm, D. (1996). *On Dialogue*. London: Routledge.

Brookfield, S.D. (ed.) (1987). *Learning Democracy: Eduard Lindeman on Adult Education and Social Change*. Beckenham, Kent: Croom Helm.

Gandbhir, G. and Foster, B. (2015). A *Conversation With My Black Son*. *New York Times* Op-Docs (17 March). https://www.nytimes.com/2015/03/17/opinion/a-conversation-with-my-black-son.html (accessed 6 February 2018).

Horton, M. (1990). *The Long Haul: An Autobiography*. New York, NY: Doubleday.

Horton, M. (2003). *The Myles Horton Reader: Education for Social Change*. Knoxville, TN: University of Tennessee Press.

Paterson, R.W.K. (1970). The concept of discussion: A philosophical approach. *Studies in Adult Education* 2 (1): 28–50.

Smith, H. (2009). The Foxfire approach to student and community interaction. In: *Promising Practices for Family and Community Involvement during High School* (ed. L. Shumow), 89–103. Charlotte, NC: Information Age.

Wah, L.M. (dir.). (1994). *The Color of Fear* (film). Running time 90 min. Stir Fry Productions.

11

Teaching Against Color Blindness

Wendy Yanow

I am a Jewish married mother of two who grew up with middle-class values in an often poor, working-class household. I am white. From the mid-1950s to the mid-1970s I lived in a two-flat in what used to be called Chicago's Northwest Side. Albany Park, having once been a predominantly Jewish lower- to middle-class neighborhood, had become an ethnically diverse, poor working-class neighborhood, where I was exposed to a multitude of languages, incredible smells, multigenerational extended families, fabulous music, and a sense of belonging (Yanow, 2007, pp. 148–149).

In our poor working-class neighborhood, education was about sending kids to school. There existed a sense of the teacher as the supreme knower of all things education. Many parents felt that if it was presented in school it was appropriate, and for the most part they complied with those unspoken rules. But there were areas in which some parents felt compelled to be more vocal. There was the time, for example, when I was in primary school – maybe kindergarten or first grade – when we were preparing for what was still called the Christmas Assembly. I came home singing the song my class was preparing to sing at the assembly. I don't remember the title, but the words included something like "Jesus loves me…" After my mother visited the

Teaching Race: How to Help Students Unmask and Challenge Racism, First Edition.
Stephen D. Brookfield and Associates.
© 2019 John Wiley & Sons, Inc. Published 2019 by John Wiley & Sons, Inc.

school and I was no longer involved in singing that song, I remember realizing "this is who we are" (pp. 148–149).

This chapter is about teaching race within the framework of critical thinking, understood as conducting a critical examination of the assumptions that inform our interpretations and understanding of lived experience. As the opening paragraphs made plain, my own meaning making and negotiation of the world is informed by assumptions I hold as a result of my experiences. Those assumptions serve as counterpoints as I work to understand others' different experiences. I use critical race theory (CRT) as the methodology for teaching and learning through story and my theoretical framework for analyzing lived experience (Delgado and Stefancic, 2012). Methodologically, CRT teaches that to understand how white supremacy operates we need to learn from people whose everyday lived experiences are centered on dealing with racism. Analytically it challenges the notion that racism is an aberrant experience and holds that instead it is endemic in our culture. It contends that any improvement that benefits people of color in a white supremacist culture only happens if white interests are served by racial justice. For example, *Brown v. Board of Education* only transpired because US global imperialism was threatened by the glaring contradiction between America's championing of democracy as a bulwark against communism and the country's practice of Jim Crow racist segregation.

For several reasons, I have found teaching race to be one of the most compelling tasks I undertake. I have to engage learners critically in a conversation about something that some of them have come to believe is of no import. I grapple with how to teach learners to move out of their familiar frames of reference and acknowledge racial and ethnic differences and the impact those differences have on how meaning is created from those lived experiences. One of the most difficult projects is teaching learners to recognize race and difference as constructed and embedded within hierarchical structures, which, at different times, advantage some and disadvantage others. Thinking structurally is cognitively challenging if you have grown up soaked in the individualistic ideology of the United States.

Becoming racially cognizant is a nonlinear and developmental process. For whites, "the process involves becoming aware of one's 'whiteness,' accepting this aspect of one's identity as socially meaningful and personally salient, and ultimately internalizing a realistically positive view of whiteness which is not based on assumed superiority" (Lawrence and Tatum, 1999, p. 2). Part of understanding what whiteness means is becoming aware of the ideology of white supremacy and the reality of white privilege. Not surprisingly, this is strongly resisted by many whites, who feel threatened by and resentful of any suggestion that they have not earned whatever education or jobs they enjoy, and who are suspicious of the idea of affirmative action. If we are to have any hope of getting white students engaged in examining their own racism, we need to use pedagogies that are dialogical, relational, and collectively humanizing. Each of us can begin to understand another's lived experience when we critically, and with humanity, reflect upon those experiences in relation to our own.

Drawing upon the work of Derrick Bell, who uses narratives to tell "… the truth about racism without causing disabling despair" (Bell, 1992, p. ix), I present three teaching exercises in which I use story as the content foundation for teaching about race and difference. Although each of these exercises can be conducted independently as stand-alone activities, the most complex learning occurs when they are sequenced. In teaching race, we need to be aware of the importance of scaffolding, of investigating a topic in increasingly complex ways to build breadth and depth of understanding. As learners gain more knowledge we can complicate things productively, so that incrementally they become aware of multiple perspectives, contradictions, and open questions.

The first exercise draws upon the small-group writing workshop method of the Community Writing Project, a popular education-based community education program located in Chicago. The aims of the workshop, as described by Adams and Hurtig (2002), include encouraging participants to become agents in their own lives through developing critical appreciation and understanding of their own and others' experiences. Through the writing and sharing of personal story, participants learn about difference while building relationships. The relationships formed from reading about and discussing others' racialized experiences then serve as a foundation for the deeper learning provided in the next two exercises.

The second exercise involves watching, critiquing, and analyzing a documentary about a well-respected, some would say loved, elementary school teacher of poor immigrant children. This exercise is most effective when students have begun to understand race as a socially and hierarchically constructed concept and have some experience critically reflecting upon lived experience.

The third exercise is more complex and builds on the experience and knowledge gained through the first two activities. This final exercise is more directly reflective of Derrick Bell's (1992) use of chronicles to teach race by providing the opportunity to engage in a complex critical racial analysis of lived experience. As such, it is pivotal to moving students to a deeper understanding of the culturally created and endemic nature of racism. For this exercise I employ two chronicles I created, one of a black woman and the other of a white woman. Although this chapter includes a detailed summary of each chronicle, the full first-person chronicles are available for use in "Autobiography as Counter-Narrative: An Empirical Study of How Race Enters and Structures the Stories of Our Lives" (Yanow, 2007). The chronicles are designed to help students understand the long-term implications of color-blind ideology, to see racism as an endemic by-product of our culture, and to recognize the often very subtle role race plays in influencing how we ascribe meaning and value to our lived experiences.

Fostering Dialogue and Relationships Through Community Writing

At the heart of learning race is learning difference. By that I mean coming to understand that each of us is a cultural being who sees and understands the world through our own distinct cultural lens and lived experience. From a racialized perspective, our racial-group membership has implications both for how others see us and for how we see ourselves and others. For white students this awareness is often primarily subconscious, given that whiteness constitutes the norm against which all other identities and actions are measured. Our job as teachers of difference and race is to take this subconscious awareness and bring it to full consciousness. We need to help students recognize and critically reflect upon those automatic assumptions that inform their racial understandings and actions.

One of the ways we can understand ourselves better as cultural beings is through writing, particularly when we write about our experiences in a collaborative manner that entails engaging with the writing of others. When we start to recognize that our lives are racialized and we come to see others' experiences as equally racialized, our understanding of the depth and pervasiveness of race begins to deepen and change.

In Developing Cultural Understanding, my 10-week course, students begin writing together on the very first night. The opening class begins with introductions of the course, the students, and me. We start to explore what it means to be cultural beings and who each of us is as a cultural being. That discussion leads to our first writing experience. At the first meeting I am fairly prescriptive, asking students to respond to prompts such as "Who are you?," "What groups do you belong to?," and "What are your core beliefs?" Sometimes, as in my opening story for this chapter, I simply ask them to offer three quick responses to the statement "I am a…"

After 10 to 15 minutes of writing, I invite folks to share their stories. Usually one or two students will volunteer. The first thing we do when people choose to read their stories aloud is to share our appreciation by offering applause. Once students have finished sharing their narratives, I ask if there is anything else anyone would like to know. Although not usually on the first night, after a few writing sessions students may offer that they recognize their own experiences in another's story or note that their experiences are very different. These and other recognitions form the basis for building relationships and the deepening of dialogue to foster cultural understanding.

Depending upon time availability, after the first session I either allot class time for writing or I invite folks to take no more than 15 minutes at home to respond to a prompt that has emerged through our discussions from that opening session. At the beginning it is important that students see community writing not as a burden but as an opportunity to explore their lived experiences. A key point to recognize is that the direction the writing takes each week is grounded in the group's discussions. The prompts emerge as folks propose notions they would like to reflect on further. If a particular prompt doesn't interest them, students could be invited to write about something else, but in the years that I have used community writing I don't recall a time when someone wrote outside the prompt. I wonder whether this is reflective of respect for the group-writing methodology as a humanizing, relationship-building process.

Students are always encouraged to write freely as they relay the experiences elicited through responding to the prompts. But the notion of writing freely (that is, without editing) is in itself difficult for many people. Initially, it can be hard for students to step outside of the paradigm they've internalized that writing is an academic performance to be evaluated. So instead of positioning writing as *writing*, I ask instead that students just put down their stories on paper. Framing writing as telling a personal story seems to relax many people. Students just need to imagine that they're telling a story to a friend, and then convey that story through words on a page rather than in the air.

Once students begin to think about their writings as stories to be shared, the learning seems to begin. I collect all the stories and read them outside of class. I read not as a teacher, but as a colleague interested in the students' experiences and how they've shared those experiences as authors. I offer nonacademic, conversational feedback, one objective of which is to build a relationship between the student and myself. As Lawrence Lightfoot (2000) points out, listening carefully and attentively to others' stories – really hearing what they say – is one of the most fundamental ways in which we show individuals that we respect them. When teachers engage with a student's story it is an inherently humanizing experience. But it is equally humanizing for students to feel their stories are being heard by each other. So each week I type up all the stories, and, with each student's permission, everyone receives a copy of everyone else's story. This way even if folks are not comfortable reading their stories aloud they are shared. We spend about 45 minutes each week reading our stories and reflecting upon them in the context of the course material that we are studying that week.

The writing exercise continues over several weeks, while at the same time students are reading about race and other cultural constructs. Over time the prompts that emerge from class discussions begin to include probes such as "a time I felt included in a group," "a time I felt excluded," "a time I essentialized someone" (reducing an individual's complex identity to a single identifier or marker), and "a time I felt essentialized by someone else." The emergence of such prompts indicates a growing comfort level in the class, which helps to uncover the unrecognized assumptions that shape our understandings and inform our actions. In particular, the enormous impact that color-blind ideology has had on students' misunderstandings of race often starts to become evident.

Two very powerful learning challenges presented by the use of the writing workshop should be noted. First, students are challenged to examine their assumptions from whatever side of color-blind ideology they may sit; that is, whether they see race everywhere or nowhere at all. In my writing workshop I encourage all students to examine their racialized experiences as presented through the class-identified prompts. I want to avoid the situation of only people of color being expected to share their experiences with racism. Following the prompts above, white students are just as likely to explore experiences of previously unrecognized white privilege as students of color are to explore experiences as receptors of unintended racism. And students of color also explore times in which they assumed a white privilege perspective from someone, only to find that perspective to not be the case.

The second challenge presents itself when white students begin to understand how white privilege has influenced their lived experiences. Becoming aware of what it means to be white and the advantages of living in a white dominant culture usually elicits a measure of guilt and shame. Here I need to help prevent people who are recognizing their unacknowledged collusion in white supremacy from falling into a nonproductive state of despair or self-blame. One of the most important moments in class happens when white students start to recognize the extent of unintended racism and its impact on both the receiver and the perpetrator. That recognition is a first step in understanding the negative power of color-blind ideology.

Every time I conduct the writing workshop, at least once during our class a white student explains how his/her/their perspective on the existence and impact of racism on students of color has shifted. Students of color have responded respectfully as they begin to understand the enormous and usually unacknowledged power and impact that color-blind ideology has on white students' inability to recognize white experience as racialized and privileged. In a recent class, a student of color shared that he looked forward to each week's class because he could talk about experiences that actually happen to him and know that he would be listened to respectfully and understood. Others expressed their appreciation for the class being a space in which they could share racialized experience with white folks, knowing (because of what they've heard and read in their stories) that those students were becoming more racially aware. Students of color typically breathe a sigh of relief when whites start to acknowledge previously unrecognized and complicit racist behavior. Instead of blaming them for past sins, they value them for being willing to confront honestly the reality of their racialized lives. The humanizing impact of writing and sharing our life stories together seems to be a productive way to foster dialogue and build trust within the classroom. Hearing and learning from difficult stories are clearly the beginnings of a shift in perspective.

Critical Documentary Analysis

The Hobart Shakespeareans is a documentary about an inner-city teacher of poor Latino and East Asian children in California. The documentary presents a supposedly uplifting story of an extraordinarily hardworking and dedicated teacher of poor immigrant inner-city children who uses Shakespeare to teach children that if they engage in hard work and sacrifice and are kind to one another, they may one day be able to achieve the American Dream. In the teacher's mind this includes moving out of their neighborhoods to somewhere nicer (Stuart, Rotaru, and Thirteen/WNET, 2005).

I have used this documentary in a few different graduate level adult-education courses as a tool to examine how our educational systems serve as mechanisms to socialize students into cultural (mis)understanding. By applying their developing skills of critical thinking and analysis to the documentary, students begin to recognize how dominant ideologies can be perpetuated, often without recognition or intention by those engaged in hegemonic practices. Before students view the documentary, I explain that the assignment is one of *critical* analysis. I remind the students that critical thinking involves reflecting on the assumptions that inform our thinking, and that one helpful way to begin that process is to examine the assumptions that likely inform the decisions made by others. I tell them that in this case I want them to focus on the teacher in the documentary. I suggest that as they view the film they simply take notes on things the teacher says to the children and shares with the viewers about the children.

In an opening scene, the teacher, Raif Esquith explains, "This is about 50 kids who work unbelievably hard and defy the culture both of their neighborhood and of their (home) country. They immerse themselves in a culture where people are good to each other, where hard work matters and character matters even more" (Stuart, Rotaru, and Thirteen/WNET, 2005). A few moments later we see him leaving for work, with the time 5:45 a.m. on the screen, and in the final scene of the documentary, we see him heading home from work – also in the dark. This is a documentary that celebrates what Esquith describes as characteristics that are often otherwise associated with white, middle-class, Christian-American values. He teaches his students that being American includes celebrating holidays such as Halloween and Christmas and playing baseball, and that the money one earns determines where and how well one lives. At least within the documentary, Esquith does not appear to center anything about the students' lived experiences that is not presented as negative, and, from a white, middle-class, Christian perspective, missing from what counts as a life well lived.

As we watch the documentary, we see Esquith introduce the children to what he describes as American culture by teaching them about baseball, capitalism, Halloween, Christmas, and travel. He explains that he wants them to be American and experience the "good life." All students in Esquith's classroom are assigned jobs, and all students pay rent for their desks. Raif explains, "… the ones closest to the front are more expensive. If they don't do their job, they don't get paid." While on a class trip to Washington, DC, Esquith adds, "We stay at nice hotels. We eat at nice restaurants because I want the children to understand the life they are working for…Children are more likely to eat well if there are more things on the menu…" While on the bus on the last day of their trip, he says, rather sarcastically, "It's the last day…now you get to go back to Hobart…Hobart food…and all those nice people there…and your nice neighborhood." As he says this to the children, they interject with cheerful responses of "No!"

Following the viewing of the documentary, students are broken into small groups to work on a critical analysis. Because of how uplifting the story appears, it can take students a moment to get past seeing the Hobart children's classroom experience as anything but positive. As they chat together, one or another student generally points out that for Esquith, the children's experience is all about deficit. The deficits students feel he implies are that (1) the children's home language isn't English, (2) their parents do not appear to speak English, (3) their neighborhood is poor and dangerous, (4) they are poor, and (5) they apparently have no meaningful cultural resources. And although it isn't clear that the children are all Christian, Esquith shares that they are unlikely to receive any Christmas gift other than the one he and his wife will give each child.

Once students recognize Esquith's fundamental focus on deficits, they can begin to think about the ways in which his assumptions about the children, their families, their community, and the cultures from which they come guide the way he engages with the children. By uncovering this deficit paradigm, they start to explore how practices such as speaking English, celebrating Halloween and Christmas, and traveling to Washington, DC, privilege dominant cultural values. They begin to fit what they've learned about hegemony – the process by which people learn to embrace ideas and practices that actually harm them and serve the interests of dominant ideology – into the context of the film. The children are being encouraged, all for the apparently good reason of improving their standard of living, to celebrate values that in reality cut them off from the cultures that shape their identities.

My hope is that the critical analysis of this documentary will illustrate central notions of CRT, such as interest convergence, the permanence of white supremacy, and the role that color-blind ideology plays in maintaining whites' power. To help students make some of these connections, I encourage them to consider questions such as:

- How does Esquith either acknowledge or ignore the gifts of the children's home cultures, including their bilingual abilities?
- What cultural elements appear to be privileged or disavowed in this documentary?
- Whose story appears to be privileged in this documentary?

The task of analyzing the documentary through a critical lens is challenging on several fronts. Some students find it quite difficult to critique another teacher who clearly works incredibly hard, seems to have his student's best interests in mind, and is accomplishing some significant things in the terms in which he defines success. Throughout the documentary we witness some extraordinary shifts in the children's thinking about themselves as learners and what is possible in their lives.

Once the students have some analytical tools with which to understand how race, as a socioculturally constructed hierarchical structure, is constructed and maintained, they begin to recognize the hegemonic practices legitimized by color-blind ideology. Because Esquith never celebrates the children's first languages or home cultural practices; he acts as though they do not exist. Everything that defines who these children are is viewed as insignificant, unworthy of attention, in deficit.

Using a documentary at this intermediary stage in learning about race can be a very powerful tool. It moves students away from focusing solely on the experiences in the room and asks them to consider an actual set of practices in the outside world. Because they don't know the individuals in the film, they are freed to make all kinds of inferences and interpretations in a way that is less stressful than when they are examining each other's very personal stories. This particular documentary also presents a neatly encapsulated official story (Bell, 2010) of what is supposed to be the path to personal fulfillment in the United States today.

Juxtaposing Story and Counterstory

> If I have to jump six feet to get the same thing you have
> to jump two feet for – that's how racism works.
>
> *(Coates, 2017)*

On the surface, it isn't difficult to understand what Coates is saying in the quote above. He neatly encapsulates the structural nature of racial disadvantage in the juxtaposition of two different experiences in which disparity and disadvantage are fixed in place, unchangeable. Building on this idea of juxtaposing two very different narratives of racialized experience, the third exercise I describe explores the fundamentals of CRT and the idea of color-blind ideology through two constructed narratives of a black and a white woman. The exercise assumes that students have already developed relationships with each other and have done previous work identifying and critiquing white supremacy. The current exercise encourages students to examine the lived experiences of these two women for evidence of the way that racial inequality is endemic to our culture. At this point in their learning, students are more alert to uncovering examples of covert racism.

I begin the exercise with the counterstory of Connie, an African American woman born in Chicago in 1954 (Yanow, 2007, pp. 127–131). Before handing a copy of the story to each student, I read it aloud. Reflective of the CRT tenet to center the experiences of people of color, both stories are written in the first person. Once the students have heard the story read out loud, each receives a copy and I allocate time for reading and then discussion in small groups. For the purposes of this chapter, synopses of the stories follow.

Connie's Story

Connie's life is both extraordinary and ordinary, reflective of the era in which she lives. Connie is likeable, and we appreciate her tenacity in the face of tragedy, her intelligence, and her sheer hard work in facing the difficulties she encounters. As readers, we celebrate Connie's successes, and, if we are white, we might even quietly feel good about what her story suggests for African American opportunities since the civil rights movement.

Connie "was born in 1954 in a black, working-class neighborhood on Chicago's South Side" (Yanow, 2007, p. 127). Her father was a minister and she grew up understanding the challenges of racism and the struggles in which her community were engaged. She planned to be a civil rights lawyer when she grew up.

Although busing was available in Chicago, for the sake of safety Connie's parents insisted that she attend the local Catholic school. When she reached fifth grade, Connie's father hired her as a teacher's assistant at the Sunday school of his church. She continued to work there into college. Connie attended the University of Illinois at Chicago, where she became involved in politics and protest and where she met her future husband David.

David, also black, had grown up in the south suburbs. Together Connie and David moved to the North Side; she became pregnant, they married, and, after two years of college, Connie quit school to take care of her baby. When the baby turned two, she decided to return to work and explored opportunities at local day-care centers. She quickly found a job at a new day-care center as a teacher's aide and worked with every age group there for six years, bringing her children to work with her.

When their second child was two, David, tragically and without warning, died of a congenital heart disease. Connie moved back home with her parents and stayed for two years. Eventually, wanting her own place and for her children to have a more diverse experience, Connie moved out to the suburbs and looked for a teaching job. She quickly found a job as an aide in a mostly white but integrated day care and enrolled in community college to earn an early-childhood teaching certificate. She needed a higher salary to support herself and her two children. Once certified Connie began looking for lead teacher positions, but quickly learned she would need an undergraduate degree. Feeling she had little choice, Connie left the field and went to work for a bank, where she received limited tuition reimbursement. Her plan was to work, apply for student loans, and finish her degree in order to become a classroom teacher.

After reading but before discussion, students are offered a few moments to reflect individually on Connie's story and perhaps jot down some notes about how her experiences might reflect racialized experience. At this stage, it is not uncommon for students to focus on Connie's experiences with busing and civil rights, and the influence of the church in African American communities. In a recent experience using this exercise, a white woman looked up as she finished reading about Connie and asked, "Who moves to the suburbs for diversity?" Almost as soon as the question left her lips, the assumption that the question reflected became rather obvious. A student of color responded, "Well, we do." The asking of that question led to a critical discussion about the ways in which white experience is immediately normalized and what is often missing from our understanding about the broader community when we normalize whiteness.

Evelyn's Story

Then we turn to Evelyn's story, which I also read aloud before sharing a copy with each student.

Like Connie's life, Evelyn's life is both extraordinary and ordinary, and quite reflective of the era in which she is living. Evelyn is also likeable and we celebrate her successes, particularly as we consider the period of US history focusing on civil rights and women's rights (Yanow, 2007, pp. 124–127).

Evelyn "... was born in the summer of 1952 in a small town in Indiana" (p. 124). Her father was a political science professor at Indiana University and her mother a stay-at-home mom and would-be lawyer. Growing up in a house of intellectuals, from an early age Evelyn was learning about civil rights, the war in Vietnam, and protests. She dreamed of becoming a civil rights attorney one day.

Although the elementary schools were segregated, everyone in the town attended one high school. There, she "... became friends with all the black and ethnic students" (p. 125). Evelyn became involved in politics and protest and met her future husband, Dale. After graduating they ran off to Europe. When they returned, Evelyn and Dale got jobs and an apartment but didn't go back to school. Evelyn became an assistant in a Head Start preschool, and after a couple of early-childhood education courses she had her own class and was building a career in early-childhood education.

Dale and Evelyn married and had three children. After working at the preschool for six years, Evelyn became the assistant director, needing more education to become the director. After 17 years, Evelyn and Dale divorced and she needed a better job. So Evelyn left Head Start, which had been her only adult job, moved to Chicago, and worked for an accounting firm as the office manager. Although she had no experience, they were impressed that she had worked for so long in a "... profession known for its hard work and low pay" (p. 127).

After two years at the agency, the accountants agreed to support Evelyn's dream of becoming a civil rights attorney. Concerned about whether or not she would be accepted into law school, Evelyn was assured that, given "current affirmative action policies," there shouldn't be a problem (p. 127).

As with Connie's story, students are invited to quietly reflect individually on how Evelyn's experience might be racialized. At this point I hope that students are able to recognize white experience as racialized, but it is the juxtaposition of the two stories that has the potential to exemplify what racialized experience might mean from a white perspective. After they have heard Evelyn's story, I often invite students to return to Connie's story to more critically analyze that narrative before beginning to look for racialized perspectives in both stories. Then I conduct a short discussion reviewing CRT, in particular its tenet of racism as endemic to our culture, and I ask students to discuss how that might be reflected in these stories.

That question about the endemic nature of racism usually leads back to a comparing and contrasting of Evelyn and Connie's similar experiences, which led them in different directions. Students tease out how they think the early experiences of the two women might reflect how white supremacy operates. Simply raising questions about each woman's early life begins to inform students' understanding of the notion that racism is endemic in our society.

I ask students to consider the attitudes that each woman expresses about her K–12 educational experiences, integration, and busing. Initially it is not uncommon for white students to represent busing as a positive response in promoting civil rights, a push toward integration and a movement toward educational equity. For most white students, it becomes clear that busing didn't require that whites leave their neighborhoods. For African American students, the discussion often includes comments around the dismantling of neighborhoods as students were bused someplace else. They speak of long and potentially unsafe travel, being situated in classrooms with few African American teachers or students, and personal experiences of racism as youngsters. I also ask about Connie's work at the mostly white but integrated day-care center in the suburbs after David died. To whose advantage might it have been to hire a black teacher?

Early in both stories we learn that the childhood dream of each woman is to become a lawyer. Along the way, reality sets in and they both attain jobs in childcare, not an unfamiliar work environment for many women. Connie enters the profession with much more education and experience than Evelyn but never reaches the professional levels that Evelyn reaches. And Evelyn's success surpasses Connie's almost immediately. I ask the students to consider not only whether Connie's treatment versus Evelyn's is fair, assuming they both do their jobs well, but also whether they think Connie's treatment can be associated with race or be generalized. And I ask them if, while hearing/reading the story, they ever felt that Connie's treatment was unfair. Did they question anything about Connie's experience before they learned about Evelyn? If so, why; and if not, why not?

In their initial responses to Connie's story, no one is terribly surprised at the levels she achieves. And, read by itself, they might not be surprised at the story of Evelyn's advancement in early childhood and its celebration of a white woman who spends so many years in a helping profession. But with the juxtaposition of story and counterstory, the students find it difficult to be complacent about the different experiences each woman had. If we can suggest that Connie's experience of less achievement within the profession might be a result of race, can we also consider whether Evelyn's experience might reflect the influence of race? And what about the argument that race could not have influenced Evelyn's experience because whiteness often isn't even considered a racial identity? These are some questions that can be addressed in this examination of a story and a counterstory. What has been presented here will get the learning discussion started.

Conclusion

Each of the exercises presented above seeks to teach the CRT tenet that racism is pervasive and endemic in the United States, and that one of the ways that situation is secured is through the widespread acceptance of color-blind ideology. I believe that teaching this material requires an initial building of relationships through the use of dialogue. The three activities I describe are designed to constitute a humanizing process through which students learn more and more deeply about each other's racialized experiences. If we are going to attempt to dismantle racism as a culturally constructed hierarchical structure, we are going to need to see color and recognize the impact racial identity has on our lived experiences.

References

Adams, H. and Hurtig, H. (2002). Creative acts, critical insights: Adult writing workshops in two Chicago neighborhoods. In: *Community Partnerships* (ed. E. Auerbach), 147–158. Alexandria, VA: Teachers of English to Speakers of Other Languages.

Bell, D.A. (1992). *Faces at the Bottom of the Well: The Permanence of Racism.* New York, NY: Basic Books.

Bell, L.A. (2010). *Storytelling for Social Justice: Connecting Narrative and the Arts in Antiracist Teaching.* New York, NY: Routledge.

Coates, T-N. (2017). Why Obama was different in "We Were Eight Years in Power" – extended interview. Interview by Trevor Noah, *The Daily Show*

(30 October). www.cc.com/video-clips/xio46b/the-daily-show-with-trevor-noah-ta-nehisi-coates---why-obama-was-different-in--we-were-eight-years-in-power---extended-interview (accessed 1 June 2018).

Delgado, R. and Stefancic, J. (2012). *Critical Race Theory: An Introduction*, 2nd ed. New York: NYU Press.

Lawrence, S.M. and Tatum, B.D. (1999). White racial identity and anti-racist education: A catalyst for change. In *Beyond Heroes and Holidays: A Practical Guide to K–12 Anti-racist, Multicultural Education and Staff Development* (ed. E. Lee, D. Menkart, and M. Okazawa-Rey), 45–51. Washington, DC: Teaching for Change.

Lawrence Lightfoot, S. (2000). *Respect: An Exploration*. New York: Penguin.

Stuart, M. (dir.), Rotaru, A. (ed.), and Thirteen/WNET (2005). *The Hobart Shakespeareans* (film). Running time 60 min. For Thirteen/WNET. A co-production of Mel Stuart, Thirteen/WNET and POV I American Documentary, www.pbs.org/pov/hobart/film-description (accessed 1 June 2018).

Yanow, W.B. (2007). Autobiography as counter-narrative: An empirical study of how race enters and structures the stories of our lives. PhD dissertation. National Louis University.

12

Helping Students Uncover Positionality

Dianne Ramdeholl and Jaye Jones

It was during the first month of class. The course was seminar style and filled with students interested in learning more about social, economic, and racial justice. I had noticed a curious dynamic between one of the white male students (called C here) and one of the African American male students (called Z here). Each time the African American student spoke, the white student (who identified as gay) would paraphrase, saying, "I think what you're saying is..." C would also speak longer than other students and added to the comments of other students in ways that made it seem that he was offering expert advice ("Well, I think you might want to think about..." or "At my field site, I had to step in and teach the teacher how to teach"). Z noticeably avoided that student, and during a class break, when C asked him what was wrong, Z responded that he didn't need any white saviors, that there were enough in society as it was. C returned to class in tears. During an emergency check-in (a 10-minute conference I conduct with each student after class over the course of the semester), C and I unpacked what had occurred.

As C recounted what had happened, I asked him whether he felt there was any truth to what his classmate said. He said he felt it was

Teaching Race: How to Help Students Unmask and Challenge Racism, First Edition.
Stephen D. Brookfield and Associates.

a very unfair allegation by Z. I asked him to think about how Z might have experienced his behavior. He explained that he was also from a marginalized group. I told him that Z's comments weren't negating that, and that this was not a competition based on a hierarchy of oppressions. I told him it was important to hear what Z (and other students) was saying to him. If it was true, he needed to be able to hear that. It was a difficult conversation, but afterwards C made a conscious effort to stop editorializing his classmates' conversations. He and I continued speaking about the dynamic in our check-in conversations, and he admitted that what Z had said was true, but that his editorializing hadn't been intended to be offensive. He explained that he could see that his actions carried weight based on other privilege he carried.

This made me think about how white students need space to grieve – literally and figuratively – as they move out of racial ignorance and begin to understand how "white racist complicity and black suffering [are] historically linked and currently intertwined" (Yancy, 2017). Students need to feel supported in talking through their ideas about race, because, for many, it might be the first time they're asking these questions of themselves.

This is a moment in the United States that is at best uncertain, and, more fundamentally, that is located in an era of overt fear and impending dread for black and brown bodies. Since the 2016 election of Donald Trump, this dread has become even more starkly outlined. For example, almost immediately after the election, Dianne hastily planned a teach-in with three other colleagues in response to students expressing shock, disbelief, and fear. She received an angry email from a white male student asking whether his perspective as a Trump supporter would be honored in the same way that the perspectives of those opposing Trump would be. She responded to him by saying that the teach-in was intended to offer a space to support all students, including those who had reached out to her and her colleagues to say how unsafe they felt. There was no agenda other than creating a space to talk, sharing strategies for self- and collective care, and promoting the idea that we needed to look to each other for compassion and leadership. He responded by saying that while he appreciated her response, he wouldn't be participating. He also questioned why those opposing Trump were not being labeled as racist or being demonized in the ways that he felt Trump supporters were.

This electoral line in the sand has defined the fragility, if not broken quality, of race relations in this country. The rise of Trump and his cadre of billionaire populists is the most visible expression of an institutional contempt for black and brown people. From the beginning of his administration – framed by Trump's notion of "American carnage" – the livelihoods, schools, health care, and patriotism of people of color have been directly and disproportionately challenged. Communities of color continue to be brutalized by those who are being paid to protect them. Violence in communities of color continues to be a symptom (not the cause) of poverty. Police brutality and mass incarceration are systemic policies designed to contain and squeeze an entire segment of our population – the segment born with more melanin. When people live in concentrated poverty, the trauma of it can lead to violence (Dyson, 2016). Physically and emotionally, people of color find themselves drained, more marginalized, and less hopeful about the future. This collective trauma experienced daily by people of color seems invisible to other communities for whom it isn't a daily reality. What unspoken statement does that make about whose lives are valued more in society?

This chapter reflects our work as a faculty members of color at Empire State College at the State University of New York (SUNY) and Lehman College at the City University of New York (CUNY), and explores how we continue to support students while navigating racist and exclusionary processes/structures within the academy. Although the courses we teach are different, many of the strategies we utilize in our teaching are similar and were coauthored together. We discuss the ways in which unpacking whiteness as an identity in instruction can support discussions of supremacy while also making space for people of color to share their lived realities through counternarratives (Delgado and Stefancic, 2012).

The Context for Our Work

Dianne is a faculty member of color at SUNY Empire State College in New York City and Jaye is an administrator and faculty member at CUNY Lehman College. We have always been keenly aware of the ways in which we (and others like us), as women of color, are situated in a space that is inherently unfriendly and marginalizing to us. Each day we think about (and are grateful for) all of those who have come before us and who have made it possible for us to even be able to walk here in this space. Because of our experiences we are especially committed to supporting faculty and students of color. I (Dianne) am very aware of how few of us have gone through the tenure process (the academic equivalent of hazing) and survived. According to a study by the National Center for Educational Statistics (Kena et al., 2015), 79% of current full time faculty in US universities are white. I have spoken and written about my struggling and prevailing in the tenure process and about the ways in which the academy continues to represent a space in which brown and black faculty face numerous daily microaggressions (Ramdeholl, 2016).

I (Dianne) teach in an online graduate adult-education program. My students are primarily working-class adults who are dispersed geographically. I rarely meet them in person, so the relationships I develop with them are created through a different trajectory than that of face-to-face teaching. While I teach some people of color, the majority of the students are white, working-class adults. The online context makes it much more challenging to unpack issues of race. There is less willingness to be vulnerable (with good reason, since vulnerability only comes with trust), more space for misunderstandings in reading people's words, and a diminished feeling of safety in discussing issues that are fraught.

I (Jaye) am an adjunct faculty member who teaches in a senior college that is 80% Hispanic and black/African American. Despite this, the majority of both the full-time (75%) and adjunct (65%) faculty is white. As a black female, I know I am not the person whom students – both of color and white – expect to see when they enter the classroom. Belief in the idea that white people are more capable of producing and imparting knowledge – that they should be the teachers – is an unfortunate reality that educators of color such as myself must navigate. Many students of color enter Lehman having attended public schools in the relatively segregated and under-resourced communities in which they live, which despite being filled with black and Latino students are mostly staffed by white female teachers. When they enter a culturally diverse, Hispanic-serving institution such as Lehman and find that most of their instructors are also white, belief in this pattern as a norm is reinforced, and the ways in which I maintain authority in class, structure course discussions, and respond to student inquiries is undeniably shaped by these perceptions. At the same time I continue to teach because these students – often the first in their families to go to college – both represent and nurture possibility. Indeed, by the end of the semester some of them have taken the time to tell me not only that I am their first black teacher but that my presence has made a positive difference.

As former adult-literacy community practitioners, we use adaptations of strategies that are rooted in popular education. We incorporate students' experiences into courses, so students are asked to respond to what they read *and* link it to their own lived realities, discussing with each other aspects of the texts they find surprising, agree or disagree with, and have questions about. We ask students to make predictions about the endings of texts, to write a community policy based on what they read, and to write skits about the salient points in readings. We also ask students in courses to choose a sentence (or more) from particular articles and explain why that sentence was the most important one to them, and to discuss how relevant a particular article is to the community in which they live. In assignments, students also talk about the aspects of materials that don't resonate with their lived realities and why. Students read each other's work and gain respect and compassion for their perspectives. It is this respect that proves to be a necessary foundation for the difficult conversations in which we engage over the course of the semester.

At the outset of our courses, we also discuss ground rules and having the right to disagree with other perspectives while respecting them. I (Dianne) talk to students outside of the online course space when this standard is not observed. This has only happened three times; students have, for the most part, been compassionate with each other. It is difficult to know whether this is because they understand that their grades will be impacted otherwise, or because there is genuinely some degree of consciousness-raising occurring. Both of us prioritize the development of criticality as an objective across our teaching by asking students to explore, for example, if research they are studying has been conducted ethically, is respectful to participants, and has used appropriate methodologies. Students are asked to comment on whether authors situate themselves in research and make their assumptions clear. To develop critical reading proficiencies, students choose a piece of literature opposing the stance of each piece read, so they become used to considering multiple perspectives and positions.

Exercises to Help Students Identify Positionality

Because the majority of students of color also live with the internalized understandings that their experiences are invisible, having little or no value, we begin courses exploring race and racism by focusing on positionality. Students begin thinking about their identities (who they are in the world and how they navigate it) using a lens of intersectionality. This involves thinking about gender, racial identity, socioeconomic class, physical and mental ability, sexual identity, and prior educational and work experiences, and exploring these in critical ways. We ask them to consider three questions:

1. To what extent do these different aspects of their identities offer privilege?
2. What does privilege mean and look like to them?
3. How do they navigate this landscape?

To help in this analysis we use readings about the social construction of race and the fluidity of whiteness throughout the history of the United States. This supports students in connecting race and economics. We read Michelle Alexander's *The New Jim Crow* (2012), Theodore Allen's *The Invention of the White Race* (2012), Piven and Cloward's *Regulating the Poor* (1993), and many others. Students are expected to ask questions about these materials and to point out aspects they agree and disagree with. I (Dianne) have students post reactions on the online discussion boards and ask them to respond to each other's posts. They are typically very careful in how they respond, always being positive and encouraging of each other's work instead of disagreeing. So it is up to me to disagree with something someone said by raising questions and giving examples that point to a different reality.

When discussing social-welfare policies in the Social Welfare Institutions class, I (Jaye) try to provide students with primary sources or archival footage for review. These words and images are often a stark representation of the white, male, and class privilege that infuses many of the supposedly history-making policy endeavors that are depicted. A common theme throughout the history of policy development is the notion of so-called worthy versus unworthy poor people – the worthy poor being seen as deserving of the policies and resources that help them rise above their misfortunes. These ideas are deeply connected to race, class, and gender. The perception that poor people are not only primarily black and brown but also less likely to merit support (or more prone to take advantage of public entitlements) is something that is challenged through our work in the class.

Incorporating and Validating Students' Experiences

It is important to recognize that students and people of color – not professors – are the greatest experts on their own learning. As an instructor, I (Dianne) have come to understand that one of the most effective ways I can teach is to support students in placing their own experiences at the center of their own learning. In each assignment, there is space for students to connect their own experiences to the text and to weave their lived realities into discussions. Students of color often share with me that they appreciate a way of teaching that values their counternarratives and honors them as having the same value as texts from so-called experts. Students of color give examples of regular microaggressions, of the ways in which their knowledge is discounted on a daily basis because of their brown and black skin. Sharing stories and learning about classmates' struggles help bring the more theoretical material to life. When students learn that they have the agency to define and critique how knowledge is created, they realize they can gain insight that goes beyond textbooks, lectures, or "what I've heard."

The Learning History Paper

In any class focused on teaching race, we need to understand that we can't navigate the world only through a racialized lens and ignore gender and economic class. To help students understand intersectionality, I (Dianne) ask them to complete a learning history paper, something that I've adapted from my time as a doctoral student in adult education at National Louis University. This paper asks students to discuss who they are as educators, community members, students, spouses, and parents through their experiences as seen through the lenses of race and gender. Questions students explore include:

- To what extent does your self-identified racialized identity impact how you navigate the world?
- In what ways has this impact been determined by you or for you by others?
- How does your positionality form a lens through which you view the world and your role in it?

The learning history paper is designed to develop students' understanding of the fact that they are situated in a landscape of race and that each person lives in a world resulting from the manifestations of the legacies of racism. Students are asked in different assignments (and courses) to build upon the learning history paper to make issues of positionality ever more transparent.

Probing Privilege Through Questions

For many students – especially white working-class students – thinking about racial group membership and how that does or does not offer privilege is a relatively new experience. Through reading the narratives of other students (as well as the assigned texts), a greater collective understanding of how privilege works starts to emerge. I (Dianne) interject with questions throughout the online discussions to facilitate this process. For instance, I ask for examples to illustrate racial generalizations, or how students know that something they have said is true. Often I'll ask who benefits from a perspective they posit.

At times particular students resist responding, and in an online context this often looks like radio silence in the discussion space. I then usually reach out to the student concerned privately in order to engage him/her/them. This works with varying degrees of success, but it is necessary to keep trying to reach and engage with disengaged students and to understand that none of us has been given a lot of space to talk about and think through issues of race. For everyone, race is still very much an unfinished conversation.

Sometimes white students become inadvertently defensive in their posts, praising the readings and then pointing out all of the ways in which they themselves promote equity in their lives. I then ask them to think about and respond to the issues more from a structural than an individual point of view. For example, a discussion about how individual parents choose their children's schools might be framed by a question that asks students to identify what structures support unequal, racist policies and practices in education, and how those manifest in how parents engage with the K–12 school system in New York City.

In another course – Introduction to Qualitative Research – I (Dianne) teach, students are asked to use a lens of positionality to discuss the ways in which they are situated in their research by addressing two questions:

1. Who will most benefit from this research?
2. How does your understanding of race, class, and gender inform/impact your understanding of this research process?

Interwoven throughout the course is work by activists and academics such as Grace Lee Boggs (2012), Angela Y. Davis (1990), Robin D.G. Kelley (2002), Michael Eric Dyson (1996), Eddie S. Glaude Jr. (2016), and Brittany Cooper (2017), as well as articles and chapters from adult-education scholars such as Scipio Colin III and Talmadge Guy (1998), Vanessa Sheared (2010), and Lisa Merriweather (2004). These readings all support students' understandings of race, class, and gender and their manifestations in education. I am trying to help students encounter the dilemmas and contradictions of living in a white supremacist world while developing historically informed understandings of how race works in this country. They need to know that the history of this country is one of imperialism, with wealth gained from exploiting, brutalizing, and murdering black and brown bodies in the name of capital. Understanding this as fact is necessary if discussions are to move to deeper levels.

Some students initially express shock at the violence that occurred after the last US election, so we read about the Black Panthers and other liberation groups to gain a better historical understanding of the ways in which this country was built upon the suffering and death of black and brown people. We also study how adult education historically has been part of many popular struggles. Once they understand the history of white supremacy and the struggle to challenge and dismantle it, students are better placed to understand the underlying dynamics of this particular moment and how race has impacted their lives in both visible and invisible ways.

In the Social Welfare Institutions class that I (Jaye) teach, an important aspect of the course is to unpack how social welfare policies have been constructed and culturally positioned across time. Many students are surprised to learn that FDR's signature Social Security Act initially excluded many of the poor and people of color due to their employment status, or that the wealth gap is a result of legislative priorities that have disproportionately benefited white communities. The idea of who the *public* is when *public good* is defined has played a critical role in policy development and in how those policies are perceived by the larger society (Hannah-Jones, 2016).

Understanding that privilege is not something that is requested, but received nonetheless, is especially challenging for some students, as evidenced by comments such as "It's not our fault people are suffering...we didn't cause that" and "We can't help our skin color." I always interject and remind students that no one is asking them to be anyone else or asking them to change their skin color. None of us can be other than who we are. But starting from that place of who we are and working authentically to build solidarity as allies in racial justice struggles is a good place to start. Some students have joined groups such as the New York Collective of Radical Educators (a group of current and former public school educators and their allies) in order to focus on mobilizing communities around social justice issues that impact students, teachers, and families.

Decoding Language and Films

Both of us encourage a close analysis of textual and media representations of race. Dianne teaches a course – Racialized Narratives and Adult Education – that is designed as a close reading of texts about race. Some questions Dianne and the students unpack together include:

- Whose voices/perspectives are represented?
- Whose voices and perspectives are missing?
- Who benefits from this text and who is it most harmful to?
- Who is most directly affected by the text?
- What visions of education and the world are presented through the text?
- What specific dilemmas and contradictions are presented about race?
- What is left out or missing from the text?
- What is getting in the way of action?

I (Jaye) also encourage students to read. Students receive the majority of their information from conventional television sources, which often provide a superficial and condensed examination of complex issues. So I assign a series of scaffolded, responsive papers that are based on articles from newspapers of record about social problems that students are interested in and ask them to reflect on how a particular issue is framed as a problem using political concepts explored in the class. Each successive paper requires students to delve more deeply theoretically, and a final response paper emphasizes making conceptual connections across sources. Linking class lectures to current events such as immigration legislation impacting the Deferred Action for Childhood Arrivals policy (commonly called Daca) and the incarceration of the mentally ill reinforces the social construction of major welfare concerns. It also engages students in a process of writing to learn, which facilitates critical reflection grounded in disciplinary conventions.

In the course Adult Literacy and Social Change, we watch the film *Precious* (Daniels, 2009) and talk about the ways in which it perpetuates dominant narratives regarding race. Before we watch the film in the face-to-face course, I (Dianne) explain that there are scenes of sexual assault and violence and I let students know when those scenes come up. In my online course I let students know ahead of time that the film contains scenes that may be triggering, and if necessary they should be skipped over. Students watching the film for the first time (many watch it more than once) don't initially see or think about the ways in which dominant ideologies are perpetuated through skin color. For example, all of the heroes in the film are light-skinned people of color. Neither do students reflect on the fact that this particular film celebrates individual acts of compassion but doesn't attack structural inequities or show paths of resistance. So throughout our discussions of *Precious*, I ask how the film inadvertently reinforces what it seeks to critique.

Exploring how feature-film representations of the poor hide the reality of white poverty and fail to illuminate the historical dynamics that have led to disproportionate levels of black and brown disenfranchisement also introduces students to the political economy of racism and challenges their own stereotypes. Many students (even students of color) buy into the idea that people of color are more likely to be poor because of personal characteristics or failings – things that they can ostensibly control. So finding films and other multimedia sources that challenge this idea is critical. In this regard, important films that could be used might include *I Am Not Your Negro* (Peck, 2016), *Fruitvale Station* (Coogler, 2013), *Junction 48* (Aloni, 2016), *13th* (2016), *Which Way Home* (Cammisa, 2009), and *Do the Right Thing* (Lee, 1989).

The films shown are always connected to the larger topic of a particular module. For example, *Black Panthers: Vanguard of the Revolution* (Nelson, 2015) is part of a module on liberation movements. We ask students to watch the film and either write a review or react to a specific point made in the film, linking it to a theme in the module. Or students are told to compare and contrast two films,

or to change the ending of a film to reflect a more nuanced understanding of the current moment in race relations in the United
States. We might also pose more open-ended questions, such as:

- What moments in the film stood out for you and why?
- Were there any surprises?
- Did anything challenge what you know?
- What questions do you still have?

We might provide two films and ask students to choose one of
them and answer the questions listed above. Sometimes we extend
some of these questions and ask what we, collectively, might want
to take action against. We might also provide a number of films,
arrange students in groups, and ask group members to do a teach-in
about a film they have chosen. Films have worked particularly well
as openings to discuss issues of race in courses.

Integrating Current Events and Experiences from Outside the Classroom

Something else we consciously strive to do when teaching about racism
is to connect what is happening in communities and in the nation as a
whole to the curriculum. Given this moment, at which race remains a
potent and overtly divisive force in society, there is much to cover: the
white supremacist march in Charlottesville, the racist hate speech from
the Oval Office, the protests against travel bans, the police shootings
of unarmed people of color, and the discussions about deporting
"DREAMers" (people affected by the Daca policy). In discussions of
these events we problematize the notion of truth: Whose truth is being
proposed as the official story? How do we know something is true? Who
benefits from it being true? To what extent can multiple opposing
perspectives be privileged while preserving truth? We read different
accounts of history and discuss how they can all contain various
elements that are true. We also might study how the same headline is
analyzed in different publications to convey this point.

We often talk about the fluidity of truth and the ways in which two seemingly opposing ideas can both be true, such as the idea that someone can be a social activist as well as a racist. During this current moment in history, we read examples of how the power of social movements and people working collectively manages to effect change (Black Lives Matter is just one group of people working collectively). We discuss the importance of building alliances and collaboration and how our liberation can't and shouldn't be dependent on politicians. In understanding that history informs our current reality, we read about the Black Panther Party; the lives of Tamir Rice, Mike Brown, and countless others; and the ways in which the humanity of black and brown bodies continues to be unrecognized.

We also make connections to other forms of racism, such as Islamophobia and the systemic dehumanization of Muslims that has led to countless murders, including that of Azzedine Soufiane, Abdelkrim Hassane, and other victims in the Quebec City mosque terror attack in January 2017. While Islamophobia in Canada has a very different history than here in the United States, we strive in our courses to remember that all oppression is connected and that the humanity of black and brown bodies must always be at the forefront of our work in this area. We unpack the role the United States plays internationally in terms of how our foreign policy decides whose lives are deemed to be more valuable, whose dictatorships we prop up, and who is labeled a terrorist.

In our courses we talk about the ways that we can develop real, lived solidarity with other activists while developing well thought-out critiques of the racist, capitalistic society we live in. Students talk about the activism they're involved in within their communities and how Grace Lee Boggs's (2012) visionary organizing supports this. In visionary organizing, one is asked to think beyond protest organizing to develop well-defined critiques of the capitalist, racist, sexist society we live in and to build solidarity with alternative institutions and communities that can support the work of reimagining ourselves and thinking beyond capitalistic categories.

By undergoing a revolution of values, we can develop more capacity to be, in Boggs's terms, more *human* beings. Ideas alone can't change the world, but in changing the world ideas are transformed. Students, for the most part, find these concepts resonant. Part of this is because many of the courses I (Dianne) teach are electives in a program, so students who enroll in the courses do so because the courses cover issues they want to explore.

Our students have the common experience of being educated, so we try to show how the education system is complicit in perpetuating inequities. Anyon (1980) shows how private schooling in this country has historically served the wealthy (primarily white) population, while the upper and lower tiers of public schooling serve the middle class and poor whites, and people of color, respectively. Students are surprised when reading Anyon's (1980) article, but when they connect their own educational experiences to his analysis they recognize how education perpetuates the power of the economically advantaged in society. We hear how democratic processes and creativity are largely not taught, and how students learn there is always only one right answer to a question. The idea that they are only consumers of other people's knowledge is taught and drilled into their consciousness from a very young age, and students say that they have never conceived of themselves as producers of knowledge. The inequity of resource distribution is also starkly illustrated by students' experiences of white schools being significantly better resourced than those serving children of color.

As a social worker trained in critical adult literacy practice, I (Jaye) see the classroom as a place to situate the analysis of white supremacy in the contexts of my students' work. In their jobs my students often provide services to people of color, many of whom are interfacing with larger systems (e.g. criminal justice, child welfare) that disproportionately and negatively impact communities of color. A fair number of my students are drawn to social work because of a desire to help and advocate for vulnerable people; however, their interest in furthering their education is also tied to the sense of authority and distance this is seen as providing. They will be "different" from the people in need that sit across from them. Helping students unpack the connections between poverty, wealth, and racism not only builds their content knowledge but can heighten the sense of compassion they have for those who are struggling. Contextualizing poverty has the potential to lead to practice, research, and advocacy that is more authentic and holistic, and which honors our collective humanity.

Conclusion

In whatever ways possible, we must keep shining spotlights on the brutality inflicted on black and brown bodies. Currently, destructive lies about communities of color are being repeated without attribution and presented as truth. This adaptation to so-called alternative facts has filtered into the academy and made it physically unsafe for some faculty and students of color. The contempt for informed dialogue, engaged reflection, and the exchange of ideas – especially around race and privilege – has silenced dissent and led universities to censor faculty and even rescind academic job offers (as, for example, with Saida Grundy and Steven Salaita). So we must speak and write about racism wherever we go. We must push back against it in any way we know how, use any privilege we have to unmask it, and struggle against it where we stand. This struggle is about power, which will concede nothing without demand, making it clear that structures of oppression and privilege must be forcefully called out if they are to be eliminated (Berger, 2017).

As long as there is unequal value placed on the lives of members of different groups (with black and brown skin always on sale for at least half price), racism continues. As educators, we have to support consciousness-raising around this issue. We have to be able to name white privilege and white supremacy when we see it and work toward dismantling it. We also need to do the difficult work of looking at the ways in which we hide our own racism (mostly inadvertently) under the guise of liberalism. We need to find ways to unpack our own thinking before we can attempt to teach about it.

This unpacking can't be accomplished individually. We would suggest joining collectives in which practitioner-scholars grapple with the issue of white supremacy as a group and push back while being supportive of each other – in effect being each other's mirrors.

Educators of color, in particular, need to have culturally relevant spaces in which they can debrief, since they face racialized onslaughts that can be particularly devastating in terms of both emotional well-being and career potential. Digital and online communities might also be resources for those who work in places where few people of color reside; advocacy and support can be potentiated through global connections that reduce one's sense of isolation and leverage resources.

Although we need to challenge students when they shy away from expressing how they feel about race, we also must understand that they haven't inhabited spaces in which they can explore its complexity. So in an important sense, they genuinely may not know how they feel. Students will not always feel comfortable during these moments of exploration, and we need to help them recognize and accept this fact. There is no point in preaching to them if it only results in their alienation. Our courses ought to be viewed as one long conversation that avoids static dogmatism. Classrooms, courses, and other social justice spaces can't be truly revolutionary if there isn't space for people to grow.

When assessing students, we also need to find ways to challenge the unrecognized white, Eurocentric epistemology that privileges text, linearity, and positivism. Assignments and assessments in courses should give students multiple access points to content and knowledge. Students need to feel the difference, not just read about it. Creative and artistic representations of research, responding to case studies/readings, reviewing films, keeping journals, and envisioning theories as characters and writing skits about them can all invite students to step away from the Eurocentric standard. We can set an example of always being open to questions and showing that we take seriously what all our students ask and say. Instead of using essays as benchmarks to gauge excellence (which privileges one way of knowing), we can create assignments that honor different learning styles and ways of knowing.

As teachers, we both strive to be compassionate in helping people navigate these learning processes. Teaching about race, racism, privilege, and white supremacy is difficult work, and its emotionally laden nature means we need to be equally emotionally responsive. We are not therapists, but we do need to know when and how to help students access additional supports if they need it. We all have the tools to co-create a lovelier, more equitable society, in which being treated with dignity is the basic right of everyone, not just those who have the least melanin. We must put these ideas into practice in a committed way as if all of our lives depended on it, because they do.

References

Alexander, M. (2012). *The New Jim Crow: Mass Incarceration in the Age of Color-blindness*. New York, NY: New Press.

Allen, T.W. (2012). *The Invention of the White Race*, 2nd ed. London: Verso.

Anyon, J. (1980). Social class and the hidden curriculum of work. *Journal of Education* 162 (1): 67–92. doi:10.1177/002205748016200106.

Berger, D. (2017). Black genealogies of power: Seven maxims for resistance in the Trump years. *Black Perspectives* (28 February). https://www.aaihs.org/black-genealogies-of-power-seven-maxims-for-resistance-in-the-trump-years (accessed 1 June 2018).

Boggs, G.L. (2012). *The Next American Revolution: Sustainable Activism for the Twenty-First Century*, rev. ed. Berkeley, CA: University of California Press.

Colin, S.A.J., III and Guy, T.A. (1998). An Africentric interpretive model of curriculum orientations for course development in graduate programs in adult education. *PAACE Journal of Lifelong Learning* 7: 43–55.

Cooper, B. (2017). *Beyond Respectability: The Intellectual Thought of Race Women*. Urbana, IL: University of Illinois Press.

Davis, A.Y. (1990). *Women, Culture, and Politics*. New York, NY: Vintage Books.

Delgado R. and Stefancic, J. (2012). *Critical Race Theory: An Introduction*, 2nd ed. New York, NY: NYU Press.

Dyson, M.E. (1996). *Race Rules: Navigating the Color Line*. New York, NY: Basic Books.

Dyson, M.E. (2016). *The Black Presidency: Barack Obama and the Politics of Race in America*. New York, NY: Houghton Mifflin.

Glaude, E.S., Jr. (2016). *Democracy in Black: How Race Still Enslaves the American Soul*. New York, NY: Crown.

Hannah-Jones, N. (2016). The end of the postracial myth. *New York Times Magazine* (15 November). www.nytimes.com/interactive/2016/11/20/magazine/donald-trumps-america-iowa-race.html?mcubz=3 (accessed 1 June 2018).

Kelley, R.D.G. (2002). *Freedom Dreams: The Black Radical Imagination*. Boston, MA: Beacon Press.

Kena, G., Musu-Gillette, L., Robinson, J. et al. (2015). *The Condition of Education 2015* (NCES 2015-144). Washington, DC: US Department of Education, National Center for Education Statistics. https://nces.ed.gov/pubsearch/pubsinfo.asp?pubid=2015144 (accessed 1 June 2018).

Hunn, L. (2004). Africentric philosophy. *Promoting Critical Practice in Adult Education* 2004 (102): 65–74.

Merriweather Hunn, L. (2004). Africentric philosophy. *Promoting Critical Practice in Adult Education* 2004 (102): 65–74.

Piven, F.F. and Cloward, R. (1993). *Regulating the Poor: The Functions of Public Welfare*, rev. ed. New York, NY: Vintage.

Ramdeholl, D. (2016). Eating fire while walking on broken glass: An auto-ethnography of one adult educator's tenure process. Adult Education Research Conference, Charlotte, NC. Manhattan, KS: New Prairie Press. http://newprairiepress.org/aerc/2016/papers/33 (accessed 9 April 2018).

Sheared, V., Johnson-Bailey, J., Colin, S.A.J., III, et al. (eds.). (2010). *Handbook of Race and Adult Education: A Resource for Dialogue on Racism*. San Francisco, CA: Jossey-Bass.

Yancy, G. (2017). It's black history month. Look in the mirror. *New York Times* The Stone (9 February). https://www.nytimes.com/2017/02/09/opinion/its-black-history-month-look-in-the-mirror.html (accessed 1 June 2018).

13

Using Digital Storytelling to Unearth Racism and Galvanize Action

Mary E. Hess

Humans are storying beings. We tell stories to make sense of our lives, to understand ourselves, and to build relationships with the people around us. Stories tell us about racial identities and communicate taken-for-granted beliefs about race. In a white supremacist world, the dominant ideology's story is that white people are in positions of authority because of their inherent intelligence. The story of meritocracy tells us that people are where they are solely because of their abilities. Because racism constructs and distorts stories in multiple ways, teachers need to think carefully, clearly, and self-reflectively about those they share with students and about the spaces they create for students to listen carefully to others' stories.

The question I want to explore in this chapter – Can digital media support transformative learning around race and racism? – is an urgent one. In the immediate aftermath of voting events that took place in 2016 – Brexit and the US presidential election, in particular – there was widespread concern about the impact of digital media on perceptions of reality (Brooks, 2017; Davies, 2017). Since then, that concern has grown exponentially, as people all

Teaching Race: How to Help Students Unmask and Challenge Racism, First Edition.
Stephen D. Brookfield and Associates.
© 2019 John Wiley & Sons, Inc. Published 2019 by John Wiley & Sons, Inc.

over the world struggle to come to grips with the violence that is erupting around the explicit racism and xenophobia embodied in public demonstrations.

Lee Anne Bell et al. (2009) identify four kinds of stories that shape learning in the area of race – stock stories, concealed stories, resistance stories, and counterstories:

> We begin with *stock stories* because they are the most public and ubiquitous in dominant, mainstream institutions (such as schools, government, workplaces, and the media), and because the other story types critique and challenge their presumption of universality. Thus, they provide the ground from which we build our analysis.
>
> *Concealed stories* coexist alongside stock stories but most often remain in the shadows, hidden from public view. Though invisible to those in the dominant society, concealed stories are often circulated, told, and retold by people on the margins whose experiences and aspirations they express and honor, and they provide a perspective that is often very different from that of the mainstream.
>
> *Resistance stories* are "… stories, both historical and contemporary, that tell about how people have resisted racism, challenged the stock stories that support it, and fought for more equal and inclusive social arrangements."
>
> *Counterstories* "… are new stories that are deliberately constructed to challenge the stock stories, build on and amplify resistance stories, and offer ways to interrupt the status quo and work for change. Such stories enact continuing critique and resistance to the stock stories and enable new possibilities for inclusive human community."
>
> (Bell, Roberts, Irani, and Murphy, 2008, pp. 8–9)

In this chapter I explore how paying attention to these four kinds of stories in the domain of digital media can help us to support learning that moves beyond mere cognitive recall to thoughtful and compassionate action against racism.

I need to begin, however, by situating my own story. Audre Lorde's (1984) caution that the master's tools will never dismantle the master's house echoes through my heart. Lorde was expressing a profound concern about the erasure of crucial differences among women, and a call to be specific about social location and other forms of situatedness. Her poetry and essays broke through the stock stories with which I had grown up as a straight white cisgender woman with privilege in the upper Midwest.

In reading her work I was appalled by my own ignorance and shaken by her compelling descriptions of her experiences in the United States as a black woman, a lesbian, and an activist. But her stories did more than shake the complacent obliviousness within which I had been formed. They also invited me to pay attention to elements of my own experience that had been hidden. Lorde's fierce resistance to economic injustice evoked resonances for me of my own childhood, causing me to have new appreciation for the ways in which my mother raised my sisters and me on her own, on the margins of the small town in which I grew up. Lorde named realities that otherwise I had learned to hide, and she offered riveting stories of refusing and *resisting* that formation. I was deeply convicted by her words when I first read them as an undergraduate student, and I write this chapter hoping to honor her with pragmatic advice for continuing to resist injustice.

What might we learn from the scholars who are exploring the ways in which digital media are implicated in our meaning making? Such scholars are no longer speaking about so-called alternative facts, but have even gone so far as to use terms such as *facts* and *antifacts* (Kelly, 2016, p. 279). In the midst of the swirl of sharply contested descriptions of experience, are there ways in which digital media can support transformative learning, particularly that aimed at dismantling racism? Are there ways to engage the stock stories that come at us with the strength of a fire hose?

There are two theoretical frames in particular that have helped me to stay focused and effective in designing learning and sharing stories that draw students beyond their early socialization and into more complex and effective engagement with systemic racialization. They are described next.

The Dynamics of Transformation: Confirmation, Contradiction, Continuity

The first theory has to do with the dynamics of confirmation, contradiction, and continuity, which are described so well in the work of Robert Kegan (1982, 1994). Kegan suggests that transformative learning – particularly those factors that shape people's identity personally and in community – moves through an ongoing cycle of confirmation, contradiction, and continuity.

Confirmation has to do with understanding the space in which learning begins. In my contexts, that dynamic requires recognizing that the people with whom I am working – often predominately white and immersed in middle-class US and Christian cultures – have little or no conscious analysis of race. Until and unless I can demonstrate to them that I have empathy for the spaces they inhabit and the meaning they are currently making, trust is difficult to establish. Am I speaking in a language they understand? Am I demonstrating respect for their meaning making, even if I believe that meaning to be dangerously narrow? Have I named the stock stories with which they are familiar clearly enough, and do I understand their internal logic?

The second step is a process that Kegan labels *contradiction*, and which Mezirow's (2000) theory of transformative learning describes as encountering a disorienting dilemma – that is, a moment of dissonance when a stock story, such as "play by the rules, work hard, and you'll be rewarded," is contradicted by a disorienting reality, such as an arbitrary layoff. While this is a step that people might stumble into without any outside intervention, it comes more often from a moment in which a teacher deliberately offers a challenge to default meaning making. I am convinced that the dynamics of which Bell et al. (2008) speak when they talk about how concealed stories can "provide a perspective that is often very different from that of the mainstream" (p. 8) are the dynamics that arise when white students first begin to catch a glimpse of how stock stories have obscured their listening, their perception. Audre Lorde's work, for instance, lifted up for me a set of stories and experiences that had been concealed in the stock stories with which I grew up. Inviting students to confront stock stories through engaging with concealed stories is something I have done most often with digital media, as I will describe in a moment. Regardless of how this process arrives however, such contradiction is usually experienced as difficult, even painful, for a learner. It disrupts taken-for-granted meanings and breaks open new possibilities.

For such learning to become integrated into a person's life and really take root, the third step in the process – *continuity* – is crucial. Without finding continuity, without some form of process that offers rich resources for drawing people into deeper, more inclusive community, students can get caught up in what John Hull (1985) calls "ideological enclosures" (p. 80). Such enclosures are built on a process of foreclosing meaning, which causes a retreat into the dogmatic certainty of a previous frame rather than an advance into a transformed and transforming space. Helms's (1993) work on racial identity development notes that whites will often retreat back to an earlier stage of racial identity development (what she labels the *contact* stage, which is characterized by a belief in color blindness) in the absence of some form of community support that endorses the disintegration of earlier worldviews.

In the contexts in which I teach, the state of being confined in ideological enclosures is often described as fundamentalism, a term closely associated with religious belief. But fundamentalism can be described more generally as a strict adherence to a set of assertions that prohibits further learning. Continuity opens up learning, providing for the sharing of a person's or a community's story in a way that elicits empathy for where the story began. Continuity also provides sustenance and resilience for the story's evolution into what might once have been considered unimaginable: a future of deeper and wider community. Continuity can emerge, for example, when a person with white privilege is able to recognize both the destructive and oppressive elements of that privilege *and* move into a community committed to antiracism. Continuity encompasses taking on a new trajectory of meaning, whose acknowledgement of systemic racism both recognizes one's early formation and at the same time commits to dismantling the privileges associated with it. Continuity emerges most often with what Bell et al. (2008) describe as "resistance" stories and "counterstories."

So, confirmation, contradiction, continuity.

There is one other theoretical frame I want to offer as we think about stories, and particularly digital stories, as a resource in transformative learning around race and racism. That frame has to do with attending to the shifts taking place all around us in the midst of digital media. These are the shifts that are deeply problematic in our political processes, but they also hold potential for constructive transformation.

Digital Shifts: Authority, Authenticity, Agency

One of the most potent shifts that has been catalyzed by digital media has to do with how we understand authority. Many of the more enduring forms of structural authority, whether understood as expertise, institutional role, or identity, are being dramatically flattened (Hoover, 2016). The recent upwelling of fake news, for example, is but one symptom of a more difficult challenging of *all* news media. This blanket rejection of credibility and authority creates profound dangers for civil society. In the past, professional journalists and the news media they worked for could assume a basic respect for their reporting by virtue of their institutional structures. In our current contexts, widespread skepticism about institutions and the ubiquitous nature and immediacy of digital information mean that more and more people are refusing to grant any credibility, let alone authority, to professional news organizations. Instead, many people prefer to posit a false equivalence between websites that publish information absent any verification and websites, such as those of the *New York Times* and the *Wall Street Journal*, that continue to maintain specific professional practices. Indeed, given the fire hose of data constantly being showered upon us, the perception that we are living in a post-truth world becomes ever more palpable.

In the midst of these challenges, people are increasingly turning to personal evaluation, to networks of friends, and to peer relationships, as well as to other experientially laden criteria, to weigh authority and determine credibility. People's particular bubbles are filled with the *stories* that we share with each other. In this environment, determinations of authority are largely filtered through an assessment of the authenticity of the meaning being made (the second shifting element). Authenticity is a slippery concept, in part because it has such strongly emotional components but also because its opposite – manipulation – is so much a part of our wider contexts. People grow up in the midst of sharply neoliberal frameworks in which competition and marketing are ever present. In such contexts we need highly calibrated bullshit detectors to thrive, but it can be difficult to determine if such detectors are discarding relevant and credible information along with false and misleading information. You need only sample results from the *Wall Street Journal's* Blue Feed, Red Feed application to see how sharply differing versions of reality – sharply contrasting stories, if you will – are being shared out. Alternatively, watch how MSNBC and Fox News decode a presidential press briefing in real time.

The third element that is shifting – that of agency – holds the potential to curb the most dangerous excesses of the first two dynamics, but it is also the element that is least often directly and explicitly explored. What does it mean to have agency in an era of digital media? As Maria Popova (2014) points out, often people feel compelled to "have an opinion" to demonstrate agency, even when they have little context and even less credible information upon which to draw. It is as if the ladder of inference that once stretched upward from data to information to knowledge to wisdom has been truncated, with people rarely climbing as far as knowledge, let alone all the way up to wisdom.

Having an opinion is a very individualized and perhaps even passive form of agency. It is almost an oxymoron: passive agency. Yet in the world of rapidly changing contexts, having an opinion that is expressed via social media becomes part of how people shape their identities – and that indeed is a form of agency. In *One-Dimensional Man*, Herbert Marcuse (1964) urged that citizens engage in a great refusal to be seduced by consumerism and the legitimacy of representative democracy. In digital terms, the great refusal is to stay off social media, something that invariably marks you as antediluvian and without identity.

Absent any awareness of (let alone experience with) collective forms of agency, most people are schooled into a kind of identity creation that takes shape primarily through consumption. You may define yourself by what you watch (e.g. specific popular culture within situated echo chambers), by what you wear, by what you drive, even by the causes to which you donate. Notice how many of these identities are shaped by story. You gain agency with your friends by participating in discussions about your favorite music, films, YouTube channels, etc. You demonstrate your identity – that is, you shape your story, you have agency over your own self-creation – through what you wear and the messages your clothing and hairstyle signal. You can experience agency through being a fan of a sports team – when your team wins, you win. In this world of digital social media, you can exercise agency via the specific causes you like and that you share on Facebook.

Indeed, for many people individual agency is experienced almost entirely in terms of individual symbolic storying and consumption. The opening episode of the smart BBC TV series *Black Mirror* depicts a society in which self-worth and the possibility of exercising agency is defined by the number of likes and the personal ratings one receives via social media. Yet in the midst of this dystopian alarm there is an opening within digital media through the affordances offered by such media for new ways to have agency; to create, produce, circulate, contest, and resist stories; and to participate in particular forms of identity construction (Campbell, 2011). Systemic racism produces white privilege as well as internalized racism, but people can collectively resist such destructive forms of socialization.

Seeing Systems

We can now attend to how both of these conceptual frames – *confirmation, contradiction, continuity* and *authority, authenticity, agency* – are particularly useful in exploring how digital media can function in transformative ways.

In order to engage racism directly, confronting it and reshaping our frames of meaning making and action, we need to perceive racism systemically. We need to understand that race is a social construction and how that social construction has become deeply embedded throughout the systems in which we live and throughout the stories that we tell ourselves. Part of the challenge of confirming the reality that we and our students live in has to do with being able to perceive this embedding. We need help to uncover the stock stories, as well as the concealed, resistance, and counterstories. Here is where there is an opening for digital media to create opportunities for disruption and contradiction of default meaning making.

#BlackLivesMatter

In the past four years, one very concrete example of the power of social media to mobilize *communal* agency has come through the use of the hashtag BlackLivesMatter. There are many reasons why this hashtag has been such a catalyst, but let me point to three that connect to my argument here. First, the hashtag had its beginning in a basic assertion, in telling a story that connected with the anger, fear, and loss that was so evident in the aftermath of George Zimmerman being acquitted of the murder of Trayvon Martin.

It had *authority* because it expressed an *authentic* response and offered an immediate form of *agency*. It was an emotional outlet, but one which, given the affordances of Twitter, made possible a networking among disparate people and ultimately a catalyst for rallies, vigils, and other kinds of public assembly. Hence it embodied authority, authenticity, and agency.

At the same time, as the hashtag spread throughout various contexts it also provoked a backlash from people who had no personal experience with which to connect to the outrage, people who lived only within the stock stories. It is an irony that did not go unnoticed, that the very assertion that black people mattered (the heart of the hashtag's meaning) was experienced by many white people as a deliberate attempt to exclude them (that is, white people). This is but one example of how systemic racism functions — it makes it possible for white people to continue to see themselves as the default center, as the key arbiters of all that is purportedly normal, and as the only authors of the dominant stock stories. In that mind-set, anything that names a different reality is somehow special, exotic, and marginal, or in some other way atypical. Othering such a frame is an effective ruse for *concealment*. Refusing to see the contradictions at work, and with little access to alternative frames of meaning, many white people responded to #BLM with ill-tempered resistance rather than with an open-hearted willingness to hear the stories of police brutality communities of color were experiencing.

Confronting such destructive socialization has to begin with white people grasping how this narrowing of our perceptions hurts us. The hurts, the very brutal realities of systemic racism's impacts on people of color harm our interdependent, shared relationality. This is perhaps the most compelling personal reason why white people need to work on dismantling racism. Yet as Robin DiAngelo (2011) points out, many white people have been led into a state of white fragility, which all too often turns initial attempts to engage with us on the issue of racism into an opportunity for us to make the conversation into a space in which white people are centered – a space in which we express emotions such as sadness and guilt rather than moving into active advocacy against racism.

Quite rightly, the stories of those who have been marginalized by a system of oppression ought to take center stage. Still, we have to begin somewhere, and for white people the first part of the process – confirmation of our personal grief, anger, and guilt as we realize how systemic racism functions – is a step that needs to happen (Hess, 2016). This is a place in which white people can work with white people, in which those of us who are just a little further along the antiracism road can share how it has helped us to perceive the damage of stock stories, how it is actually empowering and liberating to see racism as a *systemic* problem, and to find ways to move in resistance to it. National networks such as Showing Up for Racial Justice and groups such as San Francisco's European-American Collaborative Challenging Whiteness can provide the continuity Kegan (1994) urged as necessary for people to experiment with new conceptions of whiteness.

For people of color to continually put themselves into spaces in which they teach white folks about racism is exhausting and even debilitating for these teachers. But drawing upon the digital stories that people of color have voluntarily shared with the world offers students in predominately white contexts the opportunity to hear from people experiencing the sharp end of the racism stick without producing a concomitant fatigue in the people sharing the stories. There are many places to draw on such resources. The Racial Justice Collaborative in Theological Education has been collecting the short video pieces that float through social media (http://rjb. religioused.org/resources). MTV shows a steady stream of pieces on racism and cultural issues on its *Decoded* web series, most of which are narrated by Francesca Ramsey (https://www.youtube.com/ watch?v=geuIV6OoP-U&list=PLLreUsexUtEO-afC42WdPta BMQDYUEOOM). The *New York Times* has a newsletter called *Race/Related* (www.nytimes.com/newsgraphics/2016/race-related/ index.html) and NPR has the *Code Switch* podcast series (www.npr. org/sections/codeswitch). There are also many resources that are more immediately local – check in with your YWCA, your science and history museums, and your interfaith initiatives for more examples.

These personal stories of *resistance*, and even further, *counter-stories*, invite engagement beyond the narrowed perceptions systemic racism seeks to inscribe, bringing wider and more diverse experiences into awareness. Certainly using such digital pieces is only a beginning, an entry point into what needs to be deeper dialogue and ongoing, accountable relationality. It is only the beginning of conscientization, the precursor to informed collective action. Still, it can be a good beginning for whites who fear saying the wrong thing in multiracial conversations and who consequently shut themselves off from any engagement.

Of course using digital stories, like any pedagogical practice in which teaching race is concerned, is fraught with unacknowledged contradictions and unforeseen consequences. For example, Michael Wesch (2008) uses the term *context collapse* to describe the way in which digital media take stories, images, and texts from one context and float them widely across the sea of cyberspace, in the process losing much of the original context in which they were produced. A simple example would be a video blog, or vlog, which is generally one person speaking to a web camera. The framing of such speech invites a sense of intimate connection, but can obscure any accompanying awareness of the situatedness of such sharing.

Imagine watching someone close-up, for instance, as the individual shares his/her/their story, and being able to return to that story and listen to it more than once, to watch that person's face with a level of construed intimacy that would not otherwise be possible. There is a freedom invited here that is profoundly promising. It is an invitation to attend to that which has been previously concealed, to hear firsthand about resistance. At the same time, Wesch calls attention to the paradox that the anonymity of commenting on YouTube videos and the other forms of digital response to vlogs and story sharing also make possible the public performance of hatred. The difference between having digital stories function as *resistance* and *counterstories*, and having them function only to reinforce *stock stories*, is a difference that teachers can impact.

The key to overcoming context collapse for teachers in these forms of sharing is to find a way into deeper, accountable relationship through recontextualization. Facilitators can use digital videos in the beginning of an extended learning event designed to move students forward from an individualized to a systemic analysis of racism. Another approach is to turn students from simple perception toward action and advocacy by asking how stories propel us into action. Antiracist pedagogy often begins with confirmation and contradiction, by lifting up concealed stories that contradict stock stories. Offering stories of resistance and counterstories can invite people into the continuity of antiracist community building.

The educational trajectory I envision moves students beyond white fragility and a personal, or even interpersonal, response to racism and into a deeper, systemic engagement. For this to happen we certainly need to engage all four kinds of stories mentioned at the outset of this chapter. But when uncovering systemic racism and moving from an individual to a communal or collective focus, sharing counterstories and stories of resistance becomes particularly important.

Working with Stories About Race and Racism

Stories are an essential route into shifting people from an individualist to a systemic analysis, and from empathic lamentation to activism. Sharing stories in which people have found ways to engage injustice collectively is particularly important, because so many people feel as if they have very little agency in their world. These are the counterstories, which have perhaps the most power to transform.

Digital documentaries, for instance, are useful counterstories, especially when you can pair them with eyewitness accounts in person, which help to ground and recontextualize such stories. I have found it very helpful, for instance, to show the award-winning documentary *A Time for Burning* (Jersey, 1967), which documents a period of time in the history of two Lutheran churches, one black and one white, paired with a Q&A session with Vivian Jenkins Nelsen, a senior fellow at Augsburg College, whose father is in the film. For my predominately Lutheran students, the film vividly reminds them of churches they grew up in and will go on to pastor. It evokes very directly the challenging and overt racism of the 1960s, using language that all too often parallels for my students contemporary debates in the churches today about GLBTQ issues. Even as the documentary confirms the realities they are inhabiting and demonstrates that the stock stories with which they are familiar are still circulating, the film also depicts the gradual awakening of one of the central white people in the film and his impassioned desire to engage racism, providing both contradiction and continuity for them.

Another film that I've used extensively is *The Color of Fear* (Wah, 1994), which documents a multiday conversation among eight men, two of whom are white. Showing that film and then facilitating a conversation about it provides confirmation, contradiction, and continuity. Confirmation, because one of the white men in the film voices the kinds of racist concerns my white students have: the stock stories they know but often refuse to utter. Contradiction, because at the same time, men of color in the film approach that man with empathy and care while refusing to ignore his racism. His assertions are directly countered, in moving and powerful ways, by stories the other men tell, which are often stories of resistance. Continuity, because the second white man in the film acknowledges his own history of racism, but also testifies through his own counterstory to the energy and resilience that comes from moving into an antiracist identity. I can both model and extend that offer of continuity by inviting my students to join a community that is committed to dismantling racism and by inviting them to construct a self-identity that is antiracist, thus developing more agency. They can begin to see how they have been led to ignore systemic racism and how their privilege blinds them and at the same time be invited into a community that sees that recognition as the first step into deeper love and accountability.

Kegan's (1994) assertion that we need continuity resonates with Bell et. al (2008) as they write of the power of counterstories. All of these authors argue that transformative learning can never come to an end. The two documentary films described above contain rich content for continuing critical engagement. Repeatedly viewing *A Time for Burning* (Jersey, 1967), for instance, provokes serious concern about what is shown and not shown. It is all too easy to see that film as the story of a white hero and to ignore the complexity and ongoing collective organizing of the black churches present in the situation. Similarly, repeatedly viewing *The Color of Fear* (Wah, 1994) can and must complicate a viewer's meaning making. There are no women in the conversation, and issues of sexuality and gender identity are nearly absent. The challenges of intersectionality can be made more visible upon repeated viewings and deeper engagement.

Our ongoing political realities – both in the challenges of the Brexit process in the United Kingdom and of the Trump administration in the United States – offer multiple opportunities for people insulated by privilege to wake up to the challenges in our midst. The depth of shock, or at a minimum stunned surprise, that many middle-class white people feel as events unfold only serve to illustrate how little connection they have made beyond their own communities. For example, most whites are unaware of the conversation that African American parents feel required to have with their own sons about how to negotiate the times they will inevitably be pulled over or frisked by white police. In this regard, *A Conversation with My Black Son* (Gandbhir and Foster, 2015) from the *New York Times* Op-Docs section is a valuable teaching tool to help white students bear witness to racism.

In many white communities, people overwhelmingly know only stock stories. These are communities that are pervaded by a profound fear of the rise of a more diverse political and public culture. If you are living in economically marginalized settings and fear that no matter how hard you work you are falling further behind, and at the same time you feel no solidarity with (or even connection to) other marginalized communities, but only feel competitive with them, then when people you have been trained to believe are lesser than you by virtue of their social placement through race are seen as getting ahead, it is possible to feel as if you have been cheated in some way. Notice each of the clauses in that prolix sentence. Such a story is only compelling if your narrative for why you are falling behind is a personal one. You are losing out in a competitive sphere, you are losing your "right" to get ahead of others. You see race only as a personal attribute and as one of the few such privileges you have as a white person. Further, for this narrative to be persuasive you must live in settings that are highly segregated by race (as are more and more cities in the United States). And beyond that, you must have no memory of (let alone education that would explain) the history of social movements in the United States. You literally have no memory or access to stories of resistance, let alone counterstories.

The insidious stock narratives of neoliberal capitalism – that persons are individuals, not relational beings; that truth is best arrived at through competition; that value accrues only to what you do, not to who you are; that if you are not successful it is due to your own worthlessness, or to someone else's cheating (Brown, 2015) – these stock narratives effectively rule out of order a systemic analysis of the social construction of race. In order to transform these understandings, we must first "catch" what they are and find ways to bring them into direct awareness so that they can be engaged.

This is work that white people need to do with other white people, *not* because we should end up by ourselves in a white-only universe, but because the pain, longing, and disillusionment that occur need a space in which to be expressed without continuing to harm people of color. As teachers we have to demonstrate that we comprehend what the learners in our setting are feeling. Hence, we need to confirm that we are familiar with the stock stories that we hear our participants expressing and that we acknowledge the experiences framing them. Only then is it possible to develop the trust and mutual respect necessary for us to start uncovering contradictions that take root in ways that foster transformation rather than ideological enclosures. Only in the presence of transformed understanding, in the continuity offered by emancipatory historiography, can antifacts fall away as we are grasped by a larger reality.

As Brookfield (2015) has written, we cannot ask students to do what we, as teachers, have not first done in front of them. Confirmation and contradiction are necessary first steps, but as Kegan (1994) points out, without continuity there is no transformation. That continuity includes annunciation – a theological word for the announcement of the Incarnation, the angel Gabriel telling Mary that she would bear a son – a word that more broadly points to the necessity of naming, claiming, and celebrating our embodiment in this new broader, deeper community, and our commitments to dismantling racism.

Offering entry points into continuity and providing ways to sustain transformative community are two of the richest ways that digital media, documentaries, vlogs, and other forms of digital communication can be so helpful. Digital media in the twenty-first century afford more participatory elements than any previous form of technologically structured communication, and thus can invite resistance to narrowness of perception while also offering ways of celebrating and sharing – annunciating! – a transformed understanding.

The Center for Digital Storytelling, now StoryCenter, has been developing concrete ways to do this form of narrative work for a very long time. Its website has an abundance of resources for supporting this kind of transformative learning, along with thousands of digital story examples. There are also numerous examples of online curriculum materials available for free, which draw on stories to invite transformative learning. Maggie Potapchuk et al. (2005), from the Center for Assessment and Policy Development in Maryland, for instance, offer a detailed curriculum – Flipping the Script – for adults that use stories to engage white privilege and other elements of systemic racism. Bell et al. (2008) have developed a specific curriculum for the K–12 setting, The Storytelling Project Curriculum: Learning about Race and Racism Through the Arts. These author-activists are developing specific ways to build continuity through shared storytelling that invites learners into antiracist community.

In these concrete examples of the ways in which digital media can be drawn on for transformative work, there is much hope to be found. As Elizabeth Drescher (2016) writes:

> In the new media age, difference is less a distinguishing barrier between groups of individuals than it is an invitation to engage and explore the lives of diverse others… new media practices of seeing others, seeing difference, expressing difference, and being in variously distributed relationships with religiously diverse others have an effect on how people regard religious difference in increasingly overlapping zones of private and public life (p. 61).

She made this observation in the context of her work with people who claim the label "spiritual but not religious," but the more general literature of digital literacies supports this assertion:

> … The new ethic of digital literacies is "cosmopolitan" practice…[which fosters] reflexive and hospitable dispositions and habits of mind necessary for ethically motivated rhetorical and semiotic decision making in relation to wide, interactive, and potentially global audiences.

> … Cosmopolitanism is the idea that one can become, indeed should aspire to be, a citizen of the world, able to embrace local ties and commitments, but also to extend well beyond them, engaging a wider human community, even across divides of seemingly irreconcilable differences (Ávila and Pandya, pp. 64–65).

This literature – as well as my own personal experience – convinces me that inviting stories that foster creating exchanges across the too-narrowly constructed containers of our meaning making can offer profound nourishment and hope for reweaving relationship among people from vastly differing contexts and experiences. Dialogue across difference must be a major method in any effort to dismantle racism. The opportunity here is to build a cosmopolitan consciousness that fosters antiracist identities that are both centered *and* open, identities that are cognizant of social location and personal situatedness, and identities that attend to personal experience *and* systemic analysis. It is about paying attention to the confirmation, contradiction, and continuity necessary for real transformation.

References

Ávila, J. and Pandya, J. (eds.) (2013). *Critical Digital Literacies as Social Praxis: Intersections and Challenges*. New York, NY: Peter Lang.

Bell, L.A., Roberts, R.A., Irani, K. et al. (2008). *The Storytelling Project Curriculum: Learning About Race and Racism Through Storytelling and the Arts*. Barnard College Storytelling Project. www.racialequitytools.org/resourcefiles/stp_curriculum.pdf (accessed 21 January 2017).

Brookfield, S.D. (2015). *The Skillful Teacher: On Technique, Trust, and Responsiveness in the Classroom*, 3rd ed. San Francisco, CA: Jossey-Bass.

Brooks, D. (2017). The internal invasion. *New York Times* (20 January) www.nytimes.com/2017/01/20/opinion/the-internal-invasion.html (accessed 21 January 2017).

Brown, W. (2015). *Undoing the Demos: Neoliberalism's Stealth Revolution*. Brooklyn, NY: Zone Books.

Campbell, H. (2011). Understanding the relationship between religion online and offline in a networked society. *Journal of the American Academy of Religion* 80 (1): 64–93. doi:10.1093/jaarel/lfr074.

Davies, W. (2017). How statistics lost their power – and why we should fear what comes next. *The Guardian* (19 January). www.theguardian.com/politics/2017/jan/19/crisis-of-statistics-big-data-democracy (accessed 21 January 2017).

DiAngelo, R. (2011). White fragility. *International Journal of Critical Pedagogy* 3 (3): 54–70.

Drescher, E. (2016). *Choosing Our Religion*. New York, NY: Oxford University Press.

Gandbhir, G. and Foster, B. (2015). A Conversation with My Black Son. *New York Times* Op-Docs (17 March). https://www.nytimes.com/2015/03/17/opinion/a-conversation-with-my-black-son.html (accessed 6 February 2018).

Helms, J.E. (1993). *Black and White Racial Identity: Theory, Research, and Practice*. Westport, CT: Praeger.

Hess, M. (2016). White religious educators resisting white fragility: Lessons from mystics. *Religious Education* 112: 46–57. doi:10.1080/00344087.2016.1253124.

Hoover, S. (ed.). (2016). *The Media and Religious Authority*. University Park, PA: Pennsylvania State University Press.

Hull, J. (1985). *What Prevents Christian Adults from Learning?* London: SCM Press.

Jersey, B. (1967). *A Time for Burning* (documentary). Running time 57 min. Lutheran Film Associates https://archive.org/details/atimeforburning (accessed 1 June 2018).

Kegan, R. (1982). *The Evolving Self: Problem and Process in Human Development*. Cambridge, MA: Harvard University Press.

Kegan, R. (1994). *In Over Our Heads: The Mental Demands of Modern Life*. Cambridge, MA: Harvard University Press.

Kelly, K. (2016). *The Inevitable: Understanding the Twelve Technological Forces That Will Shape Our Future*. New York, NY: Penguin.

Lorde, A. (1984). *Sister Outsider: Essays and Speeches by Audre Lorde*. Trumansburg, NY: Crossing Press.

Marcuse, H. (1964). *One-Dimensional Man: Studies in the Ideology of Advanced Industrial Society*. Boston, MA: Beacon Press.

Mezirow, J. (2000). Learning to think like an adult. In: *Learning as Transformation: Critical Perspectives on a Theory in Progress* (ed. J. Mezirow), 3–34. San Francisco, CA: Jossey-Bass.

Popova, M. (2014). *Wisdom in the age of information, an animated explication*. Future of Storytelling Conference. www.youtube.com/watch?v=bjoO6Y29f7I (accessed 21 January 2017).

Potapchuk, M., Liederman, S., Bivens, D. et al. (2015). *Flipping the Script: White Privilege and Community Building*. Center for Assessment and Policy Development. www.racialequitytools.org/resourcefiles/potapchuk1.pdf (accessed 21 January 2017).

Wah, L.M. (dir.). (1994). *The Color of Fear* (documentary). Running time 90 min. Stir Fry Productions.

Wesch, M. (2008). Context collapse. Digital Ethnography. http://mediatedcultures.net/youtube/context-collapse (accessed 21 January 2017).

14

Examining Mistakes to Advance Antiracist Teaching

Bobbi Smith

Teachers who dedicate themselves to antiracist practice take their commitment seriously. After all, this is important work, full of significance for creating a world that is more just and compassionate. We want to feel we have made a difference and that all the pain and tension have been worth it. Our hope is that by transforming people in our classrooms, maybe we can make some small contribution to transforming the world outside. Because the stakes are so high, the prospect of failure is terrifying. After all, we're not training people to make widgets; we're trying to alert them to the ways in which white supremacy insinuates itself into our actions and thoughts, and how these actions and thoughts contribute to the maintenance of supremacist structures.

Putting this level of pressure on ourselves means that the thing we fear more than anything else is failing. Often this is defined as losing control of what's happening, as when racist comments start flying around the room and people start to yell at each other. Sometimes our greatest fear is of saying something racist ourselves and being embarrassed in front of the room. When the room goes totally quiet and an awkward silence seems to last forever, we can feel as if we've lost the plot. In our minds, all the careful planning and forethought we've put into a particular session seems naïve and

Teaching Race: How to Help Students Unmask and Challenge Racism, First Edition. Stephen D. Brookfield and Associates.

foolish, and we feel like complete impostors. Here we are in the role of teacher, one who is entrusted to lead others into examining their own racism, but all we feel is fraudulent and stupid.

But the essential complexity of antiracist work means it will never go the way you've planned, and that you will probably leave most of the sessions you run feeling as if all you did was to make a stream of mistakes. In this chapter I want to explore one of the most crucial aspects of antiracist pedagogy – learning from the constant mistakes we will inevitably make. To do this I focus on one particular workshop I facilitated, which represents my experiential Mount Rainier towering over the emotional topography of my practice.

The Moment

I am quivering at the front of the room, drenched in sweat, using every fricking woo-woo technique I've ever learned to keep myself from fight or flight.

The participant in front of me finishes speaking, and with my inner voice hissing, "keep your shit *together*," I calmly respond, "Thank you. Does anyone else have any comments or questions for this group?"

Another participant raises a hand, the discussion drops to a deeper level of nuance, and I slip around in my sweaty shoes.

Ejsing (2007) comments that due to our higher levels of experience in our fields of study, teachers are the power holders in the teacher–student relationship. A position that I, as the content expert and the workshop facilitator, had enjoyed until about 45 minutes prior, when I had gleefully (and with blissful ignorance of the reality that was to ensue) chucked a stick in the spokes of this power dynamic.

I had spent the previous four hours guiding just over 20 participants through an interactive antiracist workshop on themes of identity intersectionality (Crenshaw, 1989), the notion of white privilege (Frankenberg, 1999; Yancy, 2004), and the supremacist character of so-called commonsense conditioning (Sandoval, 1999). We had done think/pair/shares on what Hulko (2009) calls "the everyday and context-contingent nature of oppression and privileges" (p. 45), checked out McIntosh's (1988) backpack, pushed our chairs around for an experiential exercise to demonstrate social location (Pyle, 2014), and interrogated a paragraph lifted from the introductory section of an online learning course for its hidden assumptions and expectations (reference withheld to protect the guilty) in order to challenge existing power structures in education.

To teach skills of critical reflexivity, throughout this process I had used self-disclosure with what I imagined was the emotional sensitivity prescribed by Ejsing (2007) to create an atmosphere of "trust, safety, learning, efficiency, productivity, connection, empowerment, and community" (Kashtan, 2005, p. 573). By the time I initiated my private metabolic nightmare, participants were (in the transformative wonderland I believed I had created) critically deconstructing power and privilege in their personal and professional contexts, sensitized to implicit cultural biases in organizational practice, experiencing a degree of trust and community with both me and each other, and positioned to apply these critical reflexivity skills in their personal and professional lives.

At this point, I explained to participants that they would be forming groups of four to five members and doing an adapted version of an ideology critique, an exercise developed by Brookfield (2012). In this critique, per Brookfield, they would take a best practice that "has been designed to be helpful and empowering and examine it for ways it is experienced differently by different people in the organization, movement or community" (p. 20). During the various stages of this exercise, the groups were given the following sequence of tasks:

1. Describe the practice and brainstorm what it's supposed to mean or achieve in terms of the accepted, commonsense, dominant view.

2. Identify some of the assumptions/expectations that are implicit or explicit in the practice.
3. Examine the practice for internal inconsistencies, paradoxes, and contradictions. What are the intended objectives of the practice, as you understand them, and is there an unconscious contradicting of the intended objectives or any demonstration of hypocrisy around them?
4. Identify what is being omitted from the practice – its "structured silences and absences" – which could be some of the commonsense, unconscious assumptions or expectations that are being imposed but not acknowledged. What significant elements or information do the commonsense, unconscious assumptions and expectations lack? Who and what is excluded?
5. Look for reasons to explain why this commonsense view ignored the contradictions and omissions you found. Decide who benefits from this commonsense practice and who is most disadvantaged by it.
6. Imagine a new, alternative structure or process that is more culturally competent than the current practice.

"And the best practice you will critically analyze in this exercise," I explained, "is this one."

Cue the match.

"Using what you've learned today," I continued, "I want you to filter today's workshop through these understandings – everything I've said and done, every activity that we've undertaken, the materials we've looked at, anything having to do with the last four hours – and identify some of the ways these things could be experienced differently by different people. At the end, someone from each group will report on your analysis."

Forty-five minutes later and I am officially on fire as I facilitate a discussion on the contradictions, omissions, flaws, and weaknesses of both my own facilitation practices and the workshop that I designed, to impart to participants the very skills they are now using to tear it apart.

Planning My Transformative Wonderland

Timmins (2006) describes critical reflexivity as "personal analysis that involves challenging personal beliefs and assumptions to improve professional and personal practice" (p. 49), while Cunliffe (2004) notes that "critically reflexive practice embraces subjective understandings of reality as a basis for thinking more critically about the impact of our assumptions, values, and actions on others" (p. 407). Pedagogically, critical reflexivity is promoted as effective in antiracist education by several authors who note its necessity in understanding the complexities of racism in contemporary society (Gay and Kirkland, 2003; Howard, 2003; Husband, 2010; Sefa Dei, 1993; St. Denis, 2007).

However, despite its value, the process of critical reflexivity is inherently problematic. Gay and Kirkland (2003) discuss how often those of us trying to facilitate critical reflexivity for others do not have a clear understanding of what it entails. They describe the confusion between actual critical reflexivity – which, in their view, involves analytical introspection, continuous reconstruction of knowledge, and the transformation of beliefs and skills – and pseudo-critical reflexivity, which involves more superficial activities, such as "describing issues, ideas, and events; stating philosophical beliefs; or summarizing statements made by scholars" (p. 182). Howard (2003) comments on the arduous nature of critical reflexivity as it demands that individuals not only ask themselves challenging questions but also provide honest answers. As he states, reflection and critique of one's own thoughts and behaviors is "one of the more difficult processes for all individuals" (p. 197). Further difficulties of critical reflexivity involve the complications of standardizing any procedure around it. As a "highly contextualized process" (Gay and Kirkland, 2003, p. 182), critical reflexivity, particularly in antiracist education, must recognize the variables present in each educational experience and that thus "there can be no formula to instruct every group or class" (Bleich, 1995, p. 44).

In the session that's the focus of this chapter, my intent was to design a process whereby participants could learn the nature of critical reflexivity, specifically as it relates to furthering antiracist practice, as well as acquiring associated skills. Cognizant of the pitfalls described by others, I looked for ways to increase the efficacy of the design. According to Brookfield (2012), "When it comes to students' learning how to practice critical thinking, it seems that they constantly look to teachers to see what the process looks like. Furthermore, given the difficulties of this process, it is important that we earn the right to ask them to do it themselves by first modeling how we try to unearth and research our own assumptions" (p. 11). This is underscored by Conklin (2008), who discusses how pedagogy that contradicts itself by demanding certain kinds of social justice-oriented actions from students without modeling that behavior first creates a counterproductive learning environment.

Heeding these cautionary voices, I labored in the design phase of the session to come up with ways I could model critical reflexivity myself, thereby improving the chances of participants acquiring the skill. I made an assumption that the pedagogical strategy of self-disclosure – of divulging information about myself to participants (Cozby, 1973) would serve this intention. On the basis of this assumption, I crafted fact-based descriptions of the several years I spent becoming critically reflexive of my own practice, the techniques I used to check my practice for racism, and the surprising places in which I found evidence of it. In this way, I looked to model how critical reflexivity can be done as well as to use self-disclosure to "increase student participation, interest, understanding, and motivation" (Cayanus, 2004, p. 9). As Lannutti and Strauman (2006) have advised, I worked to ensure that my stories were "more illustrative than revealing" (p. 96) and that the content was both relevant and worked to clarify the material (Cayanus and Martin, 2008, p. 328).

However, as with critical reflexivity, the pedagogical practice of self-disclosure is also subject to tensions and trickiness. Ejsing (2007) writes about what she calls "the ethics of self-disclosure"

(p. 235). Drawing attention to the power differential between teachers and students, she points out how self-disclosure by teachers can render students vulnerable, as teachers wield the privilege of judging students' responses to stories that teachers tell. Narrating an episode of self-disclosure by her teaching partner, Hochstetler (2013) wrestles with their mutual failure to adequately support students for whom the disclosure created undue emotional stress. Emphasizing this problematic nature of self-disclosure is Tobin's (2010) practice of weighing what he calls the "pedagogical risks" versus the "pedagogical rewards" of self-disclosure (p. 197).

How Reflexivity Became Repressive

So there I was, using recommended pedagogical practices that were fraught with shortcomings to teach antiracist pedagogy, in and of itself a highly sensitive subject matter. As mentioned, I worked my butt off to address those shortcomings. I educated myself on the pitfalls and I used recommended strategies to mitigate them. However, despite these efforts, when I retrospectively consider those four hours of course work (up to but not including the moment I set myself on fire), it is apparent to me that certain limitations existed in its design.

One of the foremost inhibitors of the session to that point was the limitation of self-disclosure as a means of successfully modeling honest critical reflexivity. Husband (2010) explains the process of "necessary negotiations," whereby in designing an antiracist course to present a critical version of African American history, she was "forced to make some necessary submissions and exclusions around these issues of curriculum content" (p. 67). Speaking specifically to self-disclosure, Tobin (2010) tells about the "different performances of self" that he employs to achieve his various pedagogical goals. He identifies the "crafted, strategic" nature of his self-disclosure and how he chooses to emphasize different aspects of his personality depending on what he wants his disclosure to accomplish (p. 202). I understood the need for "necessary negotiations" in course design, particularly when navigating time constraints, and, like Tobin, deliberately crafted my stories to illustrate central concepts and realize learning objectives. However, reflecting on the implications of these processes, I am uncertain as to whether or not *describing* moments of honest critical reflexivity that happened in my past, via a process of necessary negotiations and verbal manipulation, in and of itself qualifies as *modeling* honest critical reflexivity.

A second critical limitation of the session's first four hours is rooted in this first flaw and relates to the session's ability to model its articulated intention to challenge existing power structures in education. Sefa Dei (1993) remarks that "Anti-racist education should challenge some positivist beliefs and conceptualizations about the social world" (p. 38). With regard to the session, as I crafted my self-disclosure via my word choices, emphases, and per-spectives, and in the overall way I framed the experiences that I was describing, so did I let my own biases, significantly my unex-amined ones, steer the experience that participants would have. I would argue that without facilitating an accompanying process of post-disclosure learning (Ejsing, 2007) wherein the disclosure I made could have itself been interrogated for these biases, my action (despite the thematically relevant content – how I engaged critical reflexivity to evolve my practice in antiracist ways) failed to ade-quately challenge the traditional teacher–student power dynamic. Instead, my approach reinforced my position as the knowledge authority in the antiracist classroom.

I believe it is reasonable to suggest that my disclosure, relevant in appearance due to its thematic subject matter and intended to honestly model critical self-reflexivity, actually served to under-score existing power structures in education, even while cloaking itself in the guise of responsible, emancipatory pedagogy. This is reminiscent of Ellsworth's (1989) observation that "Strategies such as student empowerment and dialogue give the illusion of equality while in fact leaving the authoritarian nature of the teacher-student relationship intact" (p. 306). hooks (1994) clarifies this point further, declaring that "It's also really important to acknowledge that professors may attempt to deconstruct traditional biases while sharing that information through body posture, tone, word choice, and so on that perpetuate those very hierarchies and biases they are critiquing" (p. 44).

In summary, in the four hours prior to lighting myself on fire, despite my intentions to offer participants antiracist education wherein I modeled my own experiences, thereby equipping them to apply critical reflexivity skills in their professional and personal lives, I had achieved some contradictory, hypocritical ends. Upon reflection, not only had I failed to adequately *model* these experiences (though I described them well enough), but my attempts to do so were further thwarted by an incomplete pedagogy that did not reflect back on itself, but rather reinforced status quo power dynamics.

Why I Struck the Match

Back to the moment when I struck the match. I had gone into the session with the intention of having participants do the ideology critique. In keeping with the previous times that I had run the session, I planned that they would discuss the questions in their groups and that afterwards we would come back together to conclude the day and strategize around real-world applications of the entire day's learning for their practices. I did not plan to facilitate a debrief of the group session with the ideology critique, let alone a plenary reporting of each group's findings. In retrospect, I have my suspicions about why I did not plan for this – the words *messy*, *unpredictable*, and *terrifying* all come to mind. What happened, however, is that on that particular day, as I introduced the exercise, I spontaneously decided that it would be worth the risk to experiment with the possibilities and add a reporting discussion component to the exercise. To use Tobin's (2010) phrasing, in that moment I decided that the pedagogical risks might be worth the pedagogical rewards and that it was worth it to find out if they were.

WTF?

As the plenary reporting discussion picked up momentum, it became clear that in the four hours previous to this activity I had made a *lot* of mistakes. Using some of the critical reflexivity tools and techniques acquired in those four hours, participants isolated my hidden assumptions and expectations, detected some of my hidden agendas, ascertained places in which I'd demonstrated privilege and power, and pinpointed people that I'd marginalized and excluded throughout. And then they proceeded to tell me all about it and engage with each other about it. There was a palpable tension in the air as they struggled initially with how honest they wanted to be – I sensed both concern for my feelings and a hesitancy to take the discussion beyond what might be considered polite.

As I did my best not to comment on their comments, not to defend, justify, or explain myself, but instead to thank them and encourage more discussion (and to not let on how excruciatingly vulnerable and uncomfortable I felt), the degree of honesty and the nuance of their critiques deepened. What began as the students evaluating the physical formatting of the room (lecture-style rows versus a First Peoples sharing circle) evolved into an analysis of the manner in which I seemed to value Western, academic scholarship over other ways of being, and the ways that this privileged my own academic interests over non-Western worldviews of, for example, the First Peoples, upon whose territory I was running this session. Someone highlighted that my own cultural competency skills seemed to be lacking, as I had failed to invite an Elder from the local territory to bear witness to the day's proceedings. Another participant pointed out how many of the conclusions that we had drawn about the paragraph from the online course concerning the manner in which it excluded and privileged certain groups were actually true of one of the key activities that I myself had assigned to participants.

As the final group offered its insights and a sense of conclusion began to overtake the discussion, several participants commented on my courage in concluding the exercise in this way. This segued into remarks from other participants about how my willingness to facilitate a discussion of this nature offered them an example of what critical reflexivity looks like in practice. Finally, there was a general consensus that the discussion had been a powerful experience of application and modeling and that participants' learning had been bolstered by it. And BAM! – one pedagogical whim and suddenly the session morphed from a flawed, hypocritical version of itself into a version of what I had intended it to be – an antiracist learning experience in which I modeled critical reflexivity and participants acquired the skills to apply what they'd learned to their own practices and lives.

Using Mistakes as Deliberate Pedagogy

As mentioned, I didn't plan this moment of pedagogical effectiveness. Even in the moment that I prescribed it, I had no idea what was going to happen and was flying by the seat of my (very hot) pants while I navigated it. Retrospectively, however, it is clear to me that I made some big mistakes in my session design, and that in my split-second decision to facilitate an interrogation of those mistakes I made use of a teaching tool that I believe warrants some discussion.

Weimer (2013) makes the point that although teachers may exert tremendous power, "they are still never completely in control of a class" (p. 93), a situation that induces in teachers a certain amount of felt vulnerability. She argues that often teachers will look for ways to reinforce their authority as a way of keeping feelings of helplessness at bay. However, with regard to the antiracist classroom, as hooks (1994) declares, "the empowerment of students cannot happen if we refuse to be vulnerable while encouraging students to take risks" (p. 21). In retrospect, as I consider the experience of facilitating a discussion by my own students of my own pedagogical hypocrisies and failings, and as I recall the exposure and resulting vulnerability that I experienced in that moment,

I find parallels between this experience and hooks's assertion. Supplementary to this is Kelley's (2009) proposal that "intentional conversations with students about our teaching mistakes may enhance learning. In certain cases, teaching about a mistake may even advance the curriculum" (p. 288). In this instance I believe a tremendous amount of participant learning occurred.

In her review of Freedman and Stoddard Holmes's edited collection of narratives by teachers with physical aspects considered "other" by society, Hochstetler (2013) summarizes the editors' claims that "teacher bodies (and student bodies for that matter) should not be dismissed or elevated in the classroom, but *acknowledged*" (pp. 41–42), owing to what Hochstetler describes as the inevitable influence of those bodies on teachers' practices. Expanding on these authors, I would argue that a similar case be made for allowing the less-tangible but inescapable presence of teachers' contradictions, hypocrisies, flaws, weaknesses, and mistakes to also show up.

Hochstetler (2013) states that "Essentially, to be blind to the body is to be blind of how we function in the hierarchies around us" (p. 43). Again, reframing this statement within the context of teachers' less-tangible but ever-present contradictions, hypocrisies, flaws, weaknesses, and mistakes further reinforces the case for weaving those same dynamics into teaching practice in ways that advance curriculum in the antiracist classroom. As I chose to stop minimizing my felt vulnerability in the classroom and allowed students to make visible and interrogate my flaws and contradictions in relation to racism and power hierarchies, so did I render those same flaws and mistakes into powerful tools for participants to investigate how we function in the hierarchies around us. I would further contend that such modeling constitutes a form of self-disclosure that, due to its real-time nature, avoids some of the pitfalls of retrospective self-disclosure discussed earlier.

With regard to teaching mistakes, Kelley (2009) asks the question, "is there a way to work with them intentionally and creatively that is pedagogically helpful?" (p. 287). Based on my experience described above, I would respond yes to that question. I would also confess that although I believe it is possible, the fact that I stumbled upon my approach in the moment, rather than planning it out beforehand, raises certain questions for me. Does teaching intentionally and creatively about my mistakes actually involve planning, and, if so, would this fall under the category of being crafted and negotiated, thereby making it ethically and pedagogically problematic? And if I don't or can't plan for teaching about my mistakes, what are the skills and qualities that I need to demonstrate in order to ensure that in those on-the-fly moments, I navigate these situations in a way that effectively advances curriculum? Ultimately, my question is: What does teaching intentionally, creatively – and I would add ethically – about my teaching mistakes in the antiracism classroom look like? I furthermore suspect that any ensuing discussion would be strengthened by asking: What does teaching intentionally, creatively, and ethically about my teaching mistakes in the antiracism classroom *feel* like? This in turn leads me to ask questions about the potential impact in the moment of those feelings on me and on participants, and about my ability to navigate those emotions while facilitating this kind of learning experience.

With all of that being said, in my own work the implications of this experience have been numerous. While I theoretically understood that my work was likely subject to the very biases I was teaching about, my suspicions were unproven (giving me latitude to refuse to address elements that were messy, unpredictable, and terrifying). Viscerally experiencing myself and my design and delivery through the eyes of participants renders that hypocritical (yet very comfortable) place unsustainable. Put another way, by incorporating this type of real-time feedback into my session design I am now accountable in ways that I was not previously. If I am committed to what I am teaching, acknowledging these dynamics publicly obliges me to address them, which not only works to progress my practice but itself becomes a powerful modeling tool.

In terms of other antiracist educators, I believe the implications for practice lie in the possibilities latent in posing questions specifically about how design and delivery relate to content. As I experienced, this generates very different experiences than questions posed simply about content. As participants engage in this sphere, the educator's own contradictions, hypocrisies, flaws, weaknesses, and mistakes are teased out, rendering them powerful opportunities for learning. As described, the response to my approach was initially characterized by participant reluctance – due, I suspect, to its probably unsafe nature: The approach was not structured to allow for anonymity. However, particularly given the ubiquitous nature of handheld devices, designing safe, anonymous opportunities for participants to engage in this terrain can be done using social media and/or apps designed for that purpose. As I experienced, this type of engagement can lead to a subversion of the power dynamics that can keep the facilitator safe from vulnerability and inject potentially unpredictable elements into the session. Being prepared emotionally and technically for these possibilities – budgeting time during planning to accommodate what may transpire when eliciting discussions of this nature – can help with the navigation of unpredictable elements.

How to Incorporate a Pedagogy of Mistakes into One's Teaching

In discussing the possibilities of working with teaching mistakes creatively, intentionally, and ethically in order to advance curriculum in the antiracist classroom, problematic elements are likely inevitable. And that, I believe, is the foundation for a pedagogy of mistakes. Put another way, as a person conditioned by a white supremacist, technocratic society who is using problematic strategies to address problematic dynamics, it is inevitable that I will be making mistakes in the classroom. To answer my earlier question – Does teaching intentionally and creatively about my mistakes actually involve planning? – I believe that it does, but not in the sense that I plan when and where to make predesigned mistakes. I would argue that deliberate or crafted mistakes, in addition to being inauthentic, would likely be characterized by a lack of vulnerability on my part and a concomitant failure to disrupt traditional power dynamics.

I discovered in the situation this chapter describes that teacher vulnerability and power reversal can be critical to the success of antiracist education. So I would offer that planning to teach from mistakes could be as simple as first accepting the reality that I am flawed and racist and therefore my teaching is flawed and racist, and then creating a structure in which students have the time and space to safely identify where and when this is happening. In terms of the nuts and bolts of delivering a lesson, that could amount to setting aside a portion of classroom time explicitly dedicated to the messy, unpredictable, and terrifying.

For example, I could dedicate the last hour of a three-hour class to this pursuit, explaining first that as part of the antiracist curriculum we're exploring we're going to do an exercise that will help students apply their critical reflection skills so that (1) they gain experience doing it in real-world situations outside the classroom, and (2) we collectively evolve the environment we are in (our shared classroom) toward greater awareness and equity. I could explain next that as a white, middle-class woman, I have been conditioned to be racist in ways that I did not have any control over but which are now my responsibility to address, and that part of taking responsibility is opening up my teaching to analysis and feedback. I could then direct them to log in to an app that I have set up previously (TodaysMeet or 81 Dash would both work), on which students can anonymously post comments and questions that show up on an overhead projector.

I would now have options about where to take the exercise. Due to my position as the teacher, I could choose comments and/or questions from the list and guide students through discussion. I believe that if I chose this format I would be maintaining a degree of control over the exercise, potentially perpetuating the traditional student–teacher hierarchy. I think a more effective format would allow students to choose which comments and/or questions they want to address and how they want to format their analysis; for example, through writing or artwork, or through discussions with partners, in groups, or as a whole class (or a combination of all of the above).

My role throughout would be to chair the exercise but not to participate, bringing me to what I believe is the crux of ethically delivering a pedagogy of teaching from mistakes. What I have described above are the mechanics of delivering an experience of this nature. However, the teacher's role (as I learned viscerally) is anything but mechanical. In listening to students critically interrogate my teaching, at any moment I may feel angry, defensive, ashamed, disappointed, embarrassed, and/or humiliated. I may feel like a terrible teacher and a terrible racist. I may feel like a terrible person. And I believe that this is where the actual work is when ethically teaching from mistakes.

Before I introduce to students the mechanical aspects described above, I need to critically reflect on what comes up for me when I feel judged and ask myself if I can realistically negotiate those feelings during classroom discussions. Will my emotional responses unnerve me to the point that I shut down the discussion either explicitly or passive aggressively? Am I likely to take revenge on students either in the moment or in the future? Am I clear on what revenge looks like? Conscious, malicious revenge can be easy to spot but subtle, covert revenge is more difficult to identify. Depending on how I answer these questions, I may be able to deliver the mechanics of teaching from mistakes but I may not be able to do it ethically.

A potential litmus test could be to have one or more colleagues observe me teaching and offer their analysis privately. I could experience a degree of vulnerability without disrupting the power dynamic of my classroom, gathering data on how I navigated the situation and extrapolating from my actions. Ultimately, I believe that the most critical qualities and skills an educator needs to teach ethically from mistakes are (1) a readiness to experience extreme discomfort while remaining grounded, visible, and present, (2) vigilance against reacting in the moment, and (3) the ability to coach myself through if I am reacting. Am I truly willing to relinquish the protection offered me by my accepted hierarchical positioning in relation to the students in order to advance antiracist curriculum? If I'm not, then I will not be able to safely and effectively offer this modality. If I am willing, then in addition to this preliminary reflective work I may want to set up some support mechanism for myself for afterwards – a safe colleague or friend who can help me debrief.

In my experience, teaching from mistakes in antiracist education is not easy, convenient, or comfortable. It required that I forfeit a degree of power that I am not accustomed to being without, and that required that I traverse this unknown and terrifying terrain while continuing to serve participants ethically. All that being said, it was worth it. In fact, it was infinitely and beautifully worth it! Seizing on that impulse to make my own teaching the subject of ideology critique offered participants an access point to learning that I would not otherwise have been able to make available. I believe the key to using this strategy is continuous self-reflection on the part of the teacher, a commitment to honesty, and a commitment to evolving antiracist education. And I believe that if we as teachers are willing to take this on and teach ethically from our mistakes, we can effectively progress antiracist education in exciting, innovative, and excruciatingly necessary ways.

References

Bleich, D. (1995). Collaboration and the pedagogy of disclosure. *College English* 57 (1): 43–61.

Brookfield, S.D. (2012). *Teaching for Critical Thinking: Tools and Techniques to Help Students Question Their Assumptions.* San Francisco, CA: Jossey-Bass.

Cayanus, J.L. (2004). Effective instructional practice: Using teacher self-disclosure as an instructional tool. *Communication Teacher* 18 (1): 6–9.

Cayanus, J.L. and Martin, M.M. (2008). Teacher self-disclosure: Amount, relevance, and negativity. *Communication Quarterly* 56 (3): 325–341.

Conklin, H.G. (2008). Modeling compassion in critical, justice-oriented teacher education. *Harvard Educational Review* 78 (4): 652–674.

Cozby, P.C. (1973). Self-disclosure: A literature review. *Psychological Bulletin* 79 (2): 73–91.

Crenshaw, K.W. (1989). Demarginalizing the intersection of race and sex: A black feminist critique of antidiscrimination doctrine, feminist theory, and antiracist politics. *University of Chicago Legal Forum* 1989 (1): 139–167.

Cunliffe, A.L. (2004). On becoming a critically reflexive practitioner. *Journal of Management Education* 28 (4): 407–426.

Ejsing, A. (2007). Power and caution: The ethics of self-disclosure. *Teaching Theology and Religion* 10 (4): 235–243.

Ellsworth, E. (1989). Why doesn't this feel empowering? Working through the repressive myths of critical pedagogy. *Harvard Educational Review* 59 (3): 297–325.

Frankenberg, R. (ed.) (1999). *Displacing Whiteness: Essays in Social and Cultural Criticism*. Durham, NC: Duke University Press.

Gay, G. and Kirkland, K. (2003). Developing cultural critical consciousness and self-reflection in preservice teacher education. *Theory Into Practice* 42 (3): 181–187.

Hochstetler, S. (2013). A teacher's terminal illness in the secondary English classroom: The effects of disclosure. *Journal of the Assembly for Expanded Perspectives on Learning* 19 (Winter): 38–48.

hooks, b. (1994). *Teaching to Transgress: Education as the Practice of Freedom*. New York, NY: Routledge.

Howard, T.C. (2003). Culturally relevant pedagogy: Ingredients for critical teacher reflection. *Theory Into Practice* 42 (3): 195–202.

Hulko, W. (2009). The time- and context-contingent nature of intersectionality and interlocking oppressions. *Journal of Women and Social Work* 24 (1): 44–55.

Husband, T., Jr. (2010). He's too young to learn about that stuff: Anti-racist pedagogy and early childhood social studies. *Social Studies Research and Practice* 5 (2): 60–75.

Kashtan, M. (2005). The gift of self: The art of transparent facilitation. In: *The IAF Handbook of Group Facilitation: Best Practices from the Leading Organization in Facilitation* (ed. S. Schuman), 573–590. San Francisco, CA: Jossey-Bass.

Kelley, M.M. (2009). The grace of teaching mistakes. *Journal of Spirituality in Mental Health* 11 (4): 282–289.

Lannutti, P.J. and Strauman, E.C. (2006). Classroom communication: The influence of instructor self-disclosure on student evaluations. *Communication Quarterly* 54 (1): 89–99.

McIntosh, P. (1988). White privilege: Unpacking the invisible knapsack. *Peace and Freedom Magazine* (July/August): 10–12.

Pyle, N. (2014). This teacher taught his class a powerful lesson about privilege (21 November). https://www.buzzfeed.com/nathanwpyle/this-teacher-taught-his-class-a-powerful-lesson-about-privil?utm_term=.ueGZw8oMqV#.sfXvM625gn (accessed 1 June 2018).

Sandoval, C. (1999). Theorizing white consciousness for a post-empire world: Barthes, Fanon, and the rhetoric of love. In: *Displacing Whiteness: Essays in Social and Cultural Criticism* (ed. R. Frankenberg) 86–106. Durham, NC: Duke University Press.

Sefa Dei, G. (1993). The challenges of anti-racist education in Canada. *Canadian Ethnic Studies* 25 (2): 36–51.

St. Denis, V. (2007). Aboriginal education and anti-racist education: Building alliances across cultural and racial identity. *Canadian Journal of Education* 30 (4): 1068–1092.

Timmins, F. (2006). Critical practice in nursing care: Analysis, action and reflexivity. *Nursing Standard* 20 (39): 49–54.

Tobin, L. (2010). Self-disclosure as a strategic teaching tool: What I do – and don't – tell my students. *College English* 73 (2): 196–206.

Weimer, M. (2013). *Learner-centered Teaching: Five Key Changes to Practice*, 2nd ed. San Francisco, CA: Jossey-Bass.

Yancy, G. (2004). *What White Looks Like: African-American Philosophers on the Whiteness Question*. New York, NY: Routledge.

15

Avoiding Traps and Misconceptions in Teaching Race

Stephen D. Brookfield

Making mistakes (as Bobbi Smith describes in Chapter 14) is inevitable in teaching race. Once the ontological realization takes hold that doing this work means you'll usually feel as if you've got things wrong, the question then becomes "So how do we fail well?" Failing well is an idea attributed to Samuel Beckett's novella *Worstward Ho* (1983), an extended meditation on the fact that nothing works in life: Our attempts to know each other fail, our efforts to communicate fail, and our search for love fails. In contemporary leadership, economic, and entrepreneurship circles, the notion of failing well has taken on a much more inspirational patina and you can buy plaques highlighting Beckett's words to hang in your office. Here the message is that individuals and organizations progress by learning from their errors, thus sharpening their competitive edge in the global economy. I often wonder how Beckett would react if he rose from his grave and showed up at a corporate retreat center to see executives being given plaques inscribed with his words.

As you might anticipate, I react strongly against such superficial rhetoric and would never dream of having an inspirational plaque on my wall (though to be fair, I do have a poster with a

Teaching Race: How to Help Students Unmask and Challenge Racism, First Edition. Stephen D. Brookfield and Associates.

quote from Paul Robeson on my office door, so maybe I should drop my pose of enlightened, smug superiority). But I also try to avoid being mired in Beckett's existential bleakness, which is hard given that I suffer from clinical depression and anxiety. I do believe we can learn from our mistakes in antiracist teaching, but not in the sense that, once studied, they can be eliminated. Instead, I see a major part of pedagogic learning as accepting failure's necessary inevitability. Yes, I will always fail in this work, always make basic errors, and always feel like an impostor. But I can learn to keep going in the face of this demoralization and not be frozen in self-loathing and second-guessing myself. I can get better at noticing the cues alerting me to the rookie errors I'm about to commit and maybe keep them in check. And, when I do make the inevitable mistakes described in this chapter, I can be quicker to point these out and limit their worst effects. Overall, I can learn to normalize failure and see it as the essential accompaniment of this work.

In this chapter I want to highlight eight of the most common misunderstandings and missteps that I see highlighted in my own teaching practice and that of other white colleagues. For each error I try to alert readers to the cues signaling that the error is about to happen. I also talk about how to conduct damage limitation, so that the conversation is not completely derailed by the error in question.

I Can Control What Happens

If there's one thing I've learned about teaching, it's that I have far less control over classroom events than I assume. Yet the concept of teachers being able to control learning undergirds pretty much all notions of effective pedagogy. Being effective is interpreted as guiding students toward predetermined learning outcomes with the resultant improvement in knowledge and skills being measured by some kind of assessment protocol. Behind this organizational practice is the Enlightenment notion that engineering control over one's environment is possible.

Yet every time I initiate a class discussion, try out a new activity, or make any attempt to get students to think critically about race, I know that what happens next is unpredictable. And the more I use classroom response systems to find out what students are thinking, the more I realize that I often have no idea at all about their inner mental landscapes. I remember co-presenting a session one afternoon in London recently and asking the audience members what they needed to happen next for us to be able to move in a more critical direction. The TodaysMeet feed immediately lit up with comments essentially saying, "Tea PLEASE!" Here I was thinking that participants' minds were dealing with the intricacies of criticality, when in fact they were focused on beverages.

When I move into analyzing a contentious issue such as racism I know I'm entering an essentially chaotic universe. So-called hot topics (Nash, Bradley, and Chickering, 2008) hit raw spots and generate strong emotional responses. The one thing I can pretty much depend on is that very quickly I'll start to feel that I'm losing control. Views will be expressed and words spoken that will either offend or inspire, and the conversation will take turns that I can't possibly anticipate. When I start to feel that I'm losing control, I know I'll hear an internal voice screaming, "Get things back on track!" If I invariably heed that scream, I am robbed of one of the greatest pleasures of teaching – the so-called teachable moment. Such moments are ones full of rich surprise. Regarding them as unfortunate aberrations to be shortened or avoided entirely means that you will lose the chance to enjoy unexpected opportunities to help your students grow.

Having your exercise of classroom control questioned can also be very interesting. When students challenge me on my perceived racism, my lack of wokeness, or what seems to them to be arbitrary or unfair behavior by me, it is inherently destabilizing. But that destabilization can be productively insurrectional. If I respond to every student challenge by cutting it off or stamping it down then not only do I dismiss the legitimacy of student criticisms, I also lose the chance to learn. Of course, how I respond to critique is crucial:

Explaining that my comments or actions weren't *really* racist is a sure way to destroy my credibility. On the other hand, saying that my actions are only being seen as racist or sexist because I didn't explain them clearly enough lets me off the hook and presents my white supremacy as simply a problem of communication. This defense mechanism implicitly blames the audience for not being sophisticated enough to understand what was really going on.

I Need to Stay Calm

Staying calm is a central tenet of white epistemology. In Eurocentric Enlightenment thought, calmness represents the triumph of logic and reason over emotion. If you are calm you are presumed to be able to exercise clear judgment and make objective decisions. If you are emotional, however, you are assumed to lose the capacity for rational thought, the result of which will be making poor decisions based on impulses, instincts, and feelings. I was brought up in England, where the cultural approval of calmness was very strong. My childhood was one in which I learned not to grumble at misfortune but to keep calm and carry on.

I have internalized patriarchy's emphasis on men as rational decision-makers to the extent that I still hear myself saying to my wife, "When you've calmed down a bit, then we can talk about this." My wife also tells me that I take great pride in never showing anger and often asks me, "What's so bad about being angry?" Of course she also tells me that rage is a defining characteristic of my personality, so you can see I'm one conflicted puppy.

This overwhelming need to always exhibit calm was drummed into me by mentors and during my graduate study. I felt that teachers who were professionals never showed surprise and always communicated the sense that they had planned for every eventuality. If an activity went completely awry, initially I would try to imply that this was how I'd intended things to go. After about 15 years of teaching, I started to question my axiomatic commitment to calmness and started to show strong emotions. The first time I cried in class was a pretty significant event for me, and it emboldened me to start owning up to how I was feeling during emotionally fraught sessions.

There are many fraught moments in race-based teaching. Students will say something so breathtakingly racist that you're momentarily stunned. At other times open hostility is expressed, as students insult each other or call you a racist. Things become raw, and unfiltered racism shatters the bourgeois decorum that hooks (1994) identifies as the norm in higher education. People cry, squirm in discomfort, and shout out in pain and anger. Alternatively, there's a heavy pall of extremely awkward silence hanging over the room.

As Lucia Pawlowski shows in Chapter 4, students can be warned that emotionally charged exchanges are normal responses to examining race and not aberrations. Whenever naked emotions are expressed, people will typically look to you, as the teacher, to take charge. I like to express my own reactions out loud. If a student shocks me with a comment, I'll say, "That really took me off guard and I'm not sure how to react. Give me a moment." Then I'll give whatever reaction seems appropriate. When deep anger is expressed I'll talk about my own reactions to it, and that I have to fight against my own tendency to either try to calm things down or to rush to a quick break so that we can compose ourselves.

However, when students berate or insult each other I can't just let it go as some kind of honest and authentic expression of pain. I have to think of the collective learning I'm trying to foster. If people are walking out because they are incensed by someone else's treatment of them, then the conversation stops dead in its tracks. In this situation I have to point out to the insulter how harsh and violent his/her/their words sounded and to ask those insulted to talk about how they are feeling. When angry participants say I'm racist or trying to shut them down, I try to point out how much airtime they've taken and ask for other voices to be heard. I express out loud to the group my internal processing of events and say how much I dislike these kinds of antagonistic situations, but also say that I recognize that they are often necessary and that I'm trying to find my way through this one so that we don't shut down and retreat to our racialized silos or bubbles.

I Must Fix Racism and Transform My Students

People go into antiracist work with activist hearts. They want to move students to an understanding of racism so that these students can go on to combat it at every opportunity. If you're a teacher on an antiracist mission, you'll want to see dramatic and profound changes in your students. There'll be a transformative imperative that drives you in your quest to fix racism.

It's easy for teachers to overestimate their influence. We're used to thinking of our classrooms as fiefdoms over which we have total control. But although we may exercise political and institutional authority over students, particularly with respect to the authority of grading, the influence we have over cognitive development is much more tenuous. Measuring your effectiveness as a teacher by the degree to which you wreak dramatic transformations in students' worldviews will set you on a path of constant disappointment. This is particularly the case if you teach courses that are part of an institutionally mandated diversity requirement.

When teaching race you should start from a working expectation of hostility, fear, and apathy. Hostility will come from students who feel that learning about race requires some kind of racial remediation. Fear will come from students who either don't trust the teacher's ability to lead them into difficult terrain or who feel so inexperienced in this area that they will be bound to say or do the wrong thing. Apathy will be evident in students who feel that race is a lot of fuss about nothing, because we now live in a post-racial world in which the evils of slavery and colonialism are purely historical curiosities. Try to remember that in working with students' learned racism you are facing a long and powerful history of ideological manipulation that's reinforced and sustained on a daily basis by institutional structures, organizational practices, and media. To expect transformation in the face of all this is pretty crazy. To keep people in conversation is itself a remarkable accomplishment, so if you're doing that you should view your practice with pride.

I've Finally Escaped Racism

In Helms's (1993) much-quoted model of white racial identity development, the final stage is that of autonomy. This is when whites experience racial self-actualization, actively challenge racism, and no longer see other racial identities as a threat. Helms herself warns against the sequencing of neat stages in her model and asks that people remember that the model is meant as a possibly helpful heuristic, not as some kind of empirical rendering of reality. Yet it's part of modernist consciousness to look for progress in life, and antiracist educators such as myself are no different from anyone else in that regard. I like to trace a developmental trajectory in my racial awareness from my early color-blind worldview to one in which I frame much of what I experience through the lens of race. This is seductive. It gives my life purpose and allows me to congratulate myself on my movement forward. This is a big mistake. Once whites like me start to think of their racial journey as over, danger signs should start to flash.

None of us like to think of ourselves as racist, particularly teachers seeking to combat its existence. The "I'm not racist anymore" perspective holds that whether or not white people choose to be racist is down to the moral strength or militant Christianity they display in fighting the system's efforts to induct them into white supremacy. This puts us right back into the individualist paradigm in which race is seen a matter of personal choice. Comments such as "Let's leave race out of this for a moment" and "Let's put questions of race aside" are actually expressions of supremacy and privilege because they are options available only to whites. One of my earliest and most enduring lessons in race was when a colleague of color told me, "For us, *everything* is race." So assume that race permeates every interaction for students and colleagues of color – how they view their self-identities, how they name themselves, what they consider to be moral or respectful behavior, how they define a good discussion or a good teacher, and so on. Thinking you can decide when to switch the racial perspective on or off reduces race to a matter of individual choice that can be exercised on a situation-by-situation basis.

As a white teacher you should never profess your freedom from racism. You can't escape complicity in racism because you constantly benefit from racist structures. You can choose to fight racist instincts and impulses in yourself and others, but you can't decide not to be a part of racism. If racism is a structural reality that's bolstered by dominant ideology, then all whites have learned all kinds of racist stereotypes at an instinctual level. This is what Raymond Williams (1977) analyzed as the structures of feeling, the emotional responses and gut instincts taught and reinforced in institutions and practices. Just acknowledge your own collusion in racism and explain how it moves in you. Try to get in the habit of mentioning (in a matter-of-fact way, not as a dramatic confession) that since you live a racist society in which white supremacy is a dominant ideology, this means that you, like other whites, have racism embedded in you.

I Understand Your Pain

I often find myself in groups in which we get to the "I understand your pain" point. This is when well-meaning and completely sincere whites try to draw an analogy between their experiences of oppression, disenfranchisement, being ignored, and feeling voiceless, and the experience of being on the receiving end of lifelong racism. People will say that their working-class backgrounds, their disabilities, or their genders mean that they are uniquely positioned to empathize with racism. If a group has been together a long time and some level of trust has developed, there may be a gentle reminder that people should be wary of making generalizations unless they've walked in another's shoes. But much more typically, these kinds of comments detonate a conversational bomb and in 60 seconds the room zooms from a state of relative calm to expressions of frustration and anger as we move quickly into the oppression Olympics.

When you bear witness to a deeply felt statement of racial pain and hurt by a person of color it is incumbent on you to sit with it and encourage others to do the same. Don't analyze it immediately or start comparing it to the kinds of pain you've experienced. Sometimes after a profound voicing of emotion I'll ask students not to say anything for a minute or so, and then I'll ask them to post what they are feeling and thinking on the TodaysMeet feed. If I want to respond I'll usually say something to this effect:

> I know that what you just shared took a lot and was very emotional for you. So thank you for being willing to put yourself out there and create a window for us into the daily workings of racism. I know there's no way I can ever have any real awareness of what you've experienced, so I won't even try to compare it to things that have happened to me. But knowing how you're affected by these kinds of racist acts is helpful for the rest of us in thinking through and strategizing how we might act if we find ourselves involved in a situation like this.

As a white teacher you should never suggest you understand how it feels to be the victim of racism. Saying you can understand something of what people of color experience because you're from the working class, have suffered under patriarchy, are disabled, have experienced religious discrimination, or something similar will come across as naïve and condescending. You lose credibility in an instant.

Please Confess Your Racism

A couple of years ago I was having dinner with a good female friend who had spent a career of 40 years engaged in literacy work in Harlem and Washington Heights in New York. She is white, and her students, who overwhelmingly were people of color, loved her for her humor, spirit, and warmth, but mostly for her tireless advocacy on their behalf. She wouldn't put up with any bullshit, and woe betide any administrator who created a bureaucratic obstacle that blocked her students' learning.

Over dinner she told me that she had recently been to a workshop on racism, and that the first thing the workshop facilitators did was to ask every white person in the room to stand up and take turns saying "I am a racist." As she recounted this event her voice shook with anger. She couldn't believe that her four decades of antiracist endeavors had just been discounted by these facilitator-strangers, who clearly didn't know anything about her. I'm guessing that the intent of the workshop's organizers was to convey the message that we are all implicated in a racist system and that we have all learned racist instincts and impulses. But my friend was so profoundly insulted that she left the workshop immediately.

Likewise, I was running a group discussion a couple of years ago and we got talking about microaggressions. I gave some examples of my own commission of these, and a white man protested that I was obsessed with race and reading all kinds of unwarranted intentions into what were in fact innocent behaviors. In the same way that Lisa Merriweather pointed out (in Chapter 7) to her Marine Corps student that he was missing the point and disregarding the pervasiveness of racism, I kept insisting that my white, male group member was unaware of how he was in fact perpetuating racism. Eventually he got so frustrated that he shouted out in frustration, "I can't say anything without it seeming racist, so I'm not going to say else anything at all."

These two instances illustrate what Foucault (1980) called *confessional practices*. The central dynamic of each of these situations was that of the confessional: Admit the error of your ways, and I, the racially cognizant expert, will grant you absolution. In courses dealing with race I see the same imperative informing how students write reflective journals summarizing their learning. They pick up the message that a journal for a course designed to engineer transformative learning about race should document significant aha moments, when the blinders of white supremacy fall away to reveal the full extent of students' collusion in racism.

This is an implicitly coercive stance. I send the message that I expect students to confess their racism, to bring their dark secret out of the shadows into the light of day and to reveal the dirty stain on their characters. This sets up a dualistic relationship of power: On one side there's an educator with an evolved understanding of racism, on the other is the naïve, ideologically blinkered student. My New York colleague who had spent four decades working against racism felt pigeonholed exactly this way in the antiracist workshop I mentioned earlier. It's true that in many situations you as a teacher or leader will be further along the journey of uncovering your own racism than many of the participants. But it's a fatal error to come across as the fully formed expert there to preach to the unenlightened masses. In their two-decade exploration of the dynamics of white supremacy, the European-American Collaborative Challenging Whiteness (ECCW; 2010) has identified disdaining and preaching to one's supposedly less-sophisticated colleagues as some of the most frequent traps that white antiracist educators fall into.

I recognize these dangers in my own practice. It's so easy for me to adopt a proselytizing mode that communicates to students or colleagues that I feel they don't realize how much racism has got its hooks into them, how many racial microaggressions they commit, and how unaware they are of their own unawareness. Coming across as an enlightened, so-called good white person (Sullivan, 2014) who has a more developed state of racial consciousness makes other white students and colleagues mistrustful and resentful of my self-assumed superiority. This is why modeling your own continuing struggle with racist instincts is so important (Brookfield, 2014). It really should be a mantra for white-on-white race work that those in leadership roles must begin by disclosing how racism lives within them and by giving plenty of current examples of microaggressions that they have enacted and racist practices that they have left unchallenged. They should talk about what they do when they catch themselves in the middle of these moments, and say that, despite their flaws, they keep trying to work in antiracist ways. As most of the authors in this book acknowledge, modeling your own engagement with understanding and combatting racism is the sine qua non for building trustful environments and brave spaces.

I Mustn't Dominate, so I'll Stay Silent

In their explication of critical humility, the ECCW (2010) identifies a white behavior they call *withholding*. This is something I've witnessed many times and is one I am particularly prone to myself. As with so many antiracist practices, this comes from a good place. Whites like me say to themselves, "Our voices are way too dominant in society and we need to privilege the voices of people of color. So the best thing we can do is shut up." After all, the ideology of white supremacy is everywhere, white epistemology and white forms of knowledge production are dominant, and whites are used to telling everyone else what to do and think. So it appears to be entirely democratic, respectful, and humane for white people like me to stay silent in multiracial groups so that the participants of color can claim their voices. This inclination is theoretically further supported by critical race theory's advocacy of counterstorytelling.

But staying silent is problematic in many ways. First, it can come from an unacknowledged position of white supremacy. This happens when white participants assume that their voices are so strong, confident, and articulate that asserting them will inevitably overpower the fledgling voices struggling to emerge from participants of color. This is condescending and patronizing, a deficit model of what multiracial dialogue sounds like. The implicit judgment is that whites' voices are so inherently superior that hearing them will cause all other contributions to pale into insignificance.

Second, whites' silence can be taken as signaling lack of interest. I remember a woman of color asking me in the early 1980s,

"Why don't you ever say anything when I speak up? You never respond to my comments." Apparently I had done nothing other than nod encouragingly when she was talking. I had interpreted that as being supportive and respectful. She had viewed it as puzzling at best, and had been left wondering exactly what I was thinking. To her it seemed as if I viewed her comments as not being worthy of some sort of response. In a way, my silence was a white power play that for her reinscribed the dynamic of white supremacy.

Third, making any substantive changes to racial equity in this country will require the development of multiracial movements and organizations. Current political parties will need to be remade, new parties will need to emerge, social movements will need to flourish, and broad coalitions and alliances will have to be built. This means that whites will need to be involved. Developing rainbow coalitions to change policies, structures, and media representations will involve whites showing, through their speech, that they are taking people of color seriously. But if you're not used to saying something in response to comments from colleagues of color, then building any kind of collective momentum is going to be seriously impaired.

Finally, I often hear white students, friends, and colleagues say, "I don't know anything about race, so I really don't have anything to contribute to the conversation." What they mean is that because they have never experienced the daily grind of racism – having their ability constantly questioned, their authority second-guessed, being followed in stores, being assumed to be the administrative assistant rather than the dean, being pulled over regularly while driving – they can't speak with any authentic voice on race. What I usually say in response to this is something like the following:

> Okay, I understand that you're not the recipient of the
> daily assault of racism, but that doesn't mean to say you
> don't have anything to contribute. After all, you are an
> expert on white supremacy. You know a lot about how

that gets disseminated as a so-called natural or common-sense view of the world. You know about the way that having little contact with people of color allows racist stereotypes to endure. You know the kinds of racial jokes made in whites-only rooms. You know how hard it is to challenge your family and friends when they speak in racist stereotypes. So your job is to teach the rest of us how white supremacy is learned and why it endures.

I'm Your Ally

The final error I want to identify is that of declaring to people of color that you are their ally. The reasons for doing this are, of course, completely understandable. You want to let people of color know that not all whites are their enemies and that they can count on some of us for support. Since white involvement in antiracist coalitions is necessary for all the reasons mentioned earlier, you want to show that this is a real possibility. You probably also want to make the stressful, difficult, and dangerous work of pushing back on racism seem a little more hopeful.

But I think there are less admirable motives behind the "I'm your ally" declaration. Speaking for myself, I know that part of me desperately wants the approval of people of color. I want to be told I'm one of the good guys and that I'm exempted from blanket condemnations of white racism. I also want to feel a flush of self-aggrandizing, self-congratulatory pleasure at saying to myself, "You know what, I *am* a good person. My mother was right." This is one of the internal seductions I fight hardest to resist, but I know that I fail in that. Colleagues of color detect my need for reassuring approval and will tell me not to get so hung up on how *I'm* feeling, because, after all, it's not really about me, is it? I take deeply to heart George Yancy's (2018) admonition that "whatever you do, please don't seek recognition for how sorry you feel" (p. 118) but to "let your mourning move you to action, to fight for a world in which whiteness, your whiteness, ceases to violate me, Black people, and people of color" (p. 118).

One of the most crushing things for me to experience is to be called a racist. I try to work with sensitivity and goodwill, but inevitably my learned racism will show. As a white person and a representative (in the eyes of students of color) of white supremacy, I must expect to be mistrusted and not let that stop me. I must also expect white colleagues to accuse me of politically correct reverse racism. When this happens, I need to remember that this is not a sign that somehow I'm failing. It comes to every white person in this work. So I try to tell colleagues getting involved in antiracist teaching or other activism for the first time to prepare themselves for being called racist. It comes with the territory.

I remember teaching a class in the early 1990s in which the only student of color declared, "I will never trust a white person". My immediate response was to say, "That's completely understandable, I don't see why you would." But the white majority in the group was shocked and demoralized by his comment and spent a lot of time and energy trying to convince him that they were different – more enlightened and worthy of his trust. It has always seemed to be that a completely valid, well-founded suspicion, skepticism, and hostility will inevitably accompany any white person's attempt to work alongside people of color in antiracist efforts. This is no comment on you personally; rather, it's a comment on the history of how white supremacy has conditioned people of color to expect whites to always pursue their own self-interest and bolster their own power. This is why critical race theory's tenet of interest convergence holds that substantial racial improvement only happens when it benefits whites (Delgado and Stefancic, 2012).

The judgment of whether or not you are an ally to people of color is completely in their hands. You should never expect to be told that you are, and you shouldn't get hung up on gauging your success by whether or not you receive that designation. Of course, if you do hear that term applied to you by colleagues or students of color you should take it as a sincere recognition that you're doing something important and worthwhile. And, for a moment, it's fine to be proud of yourself. We all need moments of recognition and affirmation to keep our energy up for the tough stuff.

But repeat after me: *Never declare yourself an ally.* No matter how strongly you are committed to that identity, keep it private. A white person who says "I'm your ally" to a person of color comes across as condescending and inauthentic. You don't become an ally by saying that's what you are. You become an ally by consistently showing up in support of people of color. You become an ally by losing something. Instead of worrying about getting approval for being antiracist, you should be putting yourself on the line. It's your job to risk institutional condemnation by doing and saying the things that people of color will suffer even more harshly for doing and saying. Your job is to lose friends, colleagues, money, employment, perks, and prestige by calling out white supremacy in yourself and other whites, and then to not have anyone notice or thank you for it.

References

Beckett, S. (1983). *Worstward Ho.* New York, NY: Grove.

Brookfield, S. (2014). Teaching our own racism: Incorporating personal narratives of whiteness into anti-racist practice. *Adult Learning* 25 (3): 89–95.

Delgado, R. and Stefancic, J. (2012). *Critical Race Theory: An Introduction*, 2nd ed. New York, NY: NYU Press.

European-American Collaborative Challenging Whiteness (2010). White on white: Developing capacity to communicate about race with critical humility. In: *Handbook of Race and Adult Education: A Resource for Dialogue on Racism* (ed. V. Sheared, J. Johnson-Bailey, S.A.J. Colin III, E. Peterson, and S.D. Brookfield, 145–157). San Francisco, CA: Jossey-Bass.

Foucault, M. (1980). *Power/Knowledge: Selected Interviews and Other Writings, 1972–1977.* New York, NY: Pantheon Books.

Helms, J.E. (1993). *Black and White Racial Identity: Theory, Research, and Practice.* Westport, CT: Praeger.

hooks, b. (1994). *Teaching to Transgress: Education as the Practice of Freedom.* New York, NY: Routledge.

Nash, R.J., Bradley, D.L., and Chickering, A.W. (2008). *How to Talk About Hot Topics on Campus: From Polarization to Moral Conversation.* San Francisco, CA: Jossey-Bass.

Sullivan, S. (2014). *Good White People: The Problem with Middle-Class White Anti-Racism*. Albany, NY: State University of New York Press.

Williams, R. (1977). *Marxism and Literature*. New York, NY: Oxford University Press.

Yancy, G. (2018). *Backlash: What Happens When We Talk Honestly About Racism in America*. Lanham, MD: Rowman & Littlefield.

Bibliography

Adams, H. and Hurtig, J. (2002). Creative acts, critical insights: Adult writing workshops in two Chicago neighborhoods. In: *Community Partnerships* (ed. E. Auerbach), 147–158. Alexandria, VA: Teachers of English to Speakers of Other Languages.

Ahmed, S. (2014). *The Cultural Politics of Emotion*. Edinburgh: Edinburgh University Press.

Alexander, M. (2012). *The New Jim Crow: Mass Incarceration in the Age of Colorblindness*. New York, NY: New Press.

Allen, T.W. (2012). *The Invention of the White Race*, 2nd ed. London: Verso.

Ambrose, S.A., Bridges, M.W., Di Pietro, M. et al. (2010). *How Learning Works: Seven Research Based Principles for Smart Teaching*. San Francisco, CA: Jossey-Bass.

Antonio, A., Change, M., Hakuta, K. et al. (2004). Effects of racial diversity on complex thinking in college students. *Psychological Science* 15 (8): 507–510.

Anyon, J. (1980). Social class and the hidden curriculum of work. *Journal of Education* 162 (1): 67–92. doi:10.1177/002205748016200106.

Anzaldúa, G. (1987). *Borderlands/La Frontera: The New Mestiza*. San Francisco, CA: Aunt Lute Books.

Applebaum, B. (2010). *Being White, Being Good: White Complicity, White Moral Responsibility, and Social Justice Pedagogy*. Lanham, MD: Lexington Books.

Arao, B. and Clemens, K. (2013). From safe spaces to brave spaces: A new way to frame dialogue around diversity and social justice. In: *The Art of Effective Facilitation: Reflections from Social Justice Educators* (ed. L. Landreman), 135–150. Sterling, VA: Stylus.

Aspen Institute (n.d.). Glossary for understanding the dismantling structural racism/promoting racial equity analysis. https://assets.aspeninstitute.org/content/uploads/files/content/docs/rcc/RCC-Structural-Racism-Glossary.pdf (accessed 6 September 2017).

Astin, A. (1993). Diversity and multiculturalism on campus: How are students affected? *Change* 25 (2): 44–49.

Ávila, J. and Pandya, J. (eds.) (2013). *Critical Digital Literacies as Social Praxis: Intersections and Challenges*. New York, NY: Peter Lang.

Baines, S. (2013). Music therapy as an anti-oppressive practice. *The Arts in Psychotherapy* 40: 1–5.

Barnett, P. (2011). Discussions across difference: Addressing the affective dimensions of teaching diverse students about diversity. *Teaching in Higher Education* 16 (6): 669–679.

Barry, P. and O'Callaghan, C. (2008). Reflexive journal writing: A tool for music therapy student clinical practice development. *Nordic Journal of Music Therapy* 17 (1): 55–66.

Beckett, S. (1983). *Worstward Ho*. New York, NY: Grove Press.

Bell, D.A. (1992). *Faces at the Bottom of the Well: The Permanence of Racism*. New York, NY: Basic Books.

Bell, L.A. (2010). *Storytelling for Social Justice: Connecting Narrative and the Arts in Antiracist Teaching*. New York, NY: Routledge.

Bell, L.A., Roberts, R.A., Irani, K. et al. (2008). *The Storytelling Project Curriculum: Learning About Race and Racism Through Storytelling and the Arts.* Barnard College Storytelling Project. www.racialequitytools.org/resourcefiles/stp_curriculum.pdf (accessed 21 January 2017).

Berger, D. (2017). Black genealogies of power: Seven maxims for resistance in the Trump years. *Black Perspectives* (28 February). www.aaihs.org/black-genealogies-of-power-seven-maxims-for-resistance-in-the-trump-years (accessed 1 June 2018).

Berry, W. (1989). *The Hidden Wound.* San Francisco, CA: North Point Press.

Bhopal, K. (2016). *The Experiences of Black and Minority Ethnic Academics: A Comparative Study of the Unequal Academy.* New York, NY: Routledge.

Black, D. (2016). Why I left white nationalism. *New York Times* (16 November). www.nytimes.com/2016/11/26/opinion/sunday/why-i-left-white-nationalism.html?_r=0 (accessed 6 September 6 2017).

Bleich, D. (1995). Collaboration and the pedagogy of disclosure. *College English* 57 (1): 43–61.

Boggs, G.L. (2012). *The Next American Revolution: Sustainable Activism for the Twenty-First Century,* rev. ed. Berkeley, CA: University of California Press.

Bohm, D. (1996). *On Dialogue.* London: Routledge.

Boler, M. (1999). *Feeling Power: Emotions and Education.* New York, NY: Routledge.

Bonilla-Silva, E. (1997). Rethinking racism: Toward a structural interpretation. *American Sociological Review* 62 (3): 465–480.

Boostrom, R. (1998). Safe spaces: Reflections on an educational metaphor. *Journal of Curriculum Studies* 30 (4): 397–408.

Boutte, G.S. and Hill, E.L. (2006). African American communities: Implications for culturally relevant teaching. *New Educator* 2 (4): 311–329.

Brookfield, S.D. (ed.) (1987). *Learning Democracy: Eduard Lindeman on Adult Education and Social Change.* Beckenham, Kent: Croom Helm.

Brookfield, S.D. (2005). *The Power of Critical Theory: Liberating Adult Learning and Teaching*. San Francisco, CA: Jossey-Bass.

Brookfield, S.D. (2012). *Teaching for Critical Thinking: Tools and Techniques to Help Students Question Their Assumptions*. San Francisco, CA: Jossey-Bass.

Brookfield, S.D. (2014). Teaching our own racism: Incorporating personal narratives of whiteness into anti-racist practice. *Adult Learning* 25 (3): 89–95.

Brookfield, S.D. (2015). *The Skillful Teacher: On Technique, Trust, and Responsiveness in the Classroom*, 3rd ed. San Francisco, CA: Jossey-Bass.

Brookfield, S.D. (2017). *Becoming a Critically Reflective Teacher*, 2nd ed. San Francisco, CA: Jossey-Bass.

Brookfield, S.D. and Preskill, S. (2005). *Discussion as a Way of Teaching: Tools and Techniques for Democratic Classrooms*. San Francisco: Jossey-Bass.

Brooks, D. (2017). The internal invasion. *New York Times* (20 January). www.nytimes.com/2017/01/20/opinion/the-internal-invasion.html (accessed 21 January 2017).

Brown, W. (1997). The impossibility of women's studies. *differences* 9 (3): 79–101.

Brown, W. (2015). *Undoing the Demos: Neoliberalism's Stealth Revolution*. Brooklyn, NY: Zone Books.

Bucholtz, Mary (1996). Black feminist theory and African-American women's linguistic practice. In: *Rethinking Language and Gender Research* (ed. V.L. Bergvall, J.M. Bing, and A.F. Freed), 267–290. New York, NY: Routledge.

Cale, G. and Huber, S. (2001). Teaching the oppressor to be silent: Conflicts in the "democratic" classroom. *Proceedings of the 21st annual Alliance/ACE Conference: The Changing Face Of Adult Learning*, Austin, TX (10–13 October 2001).

California Newsreel. (2003). Race literary quiz, http://www.newsreel.org/guides/race/quiz.htm (accessed 1 June 2018).

California Newsreel. (2003). *Race: The Power of an Illusion*. DVD, 3 episodes, 56 min. each, www.newsreel.org/nav/title/asp?tc=CN0149 (accessed 1 June 2018).

Campbell, H. (2011). Understanding the relationship between religion online and offline in a networked society. *Journal of the American Academy of Religion*. doi:10.1093/ jaarel/lfr074.

Carter, R.T. (2003). Becoming racially and culturally competent: The Racial-Cultural Counseling Laboratory. *Journal of Multicultural Counseling and Development* 31 (1): 20–30.

Cayanus, J.L. (2004). Effective instructional practice: Using teacher self-disclosure as an instructional tool. *Communication Teacher* 18 (1): 6–9.

Cayanus, J.L. and Martin, M.M. (2008). Teacher self-disclosure: Amount, relevance, and negativity. *Communication Quarterly* 56 (3): 325–341.

Chang, M., Astin, A., and Kim, D. (2004). Cross-racial interaction among undergraduates: Some consequences, causes, and patterns. *Research in Higher Education* 45 (5): 529–553.

Cisneros, S. (1987). *The House on Mango Street*. Bloomington, IN: Third Woman Press.

Coates, T-N. (2017). *Why Obama was different in "We Were Eight Years in Power" – extended interview*. Interview by Trevor Noah, *The Daily Show* (30 October). http://www.cc.com/video-clips/xio46b/the-daily-show-with-trevor-noah-ta-nehisi-coates---why-obama-was-different-in--we-were-eight-years-in-power---extended-interview (accessed 1 June 2018).

Cole, T. (2012). The white savior industrial complex. *The Atlantic* (21 March). www.theatlantic.com/international/archive/2012/03/the-white-savior-industrial-complex/254843 (accessed 13 April 2018).

Cole Robinson, C. and Clardy, P. (2010). *Tedious Journeys: Autoethnography by Women of Color in Academe*. New York, NY: Peter Lang.

Colin, S.A.J., III and Guy, T.A. (1998). An Africentric interpretive model of curriculum orientations for course development in graduate programs in adult education. *PAACE Journal of Lifelong Learning* 7: 43–55.

Collins, P.H. (1989). The social construction of black feminist thought. *Signs* 14 (4): 745–773.

Conklin, H.G. (2008). Modeling compassion in critical, justice-oriented teacher education. *Harvard Educational Review* 78 (4): 652–674.

Cook, K., Yamagashi, T., Cheshire, C. et al. (2005). Trust building via risk taking: A cross-societal experiment. *Social Psychology Quarterly* 68 (2): 121–142.

Cooper, B. (2014). In defense of black rage: Michael Brown, police, and the American Dream. *Salon* (12 August). https://urldefense.proofpoint.com/v2/url?u=http-3A__www.salon.com_2014_08_12_in-5Fdefense-5Fof-5Fblack-5Frage-5Fmichael-5Fbrown-5Fpolice-5Fand-5Fthe-5Famerican-5Fdream_&d=DwMFAg&c=tzSjEhL4u5XIh9GXWARTsBI31pp--h2kWBIadClLS_M&r=GOqrdkpfjAD2hewakGmp9myCJP68QhE-fStbECthctU&m=dCR1w-ju-vasn59vIAIQZXHo5UBNztVUd_oXhcdpPDs&s=3FeuiQSyL5qNc1PnQAkuurb-cyrvb9ADi4bzR9N9ZFM&e=http://www.salon.com/2014/08/12/in_defense_of_black_rage_michael_brown_police_and_the_american_dream (accessed 13 April 2018).

Cooper, B. (2017). *Beyond Respectability: The Intellectual Thought of Race Women.* Urbana, IL: University of Illinois Press.

Copp, M. and Kleinman, S. (2008). Practicing what we teach: Feminist strategies for teaching about sexism. *Feminist Teacher* 18 (2): 101–124.

Cozby, P.C. (1973). Self-disclosure: A literature review. *Psychological Bulletin* 79 (2): 73–91.

Crenshaw, K.W. (1989). Demarginalizing the intersection of race and sex: A black feminist critique of antidiscrimination doctrine, feminist theory, and antiracist politics. *University of Chicago Legal Forum* 1: 139–167.

Crenshaw, K.W. (1991). Mapping the margins: Intersectionality, identity politics, and violence against women of color. *Stanford Law Review* 43: 1241–1299.

Cunliffe, A.L. (2004). On becoming a critically reflexive practitioner. *Journal of Management Education* 28 (4): 407–426.

Czopp, A., Monteith, M., and Mark, A. (2006). Standing up for a change: Reducing bias through interpersonal confrontation. *Journal of Personality and Social Psychology* 90 (5): 784–803.

Dalton, H.L. (1995). Racial Healing: The Fear Between Blacks & Whites. New York, NY: Doubleday.

Davies, W. (2017). How statistics lost their power – and why we should fear what comes next. *The Guardian* (19 January). www.theguardian.com/politics/2017/jan/19/crisis-of-statistics-big-data-democracy (accessed 21 January 2017).

Davis, A.Y. (1990). *Women, Culture, and Politics*. New York, NY: Vintage Books.

Delgado, R. and Stefancic, J. (2012). *Critical Race Theory: An Introduction*, 2nd ed. New York, NY: NYU Press.

Dessel, A. and Rogge, M. (2008). Evaluation of intergroup dialogue: A review of the empirical literature. *Conflict Resolution Quarterly* 26 (2): 199–238.

DeTurk, S. (2006). The power of dialogue: Consequences of intergroup dialogue and their implications for agency and alliance building. *Communication Quarterly* 54 (1): 33–51.

DiAngelo, R. (2011). White fragility. *International Journal of Critical Pedagogy* 3 (3): 54–70.

Dorman, T. (2017). *An Afrocentric critique of race dialogues: The application of theory and practice in Africology*. PhD dissertation. Philadelphia, PA: Temple University.

Drescher, E. (2016). *Choosing Our Religion*. New York, NY: Oxford University Press.

Driver, T. (1998). *Liberating Rites: Understanding the Transformative Power of Ritual*. Boulder, CO: Westview Press.

Duffy, R.D., Blustein, D.L., Diemer, M.A. et al. (2016). The psychology of working theory. *Journal of Counseling Psychology* 63 (2): 127–148.

Dyson, M.E. (1996). *Race Rules: Navigating the Color Line*. New York, NY: Basic Books.

Dyson, M.E. (2016). *The Black Presidency: Barack Obama and the Politics of Race in America*. New York, NY: Houghton Mifflin.

Ejsing, A. (2007). Power and caution: The ethics of self-disclosure. *Teaching Theology and Religion* 10 (4): 235–243.

Ellsworth, E. (1989). Why doesn't this feel empowering? Working through the repressive myths of critical pedagogy. *Harvard Educational Review* 59 (3): 297–325

Estrada, F. (2015). The teaching alliance in multicultural counseling course education: A framework for examining and strengthening the student-instructor relationship. *International Journal of Advanced Counseling* 37: 233–247.

European-American Collaborative Challenging Whiteness (2010). White on white: Developing capacity to communicate about race with critical humility. In: *The Handbook of Race and Adult Education: A Resource for Dialogue on Racism* (ed. V. Sheared, J. Johnson-Bailey, S.A.J. Colin III, E. Peterson, and S.D. Brookfield). San Francisco, CA: Jossey-Bass.

Fanon, F. (2005). *The Wretched of the Earth* (trans. R. Philcox). New York, NY: Grove Press.

Feagin, J.R. (2013). *The White Racial Frame: Centuries of Racial Framing and Counter-Framing*, 2nd ed. New York, NY: Routledge.

Feagin, J.R. and Vera, H. (1995). *White Racism*. New York, NY: Routledge.

Fejes, A. (2016). The confessing academic and living the present otherwise: Appraisal interviews and logbooks in academia. *European Educational Research Journal* 15 (4): 395–409.

Fink, D. (2003). *Creating Significant Learning Experiences: An Integrated Approach to Designing College Courses*. San Francisco, CA: Jossey-Bass.

Foucault, M. (1980). *Power/Knowledge: Selected Interviews and Other Writings, 1972–1977*. New York: Pantheon Books.

Fox, C. (2007). From transaction to transformation: (En)Countering white heteronomativity in "safe spaces." *College English* 69 (5): 496–511.

Fox, H. (2009). *When Race Breaks Out: Conversations About Race and Racism in College Classrooms*. New York, NY: Peter Lang.

Frankenberg, R. (ed.) (1999). *Displacing Whiteness: Essays in Social and Cultural Criticism*. Durham, NC: Duke University Press.

Freire, P. (1976). *Education as the Practice of Freedom*. London: Writers and Readers Cooperative.

Freire, P. (2000). *Pedagogy of the Oppressed*, 30th Anniversary Edition. New York, NY: Continuum International (accessed 1 June 2018).

French, B.H., Adair, Z.R., and Cokley, K. (2015). As people of color formerly employed by Mizzou, we demand change. *Huffington Post* (17 November).

www.huffingtonpost.com/bryana-h-french-phd/people-of-color-employed-mizzou-demand-change_b_8584756.html (accessed 1 June 2018).

Galtung, J. (1969). Violence, peace and peace research. *Journal of Peace Research* 6: 171.

Galtung, J. (1990). Cultural violence. *Journal of Peace Research* 27 (3): 291–305.

Galtung, J. (1996). *Peace by Peaceful Means: Peace and Conflict, Development and Civilization*. London: SAGE.

Gandbhir, G. and Foster, B. (2015). *A Conversation with My Black Son*. New York Times Op-Docs (17 March). https://www.nytimes.com/2015/03/17/opinion/a-conversation-with-my-black-son.html (accessed 6 February 2018).

Gay, G. (2010). *Culturally Responsive Teaching: Theory, Research, and Practice*, 2nd ed. New York, NY: Teachers College Press.

Gay, G. and Kirkland, K. (2003). Developing cultural critical consciousness and self-reflection in preservice teacher education. *Theory Into Practice* 42 (3): 181–187.

Glaude, E.S., Jr. (2016). *Democracy in Black: How Race Still Enslaves the American Soul*. New York, NY: Crown.

Grande, S. (2004). *Red Pedagogy*. New York, NY: Rowman & Littlefield.

Gurin, P., Dey, E., Hurtado, S. et al. (2002). Diversity in higher education: Theory and impact on student outcomes. *Harvard Educational Review* 72 (3): 330–366.

Gurin, P., Nagda, B., and Lopez, G. (2004). The benefits of diversity in education for democratic citizenship. *Journal of Social Issues* 60 (1): 17–34.

Hadley, S. (2013). *Experiencing Race as a Music Therapist: Personal Narratives*. Gilsum, NH: Barcelona Publishers.

Hagarty, S. (dir.). (2012). *Dakota 38* (film). Smooth Feather Productions, https://www.youtube.com/watch?v=1pX6FBSUyQI (accessed 1 June 2018).

Hannah-Jones, N. (2016). The end of the postracial myth. *New York Times Magazine* (15 November). www.nytimes.com/interactive/2016/11/20/magazine/donald-trumps-america-iowa-race.html?mcubz=3 (accessed 1 June 2018).

Hardy, K.L. and Bobes, T. (2016). *Culturally Sensitive Supervision and Training: Diverse Perspectives and Practical Applications.* New York, NY: Routledge.

Helms, J.E. (1993). *Black and White Racial Identity: Theory, Research, and Practice.* Westport, CT: Praeger.

Henry, A. (1993–1994). There are no safe places: Pedagogy as powerful and _dangerous terrain. *Action in Teacher Education* 15 (4): 1–4.

Hess, M. (1998). White religious educators and unlearning racism: Can we find a way? *Religious Education* 93 (1): 114–129.

Hess, M. (2016). White religious educators resisting white fragility: Lessons from mystics. *Religious Education* 112: 46–57. doi:10.1080/00344087.2016.1253124.

Hill Collins, P. and Bilge, S. (2016). *Intersectionality.* Malden, MA: Polity.

Hochstetler, S. (2013). A teacher's terminal illness in the secondary English classroom: The effects of disclosure. *Journal of the Assembly for Expanded Perspectives on Learning* 19 (Winter): 38–48.

Holland, D., Lachicotte, W. Jr., Skinner, D. et al. (1998). *Identity and Agency in Cultural Worlds.* Cambridge, MA: Harvard University Press.

Holmes, J. and Remplel, J. (1989). Trust in close relationships. In: *Close Relationships* (ed. C. Hendrick). Thousand Oaks, CA: Sage.

hooks, b. (1984). *Feminist Theory: From Margin to Center.* Cambridge, MA: South End Press.

hooks, b. (1989). *Talking Back: Thinking Feminist, Thinking Black.* Boston, MA: South End Press.

hooks, b. (1994). *Teaching to Transgress: Education as the Practice of Freedom.* New York, NY: Routledge.

Hoover, S. (ed.) (2016). *The Media and Religious Authority*. University Park: Pennsylvania State University Press.

Horton, M. (1990). *The Long Haul: An Autobiography*. New York, NY: Doubleday.

Horton, M. (2003). *The Myles Horton Reader: Education for Social Change*. Knoxville, TN: University of Tennessee Press.

Horton, M. and Freire, P. (1990). *We Make the Road by Walking: Conversations on Education and Social Change*. Philadelphia, PA: Temple University Press.

Howard, T.C. (2003). Culturally relevant pedagogy: Ingredients for critical teacher reflection. *Theory Into Practice* 42 (3): 195–202.

Hu, S. and Kuh, G. (2003). Diversity experiences and college student learning and personal development. *Journal of College Student Development* 44 (3): 320–334.

Hulko, W. (2009). The time- and context-contingent nature of intersectionality and interlocking oppressions. *Journal of Women and Social Work* 24 (1): 44–55.

Hull, J. (1985). *What Prevents Christian Adults from Learning?* London: SCM Press.

Hurtado, S. (2001). Linking diversity and educational purpose: How diversity affects the classroom environment and student development. In: *Diversity Challenged: Evidence on the Impact of Affirmative Action* (ed. G. Orfield and M. Kurleander), 187–203. Cambridge, MA: Harvard Education Publishing Group.

Husband, T., Jr. (2010). He's too young to learn about that stuff: Anti-racist pedagogy and early childhood social studies. *Social Studies Research and Practice* 5 (2): 60–75.

Jersey, B. (1967). *A Time for Burning* (film). Running time 57 min. Lutheran Film Associates https://archive.org/details/atimeforburning (accessed 1 June 2018).

Johnson-Bailey, J. and Lee, M. (2005). Women of color in the academy: Where is our authority in the classroom? *Feminist Teacher* 15 (2): 111–122.

Jones, S. (2003). The right hand of privilege. The Global LeaderSHIFT ThoughtPaper. San Fransisco, CA: Jones & Associates Consulting, www.jones inclusive.com/The_Right_Hand_of_Privilege.pdf (accessed 31 May 2018).

Journal of Blacks in Higher Education. (2006). Black student graduation rates remain low, but modest progress begins to show. *Journal of Blacks in Higher Education* 50: 88, http://www.jbhe.com/features/50_blackstudent_gradrates. html (accessed 19 October 2017).

Jun, H. (2010). *Social Justice, Multicultural Counseling, and Practice: Beyond a Conventional Approach*. Thousand Oaks, CA: SAGE.

Kashtan, M. (2005). The gift of self: The art of transparent facilitation. In: *The IAF Handbook of Group Facilitation: Best Practices from the Leading Organization in Facilitation* (ed. S. Schuman), 573–590. San Francisco, CA: Jossey-Bass.

Kegan, R. (1982). *The Evolving Self: Problem and Process in Human Development*. Cambridge, MA: Harvard University Press.

Kegan, R. (1994). *In Over Our Heads: The Mental Demands of Modern Life*. Cambridge, MA: Harvard University Press.

Keith, N. (2010). Getting beyond anaemic love: From the pedagogy of cordial relations to a pedagogy for difference. *Journal of Curriculum Studies* 42 (4): 539–572.

Kelley, M.M. (2009). The grace of teaching mistakes. *Journal of Spirituality in Mental Health* 11 (4): 282–289.

Kelley, R.D.G. (2002). *Freedom Dreams: The Black Radical Imagination*. Boston, MA: Beacon Press.

Kelly, K. (2016). *The Inevitable: Understanding the Twelve Technological Forces That Will Shape Our Future*. New York, NY: Penguin.

Kena, G., Musu-Gillette, L., Robinson, J. et al. (2015). *The Condition of Education 2015* (NCES 2015-144). Washington, DC: US Department of Education, National Center for Education Statistics, https://nces.ed.gov/ pubsearch/pubsinfo.asp?pubid=2015144 (accessed 1 June 2018).

Kendall, F.E. (2013). *Understanding White Privilege: Creating Pathways to Authentic Relationships Across Race*, 2nd ed. New York, NY: Routledge.

Kennedy, R.F. (1966). Wikiquote, Robert F. Kennedy (9 May). https://en.m.wikiquote.org/wiki/Robert_F._Kennedy (accessed 25 November 2017).

King, M. L. (2003). Letter from a Birmingham jail. In: *A Testament of Hope: The Essential Writings and Speeches of Martin Luther King, Jr.* (ed. J. M. Washington), 289–302. New York, NY: Harper Perennial.

Klein, M. (2013). Cell phones, t-shirts and coffee: Codification of commodities in a Circle of Praxis pedagogy. *Peace Studies Journal* 6 (1): 31–45.

Klein, M. (2016). *Democratizing Leadership: Counter-hegemonic Democracy in Organizations, Institutions, and Communities*. Charlotte, NC: Information Age Publishing.

Kopperud, R. (n.d.). Ryan Kopperud. http://ryankopperud.com (accessed 31 July 2017).

Kumashiro, K. (2000). Toward a theory of anti-oppressive education. *Review of Educational Research* 70 (1): 25–53.

Ladson-Billings, G. (1995a). But that's just good teaching! The case for culturally relevant pedagogy. *Theory Into Practice* 34 (3): 159–165.

Ladson-Billings, G. (1995b). Toward a theory of culturally relevant pedagogy. *American Educational Research Journal* 32 (3): 465–491.

Lannutti, P.J. and Strauman, E.C. (2006). Classroom communication: The influence of instructor self-disclosure on student evaluations. *Communication Quarterly* 54 (1): 89–99.

Lawrence, S.M. and Tatum, B.D. (1999). White racial identity and anti-racist education: A catalyst for change. In: *Beyond Heroes and Holidays: A Practical Guide to K–12 Anti-racist, Multicultural Education and Staff Development* (ed. E. Lee, D. Menkart, and M. Okazawa-Rey), 45–51. Washington, DC: Teaching for Change.

Lawrence Lightfoot, S. (2000). *Respect: An Exploration*. New York, NY: Penguin.

Lederach, J.P. (2005). *The Moral Imagination: The Art and Soul of Building Peace*, 2nd ed. New York, NY: Oxford University Press.

Leonardo, Z. and Porter, R.K. (2010). Pedagogy of fear: Toward a Fanonian theory of "safety" in race dialogue. *Race, Ethnicity and Education* 13 (2): 139–157.

Lorde, A. (1984). *Sister Outsider: Essays and Speeches by Audre Lorde*. Trumansburg, NY: Crossing Press.

Ludlow, J. (2004). From safe space to contested space in the feminist classroom. *Transformations* 15 (1): 40–56.

Lyon, G.E. (n.d.). Where I'm from. Georgeellalyon.com. www.georgeellalyon. com/where.html (accessed 31 July 2017).

Mandela, N. (1994). *Long Walk to Freedom: The Autobiography of Nelson Mandela*. Boston, MA: Little, Brown.

Manglitz, E., Guy, T., and Merriweather, L. (2014). Knowledge and emotions in cross-racial dialogues: Challenges and opportunities for adult educators committed to racial justice in educational settings. *Adult Learning* 25 (3): 111–118.

Marcuse, H. (1964). *One-Dimensional Man: Studies in the Ideology of Advanced Industrial Society*. Boston, MA: Beacon Press.

Marcuse, H. (1965). Repressive tolerance. In: *A Critique of Pure Tolerance* (ed. R.P. Wolff, B. Moore, and H. Marcuse), 95–137. Boston, MA: Beacon Press.

Marcuse, H. (1978). *The Aesthetic Dimension: Toward a Critique of Marxist Aesthetics*. Boston, MA: Beacon Press.

Marschall, M. and Stolle, D. (2004). Race and the city: Neighborhood context and the development of generalized trust. *Political Behavior* 26 (2): 125–153.

McIntosh, P. (1988). White privilege: Unpacking the invisible knapsack. *Peace and Freedom Magazine* (July/August): 10–12.

McIntosh, P. (1997). White privilege and male privilege: A personal account of coming to see correspondences through work in women's studies. In: *Critical White Studies: Looking Behind the Mirror* (ed. R. Delgado and J. Stefancic), 291–299. Philadelphia, PA: Temple University Press.

McKinley Jones Brayboy, B. (2003). The implementation of diversity in predominantly white colleges and universities. *Journal of Black Studies* 34 (1): 72–86.

Merriweather Hunn, L.R. (2004). Africentric philosophy. In: *Promoting Critical Practice in Adult Education* (ed. R. St. Clair and J. Sandlin), 65–74. San Francisco, CA: Jossey-Bass.

Mezirow, J. (2000). Learning to think like an adult. In: *Learning as Transformation: Critical Perspectives on a Theory in Progress* (ed. J. Mezirow), 3–33. San Francisco, CA: Jossey-Bass.

Myers, B. (2016). Where are the minority professors? *Chronicle of Higher Education* (14 February). www.chronicle.com/interactives/where-are-the-minority-professors (accessed 19 October 2017).

Nagda, B. (2006). Breaking barriers, crossing borders, building bridges: Communication processes in intergroup dialogues. *Journal of Social Issues* 62 (3): 553–576.

Nagda, B and Zuniga, X. (2003). Fostering meaningful racial engagement through intergroup dialogues. *Group Processes & Intergroup Relations* 6 (1): 111–128.

Nash, R.J., Bradley, D.L., and Chickering, A.W. (2008). *How to Talk About Hot Topics on Campus: From Polarization to Moral Conversation.* San Francisco, CA: Jossey-Bass.

National Student Clearinghouse Research Center. (2017). *Completing College: A National View of Student Attainment Rates by Race and Ethnicity.* Herndon, VA: National Student Clearinghouse Research Center.

New York Times. (2015). A Conversation with My Black Son. *New York Times* Op Doc (March 17). Retrieved 10 January 2018 from: https://www.nytimes.com/2015/03/17/opinion/a-conversation-with-my-black-son.html (accessed 1 June 2018).

Olson, J. (2004). *The Abolition of White Democracy*. Minneapolis, MN: University of Minnesota Press.

Paterson, R.W.K. (1970). The concept of discussion: A philosophical approach. *Studies in Adult Education* 2 (1): 28–50.

Piven, F.F. and Cloward, R. (1993). *Regulating the Poor: The Functions of Public Welfare*, rev. ed. New York, NY: Vintage.

Popova, M. (2014). *Wisdom in the age of information, an animated explication*. Future of Storytelling Conference. www.youtube.com/watch?v=bjoO6Y29f7 (accessed 21 January 2017).

Potapchuk, M., Liederman, S., Bivens, D. et al. (2015). *Flipping the Script: White Privilege and Community Building*. Center for Assessment and Policy Development. www.racialequitytools.org/resourcefiles/potapchuk1.pdf (accessed 21 January 2017).

Pyle, N. (2014). This teacher taught his class a powerful lesson about privilege (21 November). www.buzzfeed.com/nathanwpyle/this-teacher-taught-his-class-a-powerful-lesson-about-privil#.xdY5XPjJxG (accessed 1 June 2018).

Ramdeholl, D. (2016). Eating fire while walking on broken glass: An auto-ethnography of one adult educator's tenure process. Adult Education Research Conference, Charlotte, NC. Manhattan, KS: New Prairie Press. http://newprairiepress.org/aerc/2016/papers/33 (accessed 9 April 2018).

Rogers, D.T. (2009). The working alliance in teaching and learning: Theoretical clarity and research implications. *International Journal for the Scholarship of Teaching and Learning* 3 (2), Article 28. 10.20429/ijsotl.2009.030228 (accessed 1 June 2018).

Rojzman, C. (1999). *How to Live Together: A New Way of Dealing with Racism and Violence*. St. Kilda, West Australia: Acland.

Rosenberg, M.B. (2003). *Nonviolent Communication: A Language of Life*. Encinitas, CA: Puddledancer Press.

Rosestone Collective. (2014). Safe space: Towards a reconceptualization. *Antipode* 46 (5): 1346–1365.

Sajnani, N. (2012). Response/ability: Imagining a critical race feminist paradigm for the creative arts therapies. *The Arts in Psychotherapy* 39: 186–191.

Sandoval, C. (1991). U.S. third world feminism: The theory and method of oppositional consciousness in the postmodern world. *Genders* 10 (Spring): 1–24.

Sandoval, C. (1999). Theorizing white consciousness for a post-empire world: Barthes, Fanon, and the rhetoric of love. In: *Displacing Whiteness: Essays in Social and Cultural Criticism* (ed. R. Frankenberg), 86–106. Durham, NC: Duke University Press.

Saslow, E. (2016). The white flight of Derek Black. *Washington Post* (15 October). https://www.washingtonpost.com/national/the-white-flight-of-derek-black/2016/10/15/ed5f906a-8f3b-11e6-a6a3-d50061aa9fae_story.html?utm_term=.71493a0a358f (accessed 6 September 2017).

Schön, D. (1983). *The Reflective Practitioner: How Professionals Think in Action.* New York, NY: Basic Books.

Sefa Dei, G. (1993). The challenges of anti-racist education in Canada. *Canadian Ethnic Studies* 25 (2): 36–51.

Shahjahan, R. (2015). Being "lazy" and slowing down: Toward decolonizing time, our body, and pedagogy. *Educational Philosophy and Theory* 47 (5), 488–501.

Sheared, V., Johnson-Bailey, J., Colin, S.A.J., III, Peterson, E., and Brookfield, S.D. (eds.) (2010). *Handbook of Race and Adult Education: A Resource for Dialogue on Racism.* San Francisco, CA: Jossey-Bass.

Singleton, G.E. (2005). *Courageous Conversations About Race: A Field Guide for Achieving Equity in Schools.* New York, NY: SAGE.

Six, F. (2005). *The Trouble with Trust: The Dynamics of Interpersonal Trust Building.* Cheltenham, UK: Edward Elgar.

Smith, H. (2009). The Foxfire approach to student and community interaction. In: *Promising Practices for Family and Community Involvement during High School* (ed. L. Shumow), 89–103. Charlotte, NC: Information Age.

St. Denis, V. (2007). Aboriginal education and anti-racist education: Building alliances across cultural and racial identity. *Canadian Journal of Education* 30 (4): 1068–1092.

Stuart, M. (dir.), Rotaru, A. (ed.), and Thirteen/WNET (2005). *The Hobart Shakespeareans (film)*. Running time 60 min. For Thirteen/WNET. A co-purocuction of Mel Stuart, Thirettn/WNET and POV I American Documentary, www.pbs.org/pov/hobart/film-description (accessed 1 June 2018).

Sue, D.W. (2010). *Microaggressions in Everyday Life: Race, Gender, and Sexual Orientation*. Hoboken, NJ: John Wiley & Sons, Inc.

Sue, D.W. (2015). *Race Talk and the Conspiracy of Silence: Understanding and Facilitating Difficult Dialogues on Race*. Hoboken, NJ: John Wiley & Sons, Inc.

Sue, D.W. and Sue, D. (2015). *Counseling the Culturally Diverse: Theory and Practice*. Hoboken, NJ: John Wiley & Sons, Inc.

Sullivan, S. (2014). *Good White People: The Problem with Middle-Class White Anti-Racism*. Albany, NY: State University of New York Press.

Tablante, C. and Fiske, S. (2015). Teaching social class. *Teaching of Psychology* 42 (2): 184–190.

Takacs, D. (2003). How does your positionality bias your epistemology? *Thought & Action* 19 (1): 27–38.

Tatum, B.D. (1992). Talking about race, learning about racism: The application of racial identity development theory in the classroom. *Harvard Educational Review* 62 (1): 1–24.

Tatum, B.D. (2003). *Why Are All the Black Kids Sitting Together in the Cafeteria? And Other Conversations About Race*. New York, NY: Basic Books.

Timmins, F. (2006). Critical practice in nursing care: Analysis, action and reflexivity. *Nursing Standard* 20 (39): 49–54.

Tobin, L. (2010). Self-disclosure as a strategic teaching tool: What I do – and don't – tell my students. *College English* 73 (2): 196–206.

Townes, E. (2006). Womanist theology. In: *Encyclopedia of Women and Religion in North American Culture*, Vol. 3 (ed. Rosemary Keller, Rosemary Skinner, and Rosemary Radford Ruether), 1165–1172. Bloomington, IN: Indiana University Press.

Trout, M. and Basford, L. (2016). Preventing the shut-down: Embodied critical care in a teacher educator's practice. *Action in Teacher Education* 38 (4): 358–370.

US Department of Education, National Center for Education Statistics. (2015). The Condition of Education 2015. NCES 2015-144. https://nces.ed.gov/pubsearch/pubsinfo.asp?pubid=2015144 (accessed 13 April 2018).

Vella, J. (2002). *Learning to Listen, Learning to Teach: The Power of Dialogue in Educating Adults*. San Francisco, CA: Jossey-Bass.

Wah, L.M. (dir.). (1994). *The Color of Fear* (documentary). Running time 90 min. Stir Fry Productions.

Wampold, B.E (2001). *The Great Psychotherapy Debate: Models, Methods, and Findings*. Mahwah, NJ: Erlbaum.

Warren, L. (2005). Strategic action in hot moments. In: *Teaching Inclusively: Resources for Course, Department and Institutional Change in Higher Education* (ed. M. Ouellet). Stillwater, OK: New Forums.

Weimer, M. (2013). *Learner-centered Teaching: Five Key Changes to Practice*, 2nd ed. San Francisco, CA: Jossey-Bass.

Wesch, M. (2008). Context collapse. Digital Ethnography. http://mediatedcultures.net/youtube/context-collapse (accessed 21 January 2017).

Wijeyesinghe, C. and Jackson, B. (eds.) (2001). *New Perspectives on Racial Identity Development: A Theoretical and Practical Anthology*. New York, NY: New York University Press.

Wildman, S.M. and Davis, A.D. (2008). Making systems of privilege visible. In: *White Privilege: Essential Readings on the Other Side of Racism* (ed. P.S. Rothenberg), 109–116. New York, NY: Worth Publishers.

Williams, R. (1977). *Marxism and Literature*. New York, NY: Oxford University Press.

Wise, T. (2005). *White Like Me: Reflections on Race from a Privileged Son*. New York, NY: Soft Skull Press.

Wright, R. (1996). *Eight Men*. New York: Harper Perennial.

Yancy, G. (2004). *What White Looks Like: African-American Philosophers on the Whiteness Question*. New York, NY: Routledge.

Yancy, G. (2012). *Look, a White! Philosophical Essays on Whiteness*. Philadelphia, PA: Temple University Press.

Yancy, G. (2015a). Dear white America. *New York Times Opinionator* (24 December). https://opinionator.blogs.nytimes.com/2015/12/24/dear-white-america (accessed 9 January 2018).

Yancy, G. (2015b). Introduction: Un-suture. In: *White Self-Criticality Beyond Anti-Racism: How Does It Feel to Be a White Problem?* (ed. G. Yancy), xi–xxvii. Lanham, MD: Lexington Books.

Yancy, G. (2017a). It's black history month. Look in the mirror. The Stone *New York Times* (9 February). www.nytimes.com/2017/02/09/opinion/its-black-history-month-look-in-the-mirror.html (accessed 9 April 2018).

Yancy, G. (2017b). *Black Bodies, White Gazes: The Continuing Significance of Race in America*. Lanham, MD: Rowman & Littlefield.

Yancy, G. (2018). *Backlash: What Happens When We Talk Honestly About Racism in America*. Lanham, MD: Rowman & Littlefield.

Yanow, W.B. (2007). Autobiography as counter-narrative: An empirical study of how race enters and structures the stories of our lives. PhD dissertation. National Louis University.

Zuniga, X., Nagda, B., and Sevig, T. (2002). Intergroup dialogues: An educational model for cultivating engagement across differences. *Equity and Excellence in Education* 35 (1): 7–17.

Index

References to figures are given in italics, e.g. *82*

Teaching Race: How to Help Students Unmask and Challenge Racism, First Edition.
Stephen D. Brookfield and Associates.
© 2019 John Wiley & Sons, Inc. Published 2019 by John Wiley & Sons, Inc.